Contents

CW00432041

Diamond
Publications

© **Copyright**

Published by Diamond Publications
PO Box 59, Bideford, Devon EX39 4YN.
Tel: 01271 860183 Fax: 01271 860064
Email: info@gethooked.co.uk   Web Site: www.gethooked.co.uk

Editor: Graham Sleeman   01566 785782
Distribution: Jane Diamond   01271 860183
Distribution: Devon - Harry Lentern   07714 438262
Advertising: Jane Diamond   01271 860183
Design & Typeset by Type High   01566 785782
Printed by Ashley House   01392 202320
Cover Pictures: Mike Weaver, Julien Busselle (Bass), Brian Gay (Perch).

Special thanks to the team at the Environment Agency, annually understanding partners and children, Veerla for 'databasing', Emma, and everyone who contributed to this, the eighth of many. Now I can go fishing!

While every effort has been made to ensure that the information in this publication is accurate at the time of going to press, the publishers cannot accept responsibility for any errors or omissions which may have occurred. Remember fisheries change hands and rules change. **Always phone if in doubt.**

ISBN 0-9527547-5-4

Introduction

Welcome...

To the eighth edition of the Get Hooked Guide to Angling in South West England

This is the fifth year we have published in association with the Environment Agency.

Once again we have contacted EVERY fishery and association, offering day ticket fishing, known to us or the Environment Agency, throughout the area. Everyone who has responded is detailed in our directory section which has increased yet again and now has over 500 entries, re-affirming our position as THE DEFINITIVE guide to angling throughout the South West of England.

May we take this opportunity to ask those who have not responded or whom we don't know of, to contact us for insertion in next year's issue, a directory entry, in the guide and on the web site, costs you nothing.

If you have access to the internet you can use the on line form to send us your details for inclusion on the web site database, or next year's guide as well as notifying us of any changes throughout the coming year. Obviously updates to the paper guide will have to wait for the next edition but the website database will be updated on a regular basis. Use of the internet is becoming more widespread within the fishing fraternity with some 170 entries in the directory contactable by Email. If technology has not caught up with you yet we find the phone or fax still works perfectly!

We have a real selection of editorials this year. The Environment Agency section covers all the latest byelaws and licencing details (you can now purchase your licence on the internet) and we have contributions from charitable organisations and several groups dedicated to improving and supporting the sport. Please take the time to read them. I know everybody just looks at the pictures on the first browse, but all of these organisations are working for you, they need your support.

Our thanks go out to all the advertisers and contributors who help us make this publication what it is. We know the advertising is successful and hope the new advertisers will benefit as much as those who have been with us from our first edition.

An annual thank you is due to the tackle shops who have helped tremendously in finding previously unknown (to us) fisheries and clubs, enabling us to make the directory so comprehensive.

We have a great selection of pictures from the fisheries again this year, thanks to everyone who made the effort and apologies for not being able to get them all in. We would like to reiterate that the vast majority of pictures are supplied by anglers and fishery owners, not professional photographers, so don't be too critical if some of them aren't pin sharp! All photos of catches from fisheries in the guide are welcome (some more of species other than Carp would be great!)

Our Web Site 'Fish Finder' contains all the information published in our directory in a fully searchable format. There is no quicker way of finding fishing in the South West. We have some links on the site and welcome further enquiries. Fishing related sites only need apply.
Point your browser at:
www.gethooked.co.uk
Or Email us at: info@gethooked.co.uk

From some of the best sea fishing to a huge, and ever increasing, variety of coarse fishing and game fishing, on stillwaters and rivers, to equal anywhere in the country. The South West has a huge amount to offer anglers from all branches of the sport.

We are sure you will find The Get Hooked Guide to Angling in the South West of England useful, informative and entertaining, whether you are local or visiting the area.

Enjoy your fishing

Graham Sleeman
Editor.

2

ENVIRONMENT AGENCY

The Environment Agency for England and Wales was established by the 1995 Environment Act and became operational on 1 April 1996.

We are one of the largest and most powerful environmental protection and regulation agencies in Europe. Our duty is to protect the environment in a way that contributes towards sustainable development through the management of air, land and water. This involves meeting the needs of the present without compromising the ability of future generations to meet their own needs.

We have specific responsibilities for water resources, pollution prevention and control, waste management, flood defence, fisheries, conservation and recreation.

Our vision is a healthy, rich and diverse environment in England and Wales for present and future generations.

A key element in this vision is looking after the important fisheries of the South West.

Fish are one of the best indicators of the state of rivers and lakes. Healthy and abundant freshwater fish stocks and populations will demonstrate the Agency's success in contributing towards its overarching duty to contribute towards sustainable development.

To help make progress, Local Environment Agency Plans (LEAPs) and salmon action plans (SAPs) are being drawn up with the help of public consultation for the whole region.

These include lists of actions for the Agency and other interested parties to protect and enhance the environment. Copies of these plans are available free of charge from Agency offices.

The work of the Agency helps fisheries in many ways. Pollution prevention, dealing with low river flows and habitat improvements are three good examples.

In addition, the Agency's fisheries staff carry out a number of vital tasks. These include:
• Controlling the pressure on fisheries through issuing licences and making byelaws
• Preventing damage to fish and fish stocks by effective enforcement of fishery laws
• Ensuring the health and abundance of fish stocks through regular fisheries surveys
• Rescuing fish when pollution incidents occur and minimising damage to fish stocks
• Stocking fish to restore and improve fisheries
• Carrying out habitat improvement
• Constructing fish passes
• Monitoring of fish stocks i.e. catch returns, juvenile surveys and fish counters
• Carrying out fisheries research to allow future improvements and developments.

Fisheries operations are organised by staff based in the Agency's four South West areas.

They can be contacted as follows:

Cornwall:
Fisheries, Ecology and
Recreation Manager
Environment Agency
Sir John Moore House
Victoria Square
BODMIN PL31 1EB
Tel: 01208 265012
Fax: 01208 78321

Devon:
Fisheries, Ecology and
Recreation Manager
Environment Agency
Exminster House
Miller Way
EXMINSTER EX6 8AS
Tel: 01392 316032
Fax: 01392 316016

North Wessex:
Fisheries, Ecology and
Recreation Manager
Environment Agency
Rivers House
East Quay
BRIDGWATER Som. TA6 4YS
Tel: 01278 484655
Fax: 01278 452985

South Wessex:
Fisheries, Ecology and
Recreation Manager
Environment Agency
Rivers House
Sunrise Business Park
Higher Shaftesbury Road
BLANDFORD DT11 8ST
Tel: 01258 483373
Fax: 01258 455998

Strategic policy and planning issues are co-ordinated by fisheries staff at the Regional Office (Manley House, Exeter).

The Region is advised by the South West Regional Fisheries, Ecology, and Recreation Advisory Committee. The Committee usually sits four times a year and its meetings are open to the public and the media. Local fisheries forums also meet in each of the four areas.

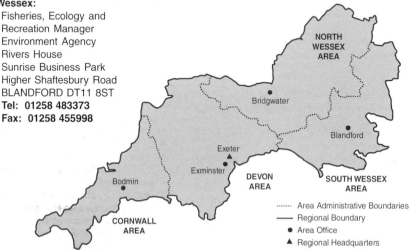

------- Area Administrative Boundaries
——— Regional Boundary
● Area Office
▲ Regional Headquarters

South Wessex 'boom boat' electric fishing on the River Frome

4

National Rod Licences

Before fishing for salmon, trout or freshwater fish (including eels) in any* water in England and Wales, it is necessary to have both a current Agency rod fishing licence and permission to fish from the owner of the fishery.

Except in waters where a general licence is in force - please check with the owner of the fishery in advance.

The area where a rod licence is required for fishing for salmon, trout and freshwater fish includes estuaries and the sea out to six miles from the shore.

In most cases a licence is not required to fish for freshwater eels in tidal water, though there are exceptions. Before fishing for eels in tidal waters, please check with your local Area Fisheries Office.

The Agency has a national rod fishing licence. This means that fishing in all regions is covered by one licence.

Licences are available for coarse fish and non-migratory trout or for all inclusive fishing, including salmon and sea trout.

The licence structure is aimed at raising approximately £14 million for essential fisheries work at a time when the Government's grant-in-aid for this area of the Agency's work is declining.

Coarse fish and non-trout

The price of the full annual licence (2001/2002) for coarse fish and non-migratory trout is £20 (£10 concessions [disabled anglers in receipt of invalidity benefit or severe disability allowance, and anyone aged 65 years and over]).

A short term coarse fish and non-migratory trout licence covers a period of eight consecutive days, giving anglers the benefit of being able to fish over two weekends. This costs £6.50 (no concessions). A one-day licence, aimed at beginners and casual anglers costs £2.50 (no concessions).

New Junior Licence

In 2001 a new full annual junior licence will be available for coarse fish and non-migratory trout priced £5.

Salmon and sea trout

The price of the full annual licence (2001/2002) for salmon and sea trout (and also including coarse fish and non-migratory trout) is £59 (concessions £29.50). An eight-day licence costs £16.50 and a one-day licence is £5.50. There are no concessions on the eight- or one-day licence.

Licences are available from every Post Office in England and Wales or from a range of local distributors. A list of these local distributors is available from the Agency offices. If necessary, you may obtain your licence by post. A form to do this is available from Agency offices.

Alternatively a 'telesales' service operates from 8am to 8pm, seven days a week, except bank holidays, for full, junior and concessionary licences. The number to ring is 0870 1662662.

It is also now possible to obtain full licences - eight and one day and the new full junior licence - through the Agency's 'on-line licensing system'. Details are available on the fisheries web site: www.environment-agency.gov.uk/fish.

Payment by credit/debit card for 'telesales' and 'online': the licence will be immediately valid as the purchaser will be provided with a reference number to quote if challenged when fishing. Proof of identity will also be needed until the full licence has been received.

The 2001/2002 licences will be valid until 31 March 2002. Licences are issued on a 12-month basis and are subject to price reviews.

The licence has the following benefits:

* You can use a rod and line anywhere in England and Wales.

* You can use up to two rods per licence, subject to the National Byelaws (see page 13) and any local rules.

Your rod licence will help the Agency to continue and improve the vital work it carries out, including:

* Management of fish stocks.
* Surveys, essential for picking up changes and problems.

5

* Improvements in fisheries and the fish's environment.
* Fish rearing and stocking of rivers.
* Rescue of fish which would otherwise be lost through drought, pollution or other causes.
* Advice on fishing and management issues.
* Protection of stocks through enforcement activities, including anti-poaching patrols.

Please note that:

1. The licence gives you the right to use a fishing rod and line but does not give you the right to fish. You must always check that you have the permission of the owner or tenant of the fishing rights before starting to fish.

2. Your licence is valuable - if it should be lost, a duplicate can be issued from PO Box 432, National Rod Licence Administration, Environment Agency, Richard Fairclough House, Knutsford Road, Warrington, WA4 1HH. A charge of £5 will be made. Please make a note of the Licence Stamp Number.

3. The licence is yours alone; it cannot be used by anyone else. Please make sure that you sign the licence before you go fishing.

4. Your licence must be produced on demand to a water bailiff of the Agency who produces his or her warrant, a police officer or any other licence holder who produces his or her licence. Failure to do so is an offence and may make you liable to prosecution (maximum fine £2,500).

5. The licence is only valid if the correct name, address and date of birth of the holder, and the date and time of issue are shown without amendments, a stamp of the correct duty is attached and the licence is signed by the holder and the issuing agent.

6. A national rod licence is not required where a general licence is in force. Please check with the owner in advance.

7. The catch return form attached to the licence for salmon and sea trout is very important. This information is required by law and you should send in a return, even if you recorded a "nil" catch. Please fill in and return the form in an envelope when your licence expires, using the FREEPOST address.

8. Details of rod fishing byelaws and angling information can be obtained from Agency offices. Fishery byelaws may vary between different Agency Regions - if in doubt, check first. Details of the main byelaws applying to the Agency in the South West can be found on pages 7 to 12.

Salmon and sea trout kelts

Salmon and sea trout which are about to spawn, or have recently spawned but not recovered, are known as unclean. Fish in either condition, if caught, must by law be returned to the water with as little damage as possible. Fish about to spawn are identifiable by the ease with which eggs or milt can be extruded from the vent.

Those having recently spawned are called kelts and can be identified from clean fish by using the comparison given below.

KELT

1. Line of back and belly parallel
2. Gill maggots almost invariably present (salmon only)
3. Distinct "corner" or change of direction in profile of body at back of skull
4. Fins invariably frayed
5. Vent suffused and easily extruded by pressure
6. Belly normally black

CLEAN

1. Back and belly convex in relation to each other
2. Gill maggots only present in previous spawners or fish which have been some time in the river
3. Head tapers into body without a break
4. Fins entire; rarely frayed
5. Vent firm and compact
6. Belly normally pale

Smolts and parr

Young salmon known as parr look very similar to brown trout and are often caught by trout anglers. These parr are destined to run the rivers in a few years as adult salmon after feeding at sea. It is an offence knowingly to take, kill or injure these parr, and any which are caught by mistake must be returned to the water.

Salmon parr can be identified from trout by using the comparison given below. In March, April and May, salmon and sea trout parr begin to migrate to the sea. The spots and finger marks disappear and the body becomes silvery in colour. They are then called smolts and must be returned to the water if caught.

SALMON PARR

1. Body slightly built and torpedo-shaped
2. Tail distinctly forked
3. A perpendicular line from the back of the eye will not touch the maxillary bone
4. Eight to twelve finger marks, even in width, well-defined and regularly placed along the sides
5. No white line on leading edge of fins
6. No red colour on adipose fin

TROUT

1. Body thicker and clumsier looking
2. Tail with shallow fork
3. A perpendicular line from the back of the eye will pass through or touch the maxillary bone
4. Finger marks less numerous, uneven in width, less defined, irregularly placed along the sides
5. Normally white line on leading edge of fins
6. Adipose fin generally coloured with orange or red.

ROD FISHING SEASONS

The "Open Seasons", i.e. the periods when it is permitted to fish, are set out in the table opposite.

★ *There is no statutory close season for coarse fish and eels in still waters, but some clubs and fishery owners may impose their own close seasons.*

Cornwall area staff attending 'egg box' rearing units - River Tamar.

FISHERY DISTRICT	MAJOR RIVERS WITHIN DISTRICT	ROD & LINE OPEN SEASON (dates inclusive) Starts	Ends
SALMON			
Avon (Devon)	Avon (Devon)	15 Apr	30 Nov
	Erme	15 Mar	31 Oct
Axe (Devon)	Axe, Otter, Sid	15 Mar	31 Oct
	Lim	1 Mar	30 Sept
Camel	Camel	1 Apr	15 Dec
Dart	Dart	1 Feb	30 Sept
Exe	Exe	14 Feb	30 Sept
Fowey	Fowey, Looe, Seaton	1 Apr	15 Dec
Tamar & Plym	Tamar, Tavy, Lynher,	1 Mar	14 Oct
	Plym, Yealm	1 Apr	15 Dec
Taw & Torridge	Taw, Torridge	1 Mar	30 Sept
	Lyn	1 Feb	31 Oct
Teign	Teign	1 Feb	30 Sept
Frome (Dorset) & Piddle		1 Mar	31 Aug
	All other rivers in North & South Wessex Areas	1 Feb	31 Aug
MIGRATORY TROUT			
Avon (Devon)	Avon (Devon)	15 Apr	30 Sept
	Erme	15 Mar	30 Sept
Axe (Devon)	Axe, Otter, Sid	15 Apr	31 Oct
	Lim	16 Apr	31 Oct
Camel	Camel, Gannel, Menalhyl Valency	1 Apr	30 Sept
Dart	Dart	15 Mar	30 Sept
Exe	Exe	15 Mar	30 Sept
Fowey	Fowey, Looe, Seaton, Tresillian	1 Apr	30 Sept
Tamar & Plym	Tamar, Lynher, Plym, Tavy, Yealm	3 Mar	30 Sept
Taw & Torridge	Taw, Torridge, Lyn	15 Mar	30 Sept
Teign	Teign	15 Mar	30 Sept
	All rivers in North & South Wessex Areas	15 Apr	31 Oct
BROWN TROUT			
	Camel	1 Apr	30 Sept
	Other rivers in Devon & Cornwall Areas	15 Mar	30 Sept
	All rivers in North & South Wessex Areas	1 Apr	15 Oct
	All other water in Devon & Cornwall Areas	15 Mar	12 Oct
	All other waters in North & South Wessex Areas	17 Mar	14 Oct
RAINBOW TROUT			
	Camel & Fowey	1 Apr	30 Sept
	Other rivers in Devon & Cornwall Areas	15 Mar	30 Sept
	All rivers in North & South Wessex Areas	1 Apr	15 Oct
	Reservoirs, Lakes & Ponds ★ No statutory close season		
GRAYLING, COARSE FISH & EELS			
	Rivers, Streams and Drains including the Glastonbury Canal	16 Jun	14 Mar
	Enclosed waters - Ponds, Lakes & Reservoirs, all other Canals ★ No statutory close season		

NATIONAL BYELAWS TO PROTECT SALMON STOCKS

National byelaws to protect spring salmon were introduced in April 1999.

A summary of the byelaws is as follows:
Mandatory catch and release of all salmon for all rivers before 16 June.
Fly and spinner only (where not already limited by existing byelaws) before June 16 for salmon fishing.

These measures replace some of the existing measures already in place.

Catch and release of salmon is mandatory to 16 June, removing the bag limit of two salmon before 1 June on the Taw and Torridge. It also supersedes any early season voluntary bag limits.

Anglers are still encouraged to fish catch and release after 16 June and especially to return any large red fish late in the season which may be "springers". The 70 cm limit in August/ September on the Taw and Torridge still applies.

Permitted baits are restricted to artificial fly and artificial lure until 16 June. Exceptions where other restrictions remain include the Taw and Torridge (fly only from April 1) and North and South Wessex (fly only before 15 May).

These national byelaws are designed as a baseline and are considered to be the lowest common denominator across the country addressing the national problem of a decline in early-run large salmon.

Measures to address other local stock problems will continue to follow a river-by-river approach based on the programme of individual salmon action plans being developed by the Agency with local fisheries interests.

PERMITTED BAITS

The use of particular baits for fishing is regulated by byelaws and in some cases additional restrictions are imposed by the fishing association or riparian owner. The byelaw restrictions are shown in the table below:
★ *This restriction only applies to water where a statutory coarse fish close season is applicable. It does not apply to stillwaters. See also section on rod fishing seasons and the note on canal close seasons (page 12).*
★★ *All references to "Trout" include migratory trout and non-migratory trout.*
★★★ *This is a change introduced in 1998.*

No spinning for trout in waters included within the Dartmoor National Park, the Exe above Exebridge, Otter above Langford Bridge, Torridge above Woodford Bridge, Bray above Newton Bridge, Mole above Alswear Bridge, Little Dart above Affeton Bridge, and the whole of the Okement, Lyn and Barnstaple Yeo.
Artificial baits which spin: When fishing for salmon or trout in the Avon (Devon), Axe (Devon), Exe, Dart, Taw and Torridge and Teign districts, use of any artificial bait which spins is restricted to those with only a single, double or treble hook. The width of the hook must not be greater than the spread of the vanes of the bait.

PERMITTED BAITS

FISHERY DISTRICT	SPECIES	BAITS (REAL OR IMITATION)
South West Region	Salmon	Artificial fly and artificial lure ONLY before 16 June
Avon (Devon)	Salmon & Trout ★★	No worm or maggot.
Axe (Devon)	Salmon & Trout	No shrimp, prawn, worm or maggot. Fly only after 31 July below Axbridge, Colyford.
Dart	Salmon	No worm or maggot. No shrimp or prawn except below Staverton Bridge. No spinning above Holne Bridge.
	Trout	Fly only.
Exe	Salmon & Trout	No worm or maggot.
Barnstaple Yeo (tidal)	All species (inc. sea fish)	No fishing
Taw & Torridge (except Lyn)	Salmon & Trout	No shrimp, prawn, worm or maggot. No spinning after 31 March. ★★★
Lyn	Trout	No worm or maggot before 1 June.
Teign	Trout	No worm or maggot before 1 June.
Camel & Fowey	Salmon & Trout	No byelaw restrictions on bait after 16 June
Tamar	Salmon & Migratory Trout	No worm, maggot, shrimp or prawn after 31 August.
North Wessex & South Wessex Areas	Salmon & Migratory Trout	Artificial fly only before 15 May.
North Wessex & South Wessex Areas	All species in rivers, drains and canals	No maggot (or pupae), processed product, cereal or other vegetable matter during the coarse fish close season. ★

8

SIZE LIMITS

Length to be measured from tip of the snout to the fork or cleft of the tail.

The size limits, below which fish must be returned, imposed by byelaws are set out in the table below. Riparian owners and fishing associations may impose further restrictions which anglers should familiarize themselves with before fishing.

SIZE LIMITS

AREA, DISTRICT OR CATCHMENT	MIGRATORY TROUT	NON-MIGRATORY TROUT	GRAYLING
Camel, Fowey, Tamar and Plym	18 centimetres	18 centimetres	N/A
Avon (Devon), Axe (Devon), Dart, Exe, Taw & Torridge, Teign	25 centimetres	20 centimetres	N/A
River Lim	N/A	22 centimetres	N/A
North Wessex (except By Brook)	35 centimetres	25 centimetres	25 centimetres
By Brook & tributaries	35 centimetres	20 centimetres	25 centimetres
South Wessex	35 centimetres	25 centimetres	N/A

TAW/TORRIDGE

Any salmon taken in August or September on Taw and Torridge which is greater than 70cm in length must be returned. This is one of the new measures to protect spring fish which may become catchable again towards the end of the season. See also **BAG LIMITS** and **PERMITTED BAITS** for other changes.

These size restrictions do not apply to:

(a) Any person who takes any undersized fish unintentionally if he/she at once returns it to the water with as little injury as possible.

(b) Non-migratory trout in any waters included within the Dartmoor National Park, the Exe above Exebridge, the Otter above Langford Bridge, the Torridge above Woodford Bridge, the Mole above Alswear Bridge, the Little Dart above Affeton Bridge and the whole of the Rivers Okement, Lyn and Barnstaple Yeo.

MANDATORY BAG LIMITS

See section on National Byelaws to protect salmon stocks (page 8).

North Wessex Area. The bag limits set out in the table below are imposed by the byelaws, however, some riparian owners or angling

RIVER OR AREA	SPECIES	PERIOD		
		24 HOURS	7 DAYS	SEASON
North Wessex	Non-migratory Trout	2	N/A	N/A
	Grayling	2	N/A	N/A

associations obtain dispensation to increase their bag limits. Anglers should familiarize themselves with bag limits before fishing. Once a bag limit has been taken, the angler may continue fishing for the same species, provided that any fish caught are returned without injury. Freshwater fish other than grayling, pike and eels may not be permanently removed from the water.

TAW & TORRIDGE

Following a public enquiry in 1997 new bag limits, as shown in the table below, were imposed for four years, commencing in 1998.

NOTE: From 1 April 1999, with the introduction of national salmon byelaws, the bag limits apply after 16 June.

RIVER OR AREA	SPECIES	PERIOD		
		24 HOURS	7 DAYS	SEASON
Taw	Salmon	2	3	10
	Migratory Trout	5	15	40
Torridge	Salmon	2	2	7
	Migratory Trout	2	5	20

VOLUNTARY BAG LIMITS

See section on National Byelaws to protect salmon stocks (page 9).

Spring salmon - In addition to the national byelaws, the Agency is encouraging salmon anglers to return any larger salmon, particularly red ones caught later in the season, as these are likely to be multi-sea-winter fish and valuable to the spawning stock. On many rivers a variety of voluntary measures have been adopted to protect fish stocks. All anglers should familiarize themselves with these rules before fishing. Details are provided on the next page.

Rivers Camel/Fowey/Lynher

For the above Cornish rivers a maximum of: Salmon- 2/day, 4/week and 10/season. Sea trout- 4/day. Please check with club/association as more stringent rules apply on certain waters.

River Tamar

Tamar and Tributaries Fisheries Association: 1 salmon/day followed by catch/release. All fish over 10 pounds returned from 1 Sept. Return red/unseasonable fish.

River Tavy

Tavy, Walkham and Plym Fishing Club: 1 salmon/day, return of all hen fish, limited fishing methods.

Rivers Plym, Tavy

Plymouth and District Freshwater Angling Association: 1 salmon/day, 3/season; 4 sea trout/day/night.

River Exe

River Exe and Tributaries Association: After 16 Aug salmon of 27.5" or over (8 pounds) to be returned unless injured, in which event, the next salmon caught **under** size limit to be returned.

Red or injured fish to be returned, no fishing by prawn or shrimp in Sept. No fish to be sold.

River Teign

Lower Teign Fishing Association: 4 sea trout/24 hours.

River Otter

All salmon to be returned. One mature sea trout and two school peal/season.

River Axe

Axe Fly Fishers: Catch and release only for salmon. Fly only.

River Avon (Hants)

Avon & Stour Riparian Owners and Wessex Salmon Rivers Trust. Catch and release only for salmon. No worm fishing.

Several river associations had not held their AGM prior to going to print. Please check with local club secretary for any voluntary measures that may have been agreed for other rivers before fishing.

CATCH AND RELEASE

With stocks of salmon under increasing pressure, the Environment Agency is seeking to do everything possible to protect the species for the future.

Catch and release is now becoming an established management technique for increasing spawning escapement, particularly where stocks are low. Salmon anglers are encouraged to consider this approach as a means of safeguarding salmon stocks in our rivers.

If you do decide to practice catch and release, the following guidelines may be useful to give your catch the best chance of surviving after you have returned it to the river:

Hooks - single hooks inflict less damage than doubles or trebles, barbless hooks are best. Flatten the barbs on your hooks with pliers.

Playing Fish - fish are best landed before complete exhaustion and therefore all elements of tackle should be strong enough to allow them to be played firmly.

Landing Fish - Fish should be netted and

Dace and chub from the Calverton national fish farm being introduced to the River Tone to boost stocks

unhooked in the water, if possible. Use knotless nets - not a tailer or gaff.

Handling and Unhooking - Make every effort to keep the fish in the water. Wet your hands. Carefully support the fish out of water. Do not hold the fish up by the tail, this may cause kidney damage. Remove the hook gently - if necessary, cut the line if deeply hooked. Take extra care with spring fish, as they are more susceptible to damage and fungal infection.

Do not under any circumstances keep a fish which is to be returned out of the water for more than 30 seconds. Physiological changes affecting survival begin within one minute.

Reviving the Fish - Support an exhausted fish underwater in an upright position facing the current. Estimate weight and length in the water. Avoid weighing. Handle the fish as little as possible. Be patient and give it time to recover and swim away on its own.

TESCO SWAP A SALMON SCHEME

An arrangement, originally negotiated with Tesco for the Hampshire Avon, by Wessex Salmon Rivers Trust, entitles an angler catching and returning a salmon after 16 June to a voucher to be exchanged for a farmed salmon. This scheme now applies to other rivers as follows: Frome, Dart, Teign, Camel, Fowey, Tavy, Lynher, Plym, Otter and Fal. Contact your local fisheries office for further details.

WILD TROUT SOCIETY

Anglers are asked to return all brown trout caught on the East Dart above Postbridge, on the Cherry Brook and the Blackbrook; while on the West Dart between Blackbrook and Swincombe they are to return fish between 10" and 16" long.

USE OF OTHER TACKLE

Use of float. The use of a float when fishing for salmon or trout in any waters within the Avon (Devon), Axe (Devon), Dart, Exe, Taw and Torridge, and Teign districts is prohibited.

Use of gaff. See section on national byelaws Phase 1.

Limit on number of rods in use. See section on national byelaws Phase 1.

Prohibition of use of lead weights. No person shall use any instrument on which is attached directly or indirectly any lead weight (except a weight of 0.06 grams or less, or one of more than 28.35 grams) for the purpose of taking salmon, trout, freshwater fish or eels in any waters within the Agency's region.

Prohibited Fishing Area - Kilbury Weir. It is illegal to take or attempt to take by any means any fish in any waters within 50 yards below the crest of Kilbury Weir on the River Dart.

LANDING NETS, KEEPNETS AND KEEPSACKS

A new national byelaw was introduced on 1 April 1998 making it illegal to use landing nets with knotted meshes or meshes of metallic material.

Similarly keepnets should not be constructed of such materials or have holes in the mesh larger than 25mm internal circumference; or be less than 2.0 metres in length. Supporting rings or frames should not be greater than 40cm apart (excluding the distance from the top frame to the first supporting ring or frame) or less than 120cm in circumference.

Keepsacks should be constructed of a soft, dark coloured, non-abrasive, water permeable fabric and should not have dimensions less than 120cm by 90cm if rectangular, or 150cm by 30cm by 40cm if used with a frame or designed with the intention that a frame be used. It is an offence to retain more than one fish in a single keepsack at any time.

The retention of salmonids (adults or juveniles) in keepnets is illegal except when specially approved by the Agency for collecting broodstock.

MINIMUM ROD LENGTH

North & South Wessex Areas. No person fishing with rod and line shall use a rod less than 1.5 metres in length (subject to review in Phase II of national byelaws).

UNATTENDED RODS

Unattended rods are prohibited for all species in all areas.

THEFT ACT

The Theft Act 1968, Schedule 1, makes it an offence for anyone to take or attempt to take fish in private waters or in a private fishery without the consent of the owner.

The Agency may bring a prosecution under this Act on its own fisheries. It cannot do so on behalf of an individual, and any fishery owner who wishes such a prosecution to be brought should consult the police or a solicitor.

ATTENTION
SALMON AND SEA TROUT ANGLERS

Your catch return is needed by 1 January each year. Nil returns are also required. Send returns to:

Environment Agency, FREEPOST, P.O. Box 60, Patchway, Bristol, BS12 4YY.

NATIONAL BYELAWS Phase I

A number of national byelaws has recently been approved. These replace or modify regional byelaws that existed before.

A summary of the new byelaws is given below.

1. The annual close season for fishing for rainbow trout by rod and line in all reservoirs, lakes and ponds has been dispensed with.

2. A close season for brown trout is to be retained on all waters.

3. Use of the gaff is prohibited at all times when fishing for salmon, trout and freshwater fish or freshwater eels.

4. The number of rods that may be used at any time is as follows:

a. One rod when fishing for salmonids in rivers, streams, drains and canals.

b. Two rods when fishing for salmonids in reservoirs, lakes and ponds (subject to local rules).

c. Up to four rods when fishing for coarse fish and eels (subject to local rules).

When fishing with multiple rods and lines, rods shall not be left unattended and shall be placed such that the distance between the butts of the end rods does not exceed three metres.

5. Catch returns for salmon and migratory trout should be submitted no later than 1 January in the following year.

6. See separate section on landing nets, keepnets and keepsacks.

NATIONAL BYELAWS Phase II

A further series of byelaw changes is being considered for introduction in 2001, including: use of crayfish as bait, fishing for crayfish, removal of fish, return of foul hooked fish, removal of fish for use as bait, minimum rod length and unattended rods.

Please check with your local area Fisheries Office for details.

COARSE FISH CLOSE SEASON ON CANALS

In March 2000 a new National byelaw removed the close season for coarse fish on canals within the region, with the exception of the Glastonbury Canal which is an open system with the South Drain.

FISH WITH ADIPOSE FINS REMOVED

As indicated on your rod licence, you may catch a fish from which the adipose fin has been completely removed. (These may carry a micro tag implanted within their nose - invisible to you.) If this occurs, you should follow the licence instructions.

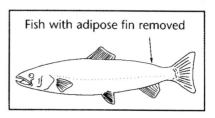
Fish with adipose fin removed

Any fish caught before 16 June without an adipose fin should be returned and reported to your local fisheries office.

* Dial 100 and ask the operator for FREEPHONE FISHWATCH. You will be put through to the Cardiff office where you should ask for the National Salmon Centre.

* Tell us your name, address and telephone number.

* Record details of your catch (where, when, size and species of fish).

* If the fish is caught after 16 June, keep the fish (or just the head) frozen if necessary and we will contact you to make arrangements for it to be inspected.

We will pay you a reward of £5 if it carries a micro tag and, of course, you keep the fish.

Details should be sent to the appropriate Area Fisheries Office.

PURCHASE AND RELEASE OF SALMON FROM LICENSED NETS

In recent years, the Wessex Salmon Rivers Trust has purchased salmon from the Mudeford nets for release to the Hampshire Avon as extra spawners to help boost stock recovery rates. Arrangements have been made for this to continue in the 2001 season.

Similar schemes have also operated on the rivers Tamar, Tavy, Lynher and Fowey, funded by a variety of sponsors including the Tamar and Tributaries Fisheries Association, Maristowe Estate and South West Water.

STOCKING FISH -
BUYER BEWARE

The Environment Agency has produced a free leaflet entitled "Buyer Beware - Your guide to stocking fish". The leaflet explains the Agency rules on fish introduction (Section 30, Salmon and Freshwater Fisheries Act 1975) and the common sense things fishery owners can do to protect themselves and their fisheries when buying/stocking fish.

Before introducing (stocking) any fish (or fish spawn) into inland waters, you must obtain written consent of the Agency. Failure to meet this obligation is a criminal offence and could lead to prosecution, with a fine of up to £2,500. In addition, the stocking of non-native species such as Wels Catfish or Grass Carp requires MAFF approval under the Import of Live Fish Act - Prohibition of Keeping or Release of Live Fish Order 1998.

Mandatory health checks will be required where fish are to be moved into rivers, streams, drains or canals, or where the risk to other fisheries is high.

Health checks will not normally be required in waters where the risk of fish escape is minimal (e.g. enclosed waters). However, there may be occasions where the Agency will still insist on a health examination.

Regardless of the Agency's requirement for health checks, it should be stressed that establishing the health of fish before any stocking is essential. The Agency encourages everyone to follow the Agency's "Buyer Beware" code. Copies of the leaflet can be obtained from any of the Agency's Fisheries Offices.

LOOK OUT! - LOOK UP!
ADVICE ON SAFE FISHING NEAR OVERHEAD ELECTRIC POWER LINES

Several people have died and others have been seriously injured whilst using fishing rods and poles near overhead electric power lines. The following advice is designed to prevent these events recurring:

i   Because rods and poles conduct electricity, they are particularly dangerous when used near overhead electric power lines. Remember that electricity can jump gaps and a rod does not even have to touch an electric line to cause a lethal current to flow.

ii   Many overhead electric power lines are supported by wood poles which can be and are mistaken for telegraph poles. These overhead lines may carry electricity up to 132,000 volts, and have been involved in many of the accidents that have occurred.

iii   The height of high voltage overhead electric power lines can be as low as 5.2 metres and they are therefore within easy reach of a rod or pole. Remember that overhead lines may not be readily visible from the ground. They may be concealed by hedges or by a dark background. Make sure you **"Look Out"** and **"Look Up"** to check for overhead lines before you tackle up and begin fishing.

iv   In general, the minimum safe fishing distance from an overhead electric power line is 30 metres from the overhead line (measured along the ground).

v   When pegging out for matches or competitions, organisers and competitors should, in general, ensure that no peg is nearer to an overhead electric power line than 30 metres (measured along the ground).

vi   For further advice on safe fishing at specific locations, contact your local Electricity Company.

vii   Finally, remember that it is dangerous for any object to get too close to overhead electric power lines, particularly if the object is an electrical conductor, e.g. lead cored fishing line, damp fishing line, rod or pole.

ENVIRONMENT AGENCY AREAS

Devon Area

Fishery Districts (Rivers in parentheses):
Avon (Avon, Erme); Axe (Axe, Sid, Otter); Dart (Dart); Exe (Exe); Taw and Torridge (Taw, Torridge, Lyn); Teign (Teign). The River Lim is included in the Devon Area.
Fisheries Officers Tel. (01392) 316032.

Cornwall Area

Fishery Districts (Rivers in parentheses):
Camel (Camel, other streams flowing into the sea on the North coast between Marshland Mouth and Lands End); Fowey (Fowey, East and West Looe, Seaton, Tresillian, other streams flowing into the sea on the South coast between Lands End and Rame Head); Tamar and Plym (Tamar, Lynher, Plym, Tavy and Yealm).
Fisheries Officers Tel. (01208) 265012.

North Wessex Area

River Catchments:
Bristol Avon (including all tributaries), Axe (Somerset), Brue, Parrett, Tone, Yeo and all other rivers, drains and streams flowing into the Bristol Channel between Avonmouth and Foreland Point.
Fisheries Officers Tel. (01278) 484655.

South Wessex Area

River Catchments:
Hampshire Avon (including all tributaries), Stour (including all tributaries), Dorset Frome, Piddle, Wey, Brit and Char and all other streams flowing into the sea between Christchurch Harbour and Charmouth.
Fisheries Officers Tel. (01258) 483373.

IN ORDER TO FISH FOR SALMON, TROUT (INCLUDING MIGRATORY TROUT), FRESHWATER FISH AND EELS IN ANY* WATERS IN THE SOUTH WEST REGION, ANGLERS WILL NEED AN ENVIRONMENT AGENCY NATIONAL ROD LICENCE AND PERMISSION FROM THE OWNER OF THE FISHERY.

ANGLERS MUST CARRY THEIR ROD LICENCES WITH THEM AT ALL TIMES WHILE FISHING.

* *Except in waters where a General Licence is in force - please check with the owner of the fishery in advance.*

ENVIRONMENT AGENCY

New fish pass at Otterton Weir - River Otter, Devon.

Take to the Hills

Mike Weaver

Spectacular scenery, miles of fishing to explore, hard-fighting wild brown trout, and a price tag that doesn't require a second mortgage - that is moorland trout fishing and here in the South West there is plenty to choose from. Head for the Dartmoor and Exmoor National Parks and you will find miles of sparkling streams, whether on the high open moors or in the deep wooded valleys that tumble down from the hills. The trout may not be very big, but there are plenty of them and, even after a day that has produced modest catches, there is something very special about wandering for hours along a wild river in unspoiled country.

But, as ever, there is a snag. Every year I meet fly fishermen who have ventured onto our moorland streams for the first time. They have enjoyed the experience and caught a fair number of wild trout but, they complain, hardly anything exceeded 15 centimetres - that's six inches in old money. Yet they have been fishing water where I know that the regulars have been taking plenty of browns from 20 centimetres up to 30 centimetres or more. So where are they going wrong and what can they do to improve their performance?

Many newcomers immediately turn to the fly pattern as the cause of their lack of success but the fly is rarely the problem. On the moors, virtually any suitable pattern will take fish, provided you fish it in the right place, at the right time, in the right way - and, above all, make sure that you have not scared every trout within reach before you even make the first cast. So here are some tips to help you make contact with the better-than-average trout that can seem to be so elusive.

Traditionally, many anglers fished the moors with three wet flies which were cast across the river and allowed to swing round on the current, but the Dartmoor and Exmoor streams are often too narrow for this method, so you are more likely to be successful when casting upstream with a dry fly, nymph or wet fly. As the trout will be facing upstream in the lively current, you have already

gone a long way towards avoiding detection by approaching the fish from behind, and wearing drab clothes and keeping off the skyline will add to your chances of success.

Newcomers waste far too much time fishing unproductive water, so here are two places to avoid like the plague. Firstly those deep still pools where you can see the trout swimming around in the depths, but they can also see you and your chances of catching them are virtually zero. And secondly there are the shallow riffles, which are easy to fish but rarely hold anything worth catching. Look out for broken water of medium pace and medium depth, with plenty of cover within easy reach. On the open moors, cover usually means boulders and the pockets and runs on a boulder-strewn stretch can be very productive. And keep on the move. Moorland trout usually come in the first cast or two, so don't waste time fishing a spot that is producing nothing. I expect to fish at least a mile of river in a three-hour session.

To get the best out of moorland fly fishing you need to master the techniques of both the dry fly and the upstream wet fly or nymph - and there are times when a combination of the two is very effective. For dry fly fishing you need a good floater like a Humpy, Elk Hair Caddis or well-hackled Adams, while for wet flies and nymphs you need look no further than traditional patterns like Pheasant Tail, Half Stone, Blue Upright, Red Palmer and Hare's Ear Nymph. These flies should be tied mainly on size 16 and 14 hooks, with a few on 18 and 12 hooks. For wet fly fishing, two flies a couple of feet apart are enough, and it is worth trying a bright floater on the dropper

17

and a drab nymph on the point, the theory being that the dropper catches the attention of the trout and the nymph fools it.

Whether wet or dry fly fishing, work slowly upstream, making a cast or two into every spot that looks likely to hold a trout, and paying particular attention to anywhere you see a fish rise. As the flies drop back towards you, always keep in touch by lifting the rod, so that when a fish takes you only need tighten to set the hook.

Upstream fishing with a dry or wet fly is best when the trout are feeding near the surface but there are times, especially early in the season, when they are almost glued to the bottom. At such times you need a fly that really bumps along the bottom and then a bead head comes into its own. A size 14 Hare's Ear or Pheasant Tail Nymph with a copper or gold bead at the head will often take trout when nothing else will, and your chances will be enhanced by an indicator on the leader to help you spot the takes. I once thought that I could spot any take without such aids but I have long since realised how many fish are missed without an indicator.

If you are planning your first outing for moorland trout, timing is vital to give you a good chance of early success. Eager to get started, many make that first attempt in March or April when the season opens, but they hardly see a fish and don't bother to try again. Even the local experts can struggle in the first few weeks so be patient and wait until late May or June. During this period, the trout normally feed all day and the tough times when the rivers become very low and clear should still be in the future.

There are always, of course, exceptions to any rule, as a day last summer was to prove. It was mid August, when the rivers are often sluggish and the trout very dour, but heavy rains had brought the Dartmoor streams into spate. The bigger rivers were still high and coloured but the tiny Cherrybrook was dropping fast and had cleared to the colour of tea. If the fish were feeding, it would be difficult to fail, so I walked downstream a mile from Upper Cherrybrook Bridge, tied a 12 Red Palmer on the dropper and a 12 Dunkeld on the point, and fished back up to the bridge through the middle of the day. The trout were immediately attracted to the two bright flies and nearly 50 trout up to 28 cm were

caught, with fish on both dropper and point on two occasions. Some mediocre outings on Cherrybrook in the past few years had made me wonder if stocks had declined, but on a day when conditions were just about perfect, the fishing was as good as it ever was.

Dartmoor and Exmoor are ideal for really stretching your legs while you are fishing and the following few examples are typical of what the energetic angler can enjoy. On a fine day it is well worth fishing up the East Dart from Postbridge, with some of the best fishing in a lovely series of small pools about a mile above the bridge. A couple of miles fishing will take you almost to Sandy Hole Pass and then you can walk directly back to your car over Broad Down, with magnificent views to the south.

Another favourite is to park at Watersmeet on the East Lyn and fish up to Rockford, ideally on a sunny day in late May when the Black Gnats are swarming over the river.

Some of the large pools will be full of trout holding just below the surface and rising to anything that looks edible, but watch out for the smaller and less obvious pockets that are often more productive.

My local river is the Teign where the stretch from Fingle Bridge up to Dogmarsh Bridge is just about right for a three-hour session. The middle part of this piece of water below Sharp Tor tumbles down through a series of rocky pools that offer some of the best trout fishing on the upper Teign.

East Dart

18

GAME

The South West Rivers Association

Whitehall's Christmas Present

(by SWRA Secretary Michael Charleston)

In offering £750,000 in matching funds to help close the salmon drift net fishery off North East England the Government has taken an unprecedented step that will help turn the tide in the international battle to save the Atlantic salmon.

In joining for the first time in partnership with the North Atlantic Salmon Fund and its private sector allies MAFF's announcement five days before before Christmas was much more important than its declared aim. It was the best Christmas present that the cause of salmon conservation could get. It's true that the money will largely be used to save the mixed stocks of fish heading for the rivers of the North East and eastern Scotland and that not one fish from South West rivers will be saved. But the gesture will do much more than assist in saving the 40,000 salmon that the 70 or so drift nets took last season.

In setting an example to other nations, it has aroused the determination of the North Atlantic Salmon Fund, its new partner, to end the commercial fishing of mixed stocks of salmon throughout the entire range of the fish and to turn the high seas feeding grounds off Greenland, Iceland and the Faroes into permanent salmon sanctuaries. It took three months longer than expected, and several letters from the South West River Association and the North Atlantic Salmon Fund to the Prime Minister, Agriculture Minister Nick Brown and Fisheries Minister Elliot Morley, before MAFF made its announcement. The delay depressed everyone.It was widely rumoured that Nick Brown was disinclined to do anything to help salmon fishing because he believed it was just 'a sport for toffs.'

We hope we helped him make up his mind by sending him a letter pointing out that this might have been true in Victorian times but that the picture was very different these days. Thanks to the co-operation of the secretaries of all the angling associations in Devon and Cornwall I was able to tell Nick Brown that out of an estimated 2,100 salmon season licence holders in the two counties. 83% were able to fish for much less money than the average soccer supporter spends.

Only 80 of the anglers paid the top rate of £255 for their fishing. The great majority, I said, paid £100 or less to fish all season and a lucky 550 of them in Cornwall could fish every day for only £35 (or £25 if they were senior citizens!) With my encouragement he got similar letters from the other salmon-fishing regions of England and Wales. Mr Brown wrote to me later saying that the Government was committed to conserving and improving salmon stocks.

Whoever, or whatever, prompted the Government's move, the fact remains that it should have an enormous spin-off for the salmon rivers of the South West. Off the west coast of the Republic of Ireland some 700 or more drift nets killed over 160,000 salmon last year.

According to some experts this annual slaughter extinguishes half of all the salmon that remain in the Atlantic. If the English drift nets go, this will be the last mass slaughter salmon have to avoid if they are to succeed in spawning. Many of these fish are not heading for Ireland itself. They are on their way to our rivers and those of Dorset and Hampshire, Wales, France and Spain. Some of them may even be American or Canadian fish.

Supported by the political implications of the British government's move, the North Atlantic Salmon Fund, which has the full support of the Atlantic Salmon Trust, the Salmon and Trout Association and America's Atlantic Salmon Federation, has arranged a 'Salmon Summit' at Limerick at the end of March. International representatives of all the nations affected by the Irish drift nets will be there to meet leaders of the netsmen and Irish government officials. As Secretary of the SWRA I have been invited to speak on behalf of the rivers of South West and Southern England.

The hopeful news is that many of the netsmen have told Orri Vigufsson, the campaigning Icelandic businessmen who is international chairman of NASF, that they are as concerned for the future of the salmon as he is. They say they would be happy to stop catching the fish in return for fair buyout terms. Since the British announcement Vigfusson, who last year honoured the SWRA by becoming its Patron, has received strong encouragement from the Faroes for the oceanic sanctuary schemes. He has visited Canada and obtained the full support of the Canadian fisheries minister and been invited to meet Irish fishery minister Frank Fahey.

Germany is trying to restore the runs that once made the Rhine the greatest salmon river of them all and its fishery minister has also offered to meet the NASF chairman. Anglers in the USA, where the Atlantic salmon is officially an endangered species, have pledged themselves to find a very large sum of money towards the international buyouts. We shall be lucky to get any further British government funds to help close or at least curb the very destructive Irish fishery. But international pressure is now focussed on Ireland to follow the British example and come up with matching funds, and not least for the sake of Irish salmon stocks.

All of us at the 'salmon summit' will be hoping to reach the basis of an agreement. Then all of us who enjoy salmon fishing, or just find enormous pleasure in seeing this extraordinary ocean rover come home to the rivers of their birth, will have to put our hands in our pockets. At the time of writing the financial details of how the international campaign have still to be finalised, but it has been suggested that every angler who can afford it should give a minimum of £50 in a once-off donation. The buyouts will have to be negotiated in stages with closure of the N.E. England nets and other much smaller mixed stocks as the first targets. Efforts are being made to persuade MAFF to include the Taw and Torridge and Tavy/Tamar/Lynher joint estuaries in this.

Then NASF's attention will be turned to removing the nets of Northern Ireland (where the fishery minister has already asked his Executive colleagues for funding) and the nets of the Irish Republic. It may not be long before we shall again be able to watch the flashing bars of silver jumping weirs and tackling any natural or manmade obstacle that lies across their path. It's just 40 years since our rivers were full of salmon. At last it really looks as if we shall be able to turn back the clock.

Almost all the omens are good. The Government has made a public declaration of its wholehearted approval of angling and its commitment to ensuring a better future for our game and coarse fish. It has accepted nearly all the 195 recommendations of the Salmon and Freshwater Fisheries Review Group, the high-powered advisory body that the previous Agriculture Minister, Jack Cunningham, appointed in April 1998 to carry out the first real review of legislation and fishery management since Victorian times.

Despite the huge volume of evidence put before the Group and the diversity of its members' interests, they ranged from fishery scientists and angling experts to a salmon netsman, they made their recommendations unanimously. Their views made such good sense that we and the other major angling organisations found very little to criticise!

The SWRA was delighted that most of its submissions were largely reflected in the recommendations. In particular our evidence obviously had a role in helping the Review Group make what we see as its four most urgent pronouncements:

• Salmon angling is of much greater economic and social importance to rural communities than netting
• The Government should provide substantial funds to help close the N.E. England drift nets
• The Government should use all available means to press the Irish government to reduce the impact of the Irish drift nets on England and Welsh salmon stocks.
• New local advisory committees should be set up and "far reaching changes" made to rectify the angling community's complaints that the Environment Agency's advisory system was not working well.

These committees would go a long way towards restoring the rights of anglers and riparian owners to have a say in how their rivers

23

are managed. The idea is now being considered by Dept of the Environment (DETR) and the SWRA has taken up DETR's invitation to submit evidence. The good news is that we, S&TA and the EA's own RFERAC all seem to agree on the need for these committees.

It's sad to be concentrating on the fate of the salmon for the third year running when wild brown trout and coarse fishermen also have problems. I assure anglers in the South West that once the measures to save the King of Fish are in place the SWRA will campaign just as vigorously for the other angling interests. So, please, bear with us a little longer!

The SWRA is the regional voice of the 17 rivers associations of Devon and Cornwall. For more information and a newsletter phone me at 01822 853293 or use my e-mail address: mwcharl@aol.com

Tony Chapman of Launceston with a 21lb 13oz fish on a 'Mike's Special'.
Tavistock Trout

VRANCH HOUSE SCHOOL FLY FISHING CHARITY CHALLENGE 2001

In aid of the Devon & Exeter Spastics Society

Pairs of anglers are invited to enter the 10th Fly Fishing Charity Challenge to raise funds for children with cerebral palsy at Vranch House School & Centre, Exeter.

The Challenge has raised a magnificent £76,590 since 1992 and raised £12,790 in 2000, nearly £3000 more than in 1999. The two top fundraisers in 2000 were Geoff Crocker of Menheniot - £1,825 and Mike Rowe of Drewsteignton - £1,380

Heats and semi-finals will take place from April to September at Bake Lakes, Bellbrook Valley, Kennick, Roadford, St. Merryn, Stithians, Tavistock, Temple, Tree Meadow and Watercress. The semi-finals are at Bake, Temple and Watercress and the finals, at Tavistock, are on the first two Sundays in October.

There are over £3,000 worth of prizes including M&S vouchers, lines, day tickets, garden statues and hooks. Entry is free provided the minimum sponsorship of £20 per person is raised. Anglers who wish to enter please contact the fisheries or Sue Gould, Marketing Manager of the Devon & Exeter Spastics Society: Tel Exeter 01392 873543.

Heat Dates:

St Merryn	Padstow	01841 533090	Sun 1st April
Bake Fishery	Saltash	0498 585836	Sun 8th April
Stithians		01209 821431	Sun 29th April
Kennick Reservoir	Bovey Tracey	01626 206027	Sun 6th May
Bellbrook Valley	Tiverton	01398 351292	Sun 13th May
Temple	Bodmin	01208 821730	Sun 24th June
Tree Meadow	Hayle	07971 107156	Sun 8th July
Roadford Lake	Okehampton	01392 873543	Sun 22nd July
Watercress	Chudleigh	01626 852168	Sun 29th July
Tavistock Trout	Tavistock	01822 615441	Sun 2nd Sept

sw lakes trust *Trout Fishing*

PREMIER RAINBOW FISHERIES

KENNICK - Nr Christow, Devon.
Permits: Self Service Kiosk
Season: 24 March - 31 October
Best Flies: Black Gnat/Montana/Damsel Nymph
Biggest Fish 1997: 10lb 14oz Rainbow.
Information: (01647) 277587
WIMBLEBALL LAKE - Nr Dulverton, Somerset.
Permits: Self Service at Hill Farm Barn
Season: 24 March - 31 October
Best Flies: Montana/Soldier Palmer/Buzzer.
Biggest Fish: 10lb 12oz Rainbow.
Information: Office hours (01398) 371372
SIBLYBACK LAKE - Nr Liskeard, Cornwall.
Permits: Self Service Kiosk at Watersports Centre
Season: 24 March - 31 October
Best Flies: Viva/Black & Peacock/Montana
Information: Ranger (01579) 342366

PREMIER BROWN TROUT FISHERY

ROADFORD - Nr Okehampton, Devon.
Permits: Angling and Watersports Centre at Lower Goodacre.
Season: 24 March - 12 October
Biggest Fish: 8lb 4oz Brown.
Information: (01409) 211514

BROWN TROUT BOAT FISHERY

TOTTIFORD - Nr Christow, Devon
BOAT ONLY
Permits: Kennick self service
Season: 15 March - 12 October
Information: (01647) 277587

INTERMEDIATE RAINBOW TROUT

STITHIANS - Nr Redruth, Cornwall.
Permits:
Stithians Watersports Centre (01209) 860301.
Sandy's Store, 7 Penryn St, Redruth (01209) 214877
Season: 15 March - 12 October
Information: Ranger (01579) 342366
WISTLANDPOUND - Nr Sth Molton, Devon.
Permits:
Post Office in Challacombe (01598) 763229.
The Kingfisher, Barnstaple (01271) 344919.
Camera & Picture, Combe Martin (01271) 883275.
Variety Sports, Ilfracombe (01271) 862039.
Season: 15 March - 12 October
Information: Ranger (01288) 321262

LOW COST RAINBOW & BROWN

BURRATOR - Nr Yelverton, Devon.
Permits: Esso Garage, Yelverton.
Season: 15 March - 12 October
Information: (01837) 871565
COLLIFORD LAKE - Nr Bodmin, Cornwall.
Permits: Colliford Tavern.
Season: 15 March - 12 October
Information: Ranger (01579) 342366
FERNWORTHY LAKE - Nr Chagford, Devon.
Permits: Self Service Kiosk
Season: 1 April - 12 October
Best Flies: Black Gnat/Invicta/G&H Sedge
Information: (01837) 871565

FREE TROUT FISHING

MELDON - Nr Okehampton, Devon.
Free to holders of a valid E.A. Rod Licence and is zoned into spinning, bait and fly.
Season: 15 March - 12 October
AVON DAM - South Brent, Devon.
Angling by spinning, fly or bait and is free to valid E.A. licence holders.
Season: 15 March - 12 October
VENFORD - Nr Ashburton, Devon.
Free to holders of valid E.A. Rod Licence and can be fished by spinning, bubble float and bait.
Season: 15 March - 12 October.
CROWDY RESERVOIR - Nr Camelford, Cornwall.
Free to holders of valid E.A. Rod Licence.
Season: 15 March - 12 October.

25

Fly Fishing for Sea Trout

Roy Buckingham

It has been said to me by several trout anglers over the years, that you must be mad to go fishing at night for sea trout. Rushing home from work, gulping down your evening meal that your partner has lovingly prepared for you, and then a quick peck on the cheek and you disappear for the rest of the night.

Over the years I have taken a great many anglers on their first sea trout fishing expedition, and have found there was an occasional angler who said their night vision was almost nil, and their casting went to pieces at night, they would not have missed it for the world, but would never do it again. Others would go out at night if accompanied by someone else, because they were scared of the dark, and that is nothing to be ashamed of. A heron screeching, a sheep coughing, or a herd of inquisitive young bullocks galloping towards you can be scary at night if you are not used to it. The majority, however, get hooked on night fishing and feverishly wait for the sea trout season to begin each year.

Most of my sea trout fishing is done on the Tamar and Lyd, one of the main tributaries. A few larger sea trout enter the lower reaches in March and April, but where I fish on the middle reaches we do not see any significant numbers until the second half of June.

If you have not fished at night before, it is always a great help to have someone who knows the water take you out during the day, and show you where the fish lie and where to cast from to avoid trees and bushes. One problem at night is knowing exactly how much line you have outside the rod tip. There is nothing more annoying than pulling your leader through the rod tip at night. An easy way to avoid this is to pull out a rod length of line, and then practise pulling off exactly a foot of line at the time. Pull off ten feet, cast it out, and then pull in ten feet, and you should still have a rod length outside the rod tip. Try it first in the daytime with your eyes closed. For night fishing I use a rod of nine or nine and a half feet that takes a size six or seven line. Most of my fishing is done with a floating line, and a leader of around nine feet tapered to eight pounds breaking strain.

Sea trout are unpredictable, so you must be prepared to change your size of fly, and sometimes your method of presentation. I well remember fishing the tail of Quarry Pool on the Tamar with my usual team of three flies. After covering all the likely places without a single touch. I changed the tail fly for a large muddler minnow, greased it up and skated it across the surface. In the next half hour I caught six sea trout all from the same spot. If I had not changed my fly, I think I would have had a blank that night.

My reasons for fishing three flies is to save time having to change the fly size, and of course the flies will fish at different depths as well. Normally I would use something like a size 12 Alexandra or Coachman on the top dropper, a

Adrian Armstead with a superb 8lb 4oz Brownie from the improving Roadford Lake.

size 8 Silver Invicta in the middle, and a big fly on the tail such as a black lure or a palmered fly such as a Zulu on a size 6 or even a 4 long-shank hook. Do not be tempted to use droppers until you feel proficient at using just one fly at night, or you could end up with one horrendous tangle in your leader.

Always try to arrive at the river in good time before it is dark, and wait until you cannot see the colour of the grass, then you can start fishing. If you cannot wait, then fish another pool as the light is fading. This can often be productive, but could spoil it for night fishing.

Sea trout will often lie in just a few inches of water at night, so always start with a short line and then gradually extend it, fishing it back on a slow retrieve. When you feel a take it could be anything from a gentle pluck to a really savage snatch, so do not strike too hard or you may end up being broken even on a strong leader.

Never leave anything lying around at night. It is surprising how your can put something down and the next moment it has disappeared on a dark night. You can buy adhesive luminous tape which can be used on nets, fly boxes, priest etc., or even a thermos flask. One angler who had fished hard for a couple of hours, decided to stop for a well earned cup of coffee, he sat down and poured his coffee into a mug. Just at that moment a sea trout splashed in the pool beside him. Creeping down to the water's edge he cast out and caught it. Feeling rather jubilant he sat down once again, picked up his now lukewarm coffee and took a large mouthful, only to spit it out again… While he was away, a large slug had crawled up his mug and decided to share his coffee ! The grass was wet with heavy dew, and when he switched his torch on, he saw that everything was covered in slugs, including the coat he was sitting on and his sandwich box.

All kinds of things happen at night. I remember sitting down at 1am to have a cup of tea. There I was, quietly sipping my tea and listening to the river in complete darkness, when my legs and bottom felt wet. We had not had rain for a couple of weeks, and the ground was bone dry… After switching on the torch I found myself sitting in the middle of the biggest fresh cow pat you have ever seen. You can imagine what my wife was thinking when she opened the back door next morning and found my trousers and a pair of white underpants stained in a sort of olive green lying on the step!

If you do not like going out at night it is perfectly possible to catch sea trout during the day. An odd fish is taken when salmon or trout fishing, but you will catch more if you fish specially for them. My normal outfit is what I use for trout. A rod of 8'5 or 9' with a size six floating line. Because sea trout are so easily scared during the day, use a leader as long as you can manage. My own formula is made up as follows. Buy a Leeda Profil Knotless salmon leader tapered to ten pounds, which I needle knot to the end of my line. To this, add 24" of 8lb, 18" of 6lb, 12" of 4lb and 3ft of 3lb. A leader tapered in this way will present the fly very gently on the water, and the heavy butt section will help straighten it out. Braided leaders tend to absorb water and will fall more heavily no matter how careful you are.

For daytime fishing I use small weighted wet flies such as coachman or black and peacock spider, or goldhead nymphs, hares ear or prince, sizes 12 and 14 or even smaller at times. On our small to medium sized rivers fish all methods upstream during the day. Wet flies and nymphs should be cast upstream or up and across and allowed to sink for three or four seconds before starting to retrieve slightly faster than the current. If there is little or no current, use the induced take method with a weighted nymph. Cast upstream and wait for the nymph to sink almost down to the bottom, and then slowly raise the rod tip, drawing the nymph up towards the surface.

Sometimes you will see them feeding on surface flies, but they can be taken on dry fly even when you do not see any rising. It is always a great advantage if you can see the fish, because if a dry fly is cast well upstream and allowed to drift over the fish, I have found this much less effective than casting into the sea trout's window of vision, which can sometimes create an immediate response. If after two or three casts the fly is refused, cast a little further upstream and retrieve the line a little faster than the current to create a wake on the surface. This will often produce a fish when all else fails.

Steve Ebdon with a 6lb 5oz Rainbow. Kennick

Summer spates will bring fresh sea trout and salmon into the rivers and, as the water is clearing, sea trout will be easier to catch under these conditions. Use a sinking line and a leader of eight or nine feet tapered to eight pounds. Size of fly will depend on the height and colour of the water. One of my own favourites is a waddington type silver stoats tail between one and two inches in length. Fish the fly downstream and across in the tails of the pools as you would for night fishing. There is no need to retrieve, in fact you might have to mend the line upstream to slow the fly down a little.

The great thing about this kind of fishing is you could catch anything from a cheeky seven inch brownie to a lively sea trout, or even the occasional salmon.

Dave Pilkington, with a night caught Sea Trout

Trout Fishing in the South Wessex Area

By Matt Carter

Rivers

The South Wessex Area encompasses many 'chalk streams' which are nationally famous for fly-fishing for trout. These include the Upper Avon at Salisbury and associated tributaries, the Rivers Frome, Piddle and River Allen a tributary of the River Stour.

Fishing access to these waters is generally controlled by local owners, estates, syndicates and in a limited way by local angling clubs.

Many of these waters are currently stocked with brown trout, however several fisheries are now turning away from this to catch and release, promoting natural production and 'wilder' fish populations. Further details regarding access are given in this guide.

Stillwaters

There are several stillwater 'put and take' fisheries spread across this area. These are generally stocked with rainbow trout although a few specialise in brown trout.

In the north of the area good stillwater fly fishing can be found at Steeple Langford Fisheries near Salisbury. In the West of the area good fly fishing can be found at the Wessex Chalk streams Ltd site near Tolpuddle.

Other notable fisheries can be found at Damerham and Rockford near Ringwood.

CONRAD VOSS BARK

1913-2000

In the late autumn of 2000, the South West lost its best-known fly fisherman with the death of Conrad Voss Bark at the age of 87. After starting as a local reporter on a London paper in 1935, Conrad went on to a distinguished career in journalism and broadcasting, his time as parliamentary correspondent for the BBC in the 1950s and 1960s making him a household name.

However, it was as a fly fisherman and angling writer that he was best known to the fishing fraternity, not only in the south west but also nationally and internationally. I well remember, at the time of his fame as a TV reporter, realising that Conrad Voss Bark was a fisherman when Trout & Salmon magazine published an article by him about Blagdon Lake some 40 years ago. Following his retirement from the BBC in 1970, he turned increasingly to writing about his great love of fly fishing and contributed countless articles to angling journals, but it was in his capacity as angling correspondent for The Times over a lengthy period that he took fishing matters to a far wider audience through his regular fishing column in that paper. He also wrote a number of fishing books including Fishing for Lake Trout, A Fly on the Water, The Encyclopaedia of Flyfishing, Conrad Voss Bark on Flyfishing, The Dry Fly - Progress since Halford and A History of Flyfishing.

For many years, Conrad was a familiar face at the Arundell Arms, the fishing hotel at Lifton owned by his wife Anne, where he contributed actively to the fly-fishing courses for which the hotel is famous. My last memory of Conrad is seeing him in the bar of the Arundell Arms in the summer of 2000 when, in spite of increasing deafness, we were able to discuss fishing matters for one last time.

Mike Weaver

Westcountry Rivers Trust

Registered Charity No. 1045806

Support the work of the Westcountry Rivers Trust today and give something back to our rivers!

On November 13th 2000 America declared that its last remaining stocks of wild Atlantic salmon are in danger of extinction and designated the fish as an endangered species. It will now be a federal offence to take salmon from any of the eight rivers of the Gulf of Maine in which the USA's only known natural populations of Atlantic salmon are struggling to survive. The US Fish and Wildlife Service and the National Marine Fisheries Service have announced the listing after a biological study that found stocks had reached "dangerously low levels".

In the UK although the mechanisms are not yet fully understood it is fair to say that urban development and a legacy of successive government's policies directed toward the intensification of agriculture is adversely affecting many of our rivers and their natural ecosystems. Our record of sustainable resource management has been poor and new threats in the form of global warming and climate change now appear to be with us.

New destabilising diseases and alien species are also having an impact. Examples include, Gyrodactylus salaris killing salmon on the continent, the invasion of Japanese Knotweed and Himalayan Balsam along our riverbanks, invasive pond weeds, Alder disease and American mink. General declines in sensitive species like salmon or indeed for that matter water voles or farmland birds are key environmental indicators that we ignore at our peril.

Like many other groups, the achievements of the Westcountry Rivers Trust have only been possible through effective working partnerships with the Environment Agency. Now the Government has announced yet further cuts in the EA's fisheries funding we must redouble our efforts and do all we can to safeguard our rivers and their biodiversity and find ways of working together ever more effectively.

New Rivers Trust headquartes

The Westcountry Rivers Trust has recently moved into new office headquarters at Lifton near Launceston, just opposite the renowned Arundell Arms Hotel. The new offices are well placed on the A30 corridor for the Rivers Trust's team to provide good coverage across the South West region and its eighteen major river catchments. Do feel free to drop in if you are in the area, the full address and contact details can be found at the end of this article.

Tamar 2000 Project

The major four year programme of restoration and rehabilitation work under the Trust's Tamar 2000 Project funded largely through MAFF and EU Objective 5B has now been completed. The innovative partnership with the Environment Agency, South West Water, the Wetlands Ecosystems Research Group, BDB Associates and others has proven a great success. The project has considerably exceeded its original targets and has demonstrated itself a key "pathfinder", developing new integrated partnership approaches to address fishery, environmental and economic issues of common concern. In particular it is the farmers that deserve the greatest credit for the project's success. Some 500 farmers and landowners received visits as part of the project with over 300 working up detailed integrated land management plans with the project's Scientific Advisory team.

- Plans cover an area of around 25,000 hectares; their aims include:
- Reduction of erosion and the sedimentation of salmonid spawning gravels
- Reduction of diffuse pollution and improvement of river water quality
- Conservation and restoration of wetlands and their function.
- Restoration of river corridor habitats
- Sustainability of local communities that maintain the river

It took a combined effort for Curtis and Josh Haling to land this 4lb 12oz Rainbow while spinning in the any method lake at Temple.

GAME

TOPP TACKLE

63 Station Rd., Taunton, Somerset TA1 1PA

Tel: 01823 282518

SPECIALISTS IN GAME FISHING EQUIPMENT

Large Fly Tying Section

We are just 5 minutes from the M5 (junction 25)
Head for the cricket ground - Railway Station.
Do not follow town centre signs.

7 Acres of Fishing on Beautiful Bodmin Moor

TROUT FISHERY

Stocked with Rainbows and Browns to double figures

On site facilities include Toilet, Hut, Refreshments, tackle for hire/sale.
Permits: **EA LICENCE REQD TO FISH.** from £5.50-2 fish to £20.50-5 fish.
Club Membership available - 10% discount on all tickets
'Any method' fishing available
Booking advised - Tel: 01208 821730 Mobile 07787 704966

Bake Fishing Lakes

Open 365 Days a Year

8am to Dusk

3 FLY LAKES

Catch and release for Rainbows & Browns to 15lb

ROD HIRE TUITION

Contact Tony Lister

E.A. ROD LICENCES AVAILABLE

Trerulefoot, Saltash, Cornwall. Tel 01752 849027 & 0498 583836
Email: tony.lister@bakelakes.co.uk. Web: www.bakelakes.co.uk

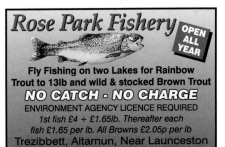

Rose Park Fishery

OPEN ALL YEAR

Fly Fishing on two Lakes for Rainbow Trout to 13lb and wild & stocked Brown Trout

NO CATCH · NO CHARGE

ENVIRONMENT AGENCY LICENCE REQUIRED
1st fish £4 + £1.65lb. Thereafter each
fish £1.65 per lb. All Browns £2.05p per lb

Trezibbett, Altarnun, Near Launceston

Tel: (01566) 86278

ORVIS ~ INNIS

Innis Moor, Penwithick, St Austell.
Open all year, 8am to Dusk, 7days a week
Three lakes totalling 15 acres
- TACKLE SHOP -
Fully Licenced Club/Hotel, B&B, Full or half board
Caravan & Camping Site
25 pitch site with toilet & shower block. Static Van available
For further information contact Mrs. P. Winch
Telephone 01726 851162
Just 1.25 miles from THE EDEN PROJECT

Bridge House Hotel

& LICENSED RESTAURANT

Salmon & Trout Fishing on the Exe

Close to Wimbleball & Clatworthy

Superb Cuisine - Sporting Breaks
All Year round trout fishing at local fisheries
£25 per person, per night including Breakfast

Bampton, Devon. Tel/Fax: 01398 331298

33

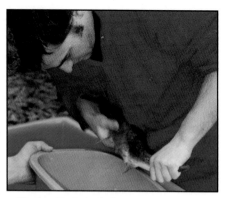

Final outputs include:

- Over 53 kilometres of riverbank fencing erected
- Over 9 kilometres of riverbank coppicing completed as part of an ongoing programme
- Erosion control measures implemented at over 90 key sites
- 6 demonstration sites established
- Over 70 salmonid spawning fords improved
- 30 obstructions to migratory fish cleared or bypassed
- Over 60 buffer strips and habitat improvement works completed

Although it is early days yet, from the EA's recent electro-fishing results there appears to be a good correlation between the type of works that have taken place and the presence respectively of both fry and parr populations. As well as benefits for both the fishery and agriculture the Trust is awaiting the outcome of a PhD study to establish the wider biodiversity changes brought about by the project.

Deep Substrate Salmon Incubation Boxes

During the development and successful trial over two years on the River Tamar of deep substrate spawning boxes many thousands of fry have been released. The spawning box programme, in partnership with the Environment Agency and the TTFA takes vulnerable salmon eggs through to fry. This winter the EA (Cornwall area) with the help of some sterling work by Bob Wellard of the Endsleigh Fishery is extending the Tamar programme and the opportunity for other associations to test this system on other Cornish rivers.

Westcountry Rivers Project (Phase I)

Focusing on the River Taw and Torridge catchments that fall within the Objective 5B area, the Westcountry Rivers Project (Phase 1) runs until April 2001, the Rivers Bray (Taw), Waldon and Lew (Torridge) are receiving priority attention. The project has been well received by farmers and fishery owners and builds on the excellent work already carried out in North Devon by the Environment Agency in partnership with riparian owners and their associations.

Around 330 farmers and river owners have joined the project and are working with the Trust's Scientific advisors and the wider community to develop sustainable catchment land management practices. It will help conserve and restore environmental quality for both people and wildlife while delivering economic gains. As in the Tamar 2000 Project this will be achieved in particular by optimising farm inputs, employing best management practices and the management and restoration of key river and wetland habitats with benefits to water quality, fisheries and other wildlife, linked to recreation and tourism development. The project will cover some 22,000 hectares and protect around 100 kilometres of river corridor. Funding is mainly through MAFF and the European Agricultural Guidance and Guarantee Fund.

Dartmoor Wild Trout Project

The Wild Trout Society and the Environment Agency have been investigating the status and requirements of wild brown trout in Devon. For the second phase of the Wild Trout Society's work on Dartmoor the Westcountry Rivers Trust were commissioned to take an in-depth look at the possible causes of declines in stocks of mature trout and to recommend solutions.

The first findings revealed that both juveniles and adults required in-stream refuge, overhanging banks, plenty of woody debris in the river and, in the case of adult fish, reasonable stream depth. It is also emerging that although trout are present in good numbers up to 15 cm, there is often a sharp drop off above that length. A contributing factor on some stretches may be the territorial nature of larger trout. In the clear water of Dartmoor streams, fish can easily see each other and that can reduce numbers in the

35

longer open pools, thus explaining the greater productivity on stretches which are broken up into numerous small pools. It may be the case that many trout over 15 cm migrate or "become" sea trout.

To address the lack of knowledge on the distribution and movement of Dartmoor trout, the Trust have undertaken a tagging study and in the summer of 2000 about 200 trout of various sizes were caught by electro-fishing on Cherry Brook and marked with a flourescent orange elastomer compound. The catch included a brown of 48 cm, demonstrating the size to which fish grow on these tiny streams.

A new catch-return card is being supplied with Duchy permits so that anglers can report the capture of tagged fish and where they were caught, and future electro-fishing surveys of the sample site will also provide data from the tagging scheme. With the Westcountry Rivers Trust's interim report now complete, the next phase is to identify which management techniques can be implemented in 2001 to improve the trout habitat.

Cornwall & EU Objective 1

The Westcountry Rivers Trust are working closely with the Environment Agency and other partners to identify opportunities for community, environmental and fisheries development projects under Cornwall's EU Objective 1 programme. Please contact the Trust office or the Environment Agency office in Bodmin for further information.

Angling 2000- an anglers token scheme

Rivers Trust Advisors working in the Tamar, Taw and Torridge catchments have identified the development of the angling resource as a valuable farm diversification income and a step towards sustainability. Individual farmers and riparian owners generally find it difficult to exploit the potential of their own small stretches of fishing but through the formation of a network marketing scheme the full potential for angler and owner may be realised.

The range of water is considerable with salmon, sea trout, grayling, trout and dace available. The only common factor being they are all wild fish. To take advantage of the Angling 2000 scheme, anglers may purchase books of tokens together with a booklet giving a full description of the scheme and the beats available including directions and where to park. At the car park for each beat there will be a post box, on arrival the angler will place the correct number of tokens into the box. To find out more about the scheme ring the Trust's new office number below or visit the web site.

Your support is vital

To continue its important work and to improve the opportunities of raising money from outside grant sources to help coarse and game fishing in the region, the Trust needs the goodwill and support of Westcountry anglers. If you can afford it, join the Westcountry Rivers Trust as a "Supporter". The Trust asks individuals to covenant £50 a year (less that £1 per week) towards its work and asks groups, clubs, businesses and organisations to covenant £100 per year. In return the Trust will send you its Newsletter and invitations to its events, river walks and other activities. You can also purchase a Westcountry Rivers Trust tie in light blue with the Trusts distinctive logo @ £10 plus £1 p&p (cheques payable to Westcountry Rivers Limited please).

For further information contact:

Westcountry Rivers Trust, Fore Street, Lifton, Devon, PL16 0AA
Telephone: 01566-784488
Fax: 01566-784404
Web address:
www.wrt.org.uk
E-mail: wrt@wrt.org.uk

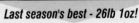

The South West Federation of Fly Fishers

West Country Federation of Fly Fishers

The South West Federation of Fly Fishers belongs to the Confederation of English Fly Fishers. The Confederation is, amongst other things, responsible for running National and International Fly Fishing Teams and Competitions. The grassroots of all the National and International Competitions are the Regional Eliminators run by Federations all over the Country.

The South West Federation runs Eliminators at Chew Valley Lake. This years dates are as follows

FIRST ELIMINATOR: SUNDAY 29 APRIL
SECOND ELIMINATOR: SUNDAY 27 MAY
FINAL ELIMINATOR: SUNDAY 24 JUNE

Competitors can ONLY enter ONE of the first two eliminators and if successful would qualify for the Final Eliminator.

Thirty competitors compete in the Final Eliminator. In 2000 there were sixteen places available for the Loch Style National, and we would hope for a similar number in 2001.

The Loch Style National in 2001 is at RUTLAND WATER on SATURDAY, SEPT 1st.

ELIGIBILITY

Anyone can enter provided that they are over 18 years of age, and have been domiciled in ENGLAND for 3 years.

Competitors can ONLY enter eliminators in ONE Region in any one year. Anyone who has previously fished at International Level for another Country is NOT eligible to fish.

If you are interested in competitive Fly Fishing, with the chance to fish for England, write to me at the address below or give me a ring.

J.A. Loud,
153/155 East Street,
Bedminster,
BRISTOL BS3 4EJ
Tel (Daytime) 0117 9872050
Tel (Evenings) 0117 9232166

The WCFFF provides eligible adults with a yearly chance to fly fish for England. Qualifiers from Devon and Cornwall compete in the National championships aiming to be in England's international squad for the following year. The spring and autumn teams fish against Ireland, Scotland and Wales in events called the Home Internationals. This is loch style fishing to International rules on stillwater.

2001 ELIMINATOR:
Wimbleball Lake
Sunday 13 May, arrive 08.45

There is also an annual river eliminator usually held each spring. Those qualifying go on to the National rivers championship seeking the chance to fish internationally on running water.

Both eliminators are routes into England's European and World teams.

The W.C.F.F.F. also runs an informal event by boat and bank at Wimbleball on Sunday 26 August 2001.

Put your name on the mailing lists!

Contact Peter Page (chairman),
Woodlands House,
Woodland,
Ashburton TQ13 7LN.
Tel/Fax 01364 654395
Email: PetePageUK@aol.com
www.wrt.org.uk
E-mail: wrt@wrt.org.uk

Trout Fly Dressing

in the West Country Tradition

John Bowden

The long tradition of West Country trout fly dressing is rooted in strong beliefs that only the finest materials should be employed to make artificial fly patterns which will consistently take trout.

West Country anglers with legendary names reinforce the evidence supporting this approach.

H.E. Cutcliffe, the surgeon whose Blue Uprights were made according to strict standards of hackle colour and quality.

The Reverend Hughes, who wrote under the nom-de-plume "Devonshire Fisherman" and tied dry flies "speckled with the gold of sunset".

R.S. Austen, the Tiverton tobacconist chiefly remembered for inventing the fly which Skues named "Tups Indispensable".

James Rowe of Barnstaple, tacklemaker, gunsmith, breeder and judge of poultry who sternly rejected hackles which today we would give our eye teeth to possess.

Claude Wade, the barrister with meticulous attention to detail in court and on the Exmoor streams.

William Heath of Dulverton, besieged by trout fishermen on the Barle for dressings of his "Olive Quill Gnat".

Fred Tout, who took over Heaths business and renamed the O.Q.G. as "Touts Beige".

And **Peter Deane**, the courageous disabled fly tying angler and inventor of the "Beacon Beige" with his inspired addition of a red game hackle.

It can be argued that the best hackles in Britain came from Devon where thousands of people bred poultry for eggs, meat, exhibitions and cockfighting. Hundreds of farmers, landowners and members of the nobility kept a run of birds carefully selected for the "pit". The best fighting cocks coincidentally produced the best hackles in shape and stiffness of fibre. Above all the colours, mainly blues and brassy duns, were superb.

The contributions made to West Country fly dressing by the famous anglers named above require deeper study and a much longer article than this so I will restrict my observations to James Rowe whose poultry breeding was very much in the Devon style. He was absolutely strict about the quality of hackles from his flock and ruthlessly culled birds which did not meet his high standards and what he saw as the proper requirements of the exhibition bench at poultry shows. Flies purchased in his Barnstaple High Street shop were dressed with hackles of prize winning standards.

Rowe's reputation as an expert breeder of poultry was widely respected and led to a demand for his services as a Judge at many poultry shows, including the great Cardiff show of 1893 which included a class of birds with specific suitability for fly dressing. Twenty eight years later Rowe's birds were still in the top rank. In the Fishing Gazette of February 19th 1921 an article entitled "May Days on Exmoor Streams" by well known angler J.H. Collins praised Rowe for his undyed true blue hackles and scarce brassy dun hackles.

The Plymouth Rock was first introduced from the U.S.A. in 1871. "British Poultry Standards", the bible for poultry breeders, records that "... the barred rock came to us as a dual purpose

NEWHOUSE FISHERY

Moreleigh, Totnes

Beginners Lake £5 plus £1.80lb for all fish caught

MAIN LAKE prices as Watercress

BIG FISH LAKE

Average Fish 9lb! £5 plus fish at £2.00lb

FLIES, ROD HIRE, TACKLE, TUITION - ALL AVAILABLE

NO E.A. ROD LICENCE REQUIRED AT BOTH FISHERIES
(Lakes covered by general E.A. Licence)

Record Rainbow 1999 - 19lb 2oz

TELEPHONE: 01548 821426

WATERCRESS FARM

WF&I

TROUT FISHERY

CHUDLEIGH, NEWTON ABBOT

NOW MANAGED BY NEWHOUSE FISHERY

RECORD RAINBOW - 19lb 15oz
RECORD BROWN - 8lb 15oz

Three crystal clear spring fed lakes stocked daily with home reared Rainbow and Brown Trout.

ALDER 'SPECIMEN' LAKE - 3lb plus
Tiger, Brown, Brook & Rainbow!
4 Fish - £30. 2 Fish - £17.

SUPPLIERS OF TOP QUALITY RESTOCKING TROUT

£20.00	5 Fish
£17.00	4 Fish
£14.00	3 Fish
£11.00	2 Fish

**FOR FURTHER DETAILS
RING (01626) 852 168**

Email: watercress.fishery@btinternet.com

41

breed, but it was developed to an exhibition ideal in which body size and frontal development were neglected in order to secure "long, narrow, finely barred feathers". There can be little doubt that Rowe exercised his skill and influence on the development of a Plymouth Rock breeding line in which the priority was superb fly dressing hackles rather than chicken meat. Rowe's aim was the classic description set out in "British Poultry Standards" - "ground colour, white with bluish tinge, barred with black with a beetle-green sheen. The barring is to be straight, moderately narrow, of equal breadth and sharply defined, to continue through the shafts of the feathers. Every feather to finish with a black tip". These were the typical Plymouth Rock barred hackles demanded by the best dressers of west country dry flies around the start of the 20th century.

Regrettably, the capes and hackles now sold as Plymouth Rock/Grizzle are inferior. I have examined hundreds in Britain, U.S.A. and Holland and have come to the sad conclusion that straight, narrow, parallel barring of the true Plymouth Rock colour has probably been bred out.

Present day barring is normally accepted as chevron shaped, rather like the stripes on a sergeant's tunic and it is very rare to find the black barring with "beetle-green sheen".

Only a tiny minority of breeders and fly dressers are concerned about straight barring. As an honourable exception the late Dave Collyer in his excellent "Fly Dressing II" declared "… the straighter the barring of black on white the better the hackle".

Modern fly tiers who are fortunate to find Plymouth Rock / Grizzle hackles which meet the requirements of "British Poultry Standards" will be on the way to dressing the Beige and the Beacon Beige to the levels of William Heath, Fred Tout and Peter Deane.

Future Flies

Over the last 25 years, Stafford Moor's reputation for quality flies was very well known, there was always a very large selection available, many of which were unique and only obtainable at the fishery and most of these were tied by Marilyn Nott.

Stafford Moor is now under new ownership but the trout anglers amongst you concerned over its new role as a coarse fishery can be assured that many of the lakes will remain stocked with the same quality trout and Marylin's flies will still be available.

She started producing a variation of montanas, then the damsels received the same treatment: there must have been over 20 patterns of cats-whisker, a selection of fritzs, daddies, pheasant tails, gold heads found their way onto most patterns, even deerhair bombs.

Marilyn also ties fully dressed salmon flies for picture frames and fishing magazine fly patterns can also be made to order.

For those special flies, try Future Flies by Marilyn Nott.

43

Tackle Review

Fly Rods

Orvis Trident TL 9ft 7pce 8wt. Rod only £635.
Kit with Battenkill Lg.Arbor/line/backing £733.

Multiple section fly rods have become popular recently and rightly so in my opinion.

Modern materials and manufacturing have eliminated the old problems of 'stiff' sections where the ferrules used to be and the action of these rods does not suffer at all. This example is no exception and the Orvis TL range have

already established themselves as top flight rods. This model continues the tradition, handles superbly and the whole lot fits in a superb leather clad rod tube measuring just 17.5". Partnered with the superb Battenkill large arbor (reviewed last year) this is an excellent 'go anywhere' outfit. Highly recommended.

Carbotec Elite 9ft 6in 3pce 7/8wt. £229

This new rod from Carbotec is an ultra light model, weighing in at just 104g. This is an excellent reservoir rod with a fairly 'tippy' action but loads of power, favouring an 8 weight line and casting excellent distance. As I've come to expect with Carbotec rods loads of power does not equate to lack of 'feel' and you get the best of both worlds. This is a true local rod, built in Exeter or Buckfastleigh and attractively finished in translucent black. Guides and reel seat are the excellent Fuji and the handle is grade A Portugese cork. At £229, including 12 months unconditional guarantee, this rod will easily compete with anything in it's class.

Orvis Trident TL 8ft 2 pce 1wt. Rod only £405.
Kit with Battenkill/line/backing £509.
Orvis 'Silver Label' version of Rod £210

This is an ultra light setup, perfect for the small river natural Brown fishing which predominates throughout the westcountry.

Finish is as you would expect from Orvis and the 'friction' reel fittings which used to be common but have been replaced by 'uplocking' devices, work perfectly and help keep the rod weight down to just 1 3/4 oz!

I can still cast an excellent length with it and presentation with such a light setup is superb.

Bruce & Walker Combi-Rod 7ft/9ft 5wt. £420

Another river trout rod with a twist. You get two interchangeable butt sections affording you two different rods. Yet again modern materials and manufacturing mean there is no discernable compromise involved in this two rods for the price of one theory.

This would perfectly suit the westcountry fly fisherman who frequents the local trout streams with the occasional foray to the local rainbow fishery where he may be a bit stretched with a 7' setup. Or maybe use the 9ft when the peal start running?

Contact the makers at...
Orvis, Exeter 01392 272599. www.orvis.co.uk
Carbotec at Exeter Angling Centre 01392 436404. www.carbotec.co.uk
Bruce & Walker 01487 813764 www.bruceandwalker.co.uk

═BRISTOL═ WATER fisheries

CHEW VALLEY LAKE
BLAGDON LAKE
THE BARROWS
LITTON LAKE

Catch rates were again very high at our fisheries in 2000, with anglers catching 3.4 trout, on average, per visit. Since over 52,000 hard-fighting rainbow and brown trout were landed over the season this meant an awful lot of enjoyable visits and a huge number of happy anglers!

We opened our new Woodford Lodge in April and it has proved to be a very popular venue. Anglers are now provided with an attractive new building housing a full scale tackle shop, a comfortable lounge and restaurant providing breakfasts, lunches and evening meals and a bar.

We continue to offer a friendly and helpful fishery service to all from the Lodge even though it is now open to the public as well as to anglers. Those seeking peace and quiet can still visit Blagdon Lodge which still caters only to anglers.

The World Fly Fishing Championships were held at Chew and Blagdon last May and were very successful with anglers from 22 countries enjoying good but testing sport in tricky conditions. Local anglers gave advice to competitors on practice days and many new friendships were forged. We enjoyed hosting the prestigious event and the standard set by our first class fisheries were warmly appreciated by all the visiting anglers.

Disabled anglers may fish from a special wheely boat, at reduced rates, at Blagdon and we have priority bank fishing spots suitable for those with limited walking ability marked out at Chew and Blagdon. Our Lodges are all accessible to wheelchair users as are the services we provide.

CHEW

at 1,200 acres, is our largest lake and it lies some seven miles due south of Bristol. It is most renowned for loch style boat fishing and has a fleet of 31 motor boats, each equipped with an outboard motor. There is plenty of room on the lake for expert and pleasure angler alike and the scenery and bird life are a real bonus for those with time to look around. May and June are usually, but not always, the best months and are the time of year when a variety of buzzers hatch and bring the trout to the surface. Casting to rising fish and hooking and playing our superb home grown rainbows, which average well over 2lbs, is the pinnacle of stillwater fly fishing.

Bank fishing can also be very good at Chew, particularly early in April, through May and June and then again in September and October. There are many miles of uncrowded lake margin to choose from and though the main season ends in mid October we continue for winter fishing up until the end of November.

BLAGDON

is 440 acres in area and has 16 rowing boats. Anglers are welcome to use their own electric outboards and a local pub operates a hire service. With no noisy petrol engines the fishery is a peaceful and beautiful place to fish. In recent seasons there have been less buzzers than at Chew but more sedges and damsel flies and the nature of the fishing is thus slightly different.

The banks provide very good sport and there are numerous hot-spots at all of which you will find ample space to cast a line. The surrounding meadows support cowslips and native orchids and overhead you will often see buzzards riding the thermals and hoards of swallows and martins competing with the trout to take the flies; fishing at Blagdon is about more than just catching fish!

THE BARROWS

are three reservoirs of 60, 40, and 25 acres lying close to Bristol on either side of the A38 some three miles out of the city. They are bank only fisheries, though we allow some float tubing

Roddy Rae returns a Salmon to the River Mole.
Highbullen Hotel

by arrangement. No.1 reservoir is brown trout only and No.2 rainbows only. No.3 contains a mixture of species. We stock slightly smaller fish, so permit prices cost less, but the Barrows perhaps provide the most reliable bank sport of all our fisheries. The evening rise can be a very profitable time with buzzer and sedge hatches giving great sport to rising fish.

LITTON LAKE.

For the second year Litton lakes will be open for public fishing. There are two lakes: the lower is 8 acres and is the main fishery stocked with rainbows and browns, while the upper is 11 acres but reduces in size through the summer and is stocked mostly with brown trout. There is a rowing boat on each lake and a permit will allow you to fish at both. The limit will be 5 trout per rod. The fishery will only be available on Fridays, Saturdays and Sundays and bookings will be made at Woodford Lodge.

PERMITS.

The centre for bookings, enquiries and tackle sales is Woodford Lodge at Chew. All kinds of permit are issued here. At Blagdon our half-timbered lodge offers a lesser range of facilities but is still a comfortable place to eat your lunch or warm up in front of a log fire and the building is staffed all morning for permits, enquiries, small tackle sales and advice. At the Barrows there is a self-service kiosk for permits and separate lavatories and shelters.

NEW OFFERS.

This year we are introducing special permit offers.

1 Any experienced angler can take a novice angler fishing on his day bank permit at no extra cost and share the catch limit. The anglers must first register with Woodford Lodge and can take advantage of the offer until the novice catches a trout.

2 In August all bank permits will be valid for two visits taken within the month.

3 In July and August if you purchase three boat permits you will be entitled to a fourth one free.

4 For people on holiday in July, August and September, we offer three mid-week boat permits at Chew or Blagdon taken within a single week, at a 15% discount.

TUITION.

We are keen to encourage all ages to take up fly fishing and offer a range of lessons backed up by half price permits for your first few visits after a lesson. Casting lessons are held on Saturday mornings and cost just £5. Following one of these you can have 2 bank permits at half price to get you going. Most beginners will need to have a full fishing lesson, (on a Saturday afternoon) in order to move on from casting to actual fishing and these cost £15 and entitle you to 4 half price permits. Our tutors hold the Stannic qualification and we will continue to give advice and help on subsequent visits for as long as it takes you to feel confident about your fishing. We can also put you in touch with private tutors and particularly recommend Mike Gleave for tuition at our lakes or elsewhere, or England International John Horsey who offers a coaching service for boat fishing at Chew or Blagdon.

We run two highly popular Beginners Days, for all ages. The first will be in late April and the second in May. These combine basic teaching with you having a go at bank and boat fishing at only £3 for juniors and £7 for adults. You also get two half price permits for your next two visits. Booking is essential.

YOUTH COMPETITION.

On Tuesday the 29th May we will hold our annual Youth Fishing Competition. Open to all anglers between 12 and 19 years, this is a boat competition at Chew with ghillies, and over £1,000 worth of prizes on offer. The entrance fee of £13 includes permits and an evening buffet. Details and booking forms from Woodford Lodge.

ENQUIRIES AND BOOKINGS.

Phone or write to Bristol Water Fisheries, Woodford Lodge, Chew Stoke, Bristol. BS40 8XH. Telephone or fax: 01275 332339 for a free brochure, for all enquiries and for bookings.

You can e-mail us at:
bob.handford@bristolwater.co.uk
or visit our web site for regular updates on the fishing at: http://www.bristolwater.co.uk

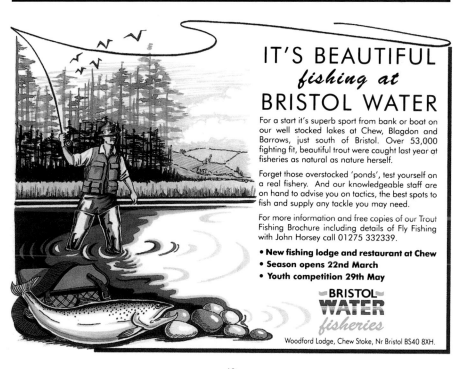

The Salmon & Trout Association

Guardians of Game Fishing since 1903

Trout, sea trout and salmon fishing are under threat from all directions. Can game angling survive? Can the game angler survive? That's up to us - and to you.

S&TA achievements

- Developed the machinery to monitor applications to abstract water or make discharges.
- Spoke for anglers in the campaign which abolished the open-ended right to abstract water.
- Persuaded the Government to review outdated fisheries legislation.
- Initiated and led the fund-raising for a legal challenge to the Scottish Executive on the sea lice issue.
- Successfully resisted the proposal to allow access to the waterside by all and sundry.
- Set up a countrywide programme to introduce young people to the joys of fly fishing.

Our priorities for the future.

- Better control of fish-eating birds.
- Force the Scottish Executive to recognize the damage caused by sea lice and bring salmon farming under independent legislation.
- Ensure that the Government acts on the key recommendations of its Fisheries Review, including:
- Speeding up the end of drift-netting for salmon
- To properly fund the Environment Agency's fisheries programmes.
- Strongly support the levying of charges on abstractors and dischargers.
- Successfully fight the game angler's corner in the competition for water and the waterside.
- During the course of 2001, double the

number of youngsters and other newcomers introduced to the sport by our fly fishing courses.

Why the S&TA needs your support

The Government and other bodies recognise the S&TA as the voice of game angling - and the more members we have, the more we'll be listened to.

Members' subscriptions pay for vital fact-finding, publicity and lobbying.

The threats to game angling are real - only by combining our efforts can we protect what we love, game anglers must speak with a united voice.

We'd be proud if you'd join us - and we're sure you'll be proud to be part of the Association. *Together we can make the difference!*

For further information on membership please contact Louise Barton on 020 7283 5838. www.salmon-trout.org

Local Contact details:

Bristol & West
Mr JS Tennant
Littlefield, Burrington, Bristol BS40 7AD
Tel: 01761 462947 (h) 01275 852143 (w)

Wessex
Mr MA Bilson
41 Cowslip Road, Pinesprings, Broadstone, Dorset, BH18 9QZ Tel: 01202 657931

Somerset
Mr CRA Hill
1 Country Cottage, Bridgehampton, Somerset BA22 4LT Tel: 01935 841558

North Devon
Mr TJC Pearkes
The Chantry, Newton House, Newton St Cyres, Exeter, EX5 5BL
Tel & Fax: 01342 851949

South & East Devon & Tamar
Mr C Hall, Higher Sticklepath Farm, Belstone, Okehampton, Devon, EX20 1RD
Tel: 01837 840420

Cornwall
Mr A Hawken, 5 Meadow Close, St Stephen, St Austell, Cornwall, PL26 7PE
Tel: 01726 822343 Fax: 01726 824175

The Salmon & Trout Association

Come and meet us at the following shows

3 - 4th March	South West Fieldsports	Shepton Mallet
17 - 19th May	Devon County Show	Exeter
28th May	Sherbourne Country Fair	Sherbourne, Dorset
30th May - 2nd June	Royal Bath & West Show	Shepton Mallet
7 - 9th June	The Royal Cornwall Show	Wadebridge

For further information please contact The Salmon & Trout Association
Fishmongers' Hall, London Bridge, London EC4R 9EL
Tel: 020 7283 5838. Fax: 020 7626 5137
www.salmon-trout.org

Tackle Review

Accessories

Peregrine Priest/Marrow Spoon - £35

Every now and then you come across a piece of tackle which functions perfectly on all levels. Such an item is this priest from Bath based Peregrine who also handcraft an excellent range of rods.

It does the job it was designed for, is superbly made and is also a thing of beauty.

To operate it you just twist the nurled brass nut, approximately one eighth of a turn, give it a flick and out pops the spoon. There is a built in stop so the spoon will not fly out and just twist the nut back to lock the spoon in position.

There are no springs or hidden parts that could get lost and the whole thing is engineered to last a lifetime. I don't think I need to explain how to use it as a priest!

Finished in silver or blue, you only buy one priest, buy this one!

Contact Roger McCourtney at Peregrine on 01761 436900

Snowbee Wading Jacket - £135

If you are looking for the ultimate Wading Jacket, look no further.

This beauty from Plymouth based Snowbee features an integral hood with elasticated draw cord and rain peak. The 3-panel hood design allows ample room for a thick scarf and hat, while for comfort, there is a rear hood adjuster strap, which can also be used to roll the hood down into a comfortable collar. Colour is an attractive dark teal.

The cuffs have an inner adjustable Neoprene cuff, plus an outer cuff with Velcro fastener. This is as waterproof as it gets! The waist is fully adjustable and the two front bellows pockets will take the largest of fly boxes and have large Velcro cover flaps plus handwarmer pockets behind. Inside there is a waterproof secure zip pocket. Strong Net D-ring on the back, plus 2

D-rings on the front. This is just one item from Snowbee's excellent range. For more see their ad on page 107.

Snowbee: 01752 334933
Or buy this and loads of other tackle on line at: www.snowbee.co.uk

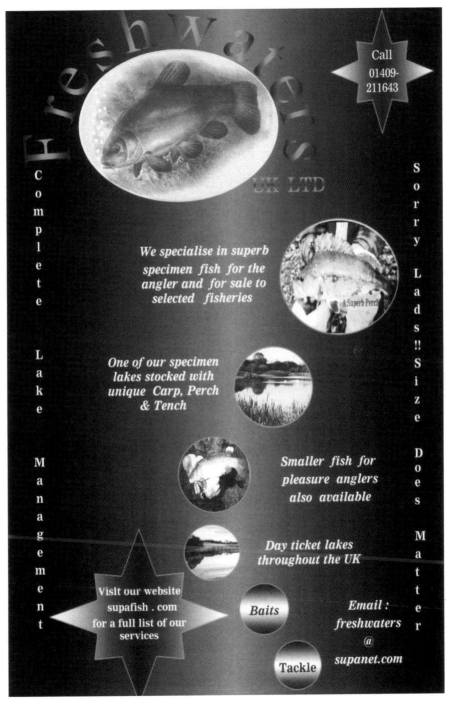
53

Young Angle

By angling photojournalist Brian Gay

Oliver Gay with a 5lb 2oz Tench

ONE of the moans I hear so many times is about the lack of younger anglers in the sport today so why is that?

Computer games have had a lot of criticism levelled at them as hogging the attention of teenagers offering more appeal than a wet day on a river! Anyone who has kids and a Playstation will know just what powerful attention grabbers they are.

Another suggestion is that fishing just isn't trendy enough for today's brand conscious teenagers and maybe to a degree that is also true, but there are a good number of fishing tackle manufacturers producing corporate wear which to some extent could satisfy that angle.

I think the major problem lies in the lack of assistance to help get youngsters on the right track. A poorly equipped youngster with no adult help left to try and catch fish on a lake by his or herself is likely to fail and with failure disillusionment follows and soon after the sport is given up.

Anyone who has an interest in angling has a duty to help young inexperienced anglers if they want the sport to exist long into the future. The danger is that if there are not enough younger anglers backing the sport the next generation could be in danger of succumbing to the anti lobby and fishing could fall by the wayside.

Okay enough of the doom and gloom so what can you do about it? The short term answer, which handled right should ensure a long term future, is to occasionally stop worrying about catching your own fish but help a youngster instead. My own experience with my 12-year-old son Oliver is that for years he was never really interested in fishing, but I never forced him into going. What swayed him was accompanying me on angling photographic assignments and a fateful cast on a friends method feeder rod which resulted in a 5 lb 2 oz tench.

I knew from the moment I dropped him back home that the worm had turned: "Mum I've caught a fish bigger than dad" he exclaimed - the seed had been sewn but had the bug bitten?

It wasn't long before Oliver along with my partner Andi's youngsters Daniel, 10, and Thomas, 5 were also keen to sample a full fishing session of their own. Now catching fish is key when youngsters go fishing, especially with a 5-year-old whose boredom threshold is low, that means a careful choice of venue, and swim.

I decided to take them to a venue where plenty of small fish could be caught in quick succession on simple tactics. Catching fish will keep their interest up, while simple rigs aid tackle handling building confidence before moving on to more advanced tactics.

I wanted somewhere that these small fish could be encouraged to feed in the margins so casting a long way was not necessary. To get them off the mark I decided that a simple small waggler taking three or four BB shot with the bulk locked around the float and just a couple of number ten dust shot spaced out down the line would lead to tangle free casting (very important when the ratio is one adult to three kids unless you want to spend all day untangling rigs!).

At this stage rods and reels were too advanced and two metres of pole for each lad was the answer. Fortunately I had enough top-sets from my pole to fulfil this requirement. Such

Rob Bullock with a 6lb 9oz Bream caught during a match on the Bristol Avon at Sutton Benger in August 2000.

a set up is about as simple as you can get the only problem then was where to go?

I knew that the Lands End Farm held lots of 2-6 oz carp in the specimen lake, a spin off of successful spawning, and that they were feeding readily so that was the scene for our first proper session. It wasn't all plain sailing however as our first choice of swims failed to produce, and the lads began to get a bit impatient. A move was called for and with the help of fishery owner Martin Duckett we moved to a pitch on the opposite bank where the wind was pushing into the reeds.

A few pellets fed into the swim soon confirmed the fish were there as they boiled in competition with each other. The three lads sat side by side, and baiting with segments of worm on the hook proceeded to experience their first taste of catching fish with float tackle.

A competitive spirit was generated and the two elder boys were concentrating hard to outscore each other. That competitiveness actually sparked their interest even more and the concentration displayed was intense - dare I say more than they apply to their computer games! A shared 30 lb catch of small carp had them hooked. "Fishing's pretty cool" and "When are we going again?" were comments confirming the bug had bitten.

Other trips to Emerald Pool at Highbridge and Westhay's Avalon both in Somerset, have seen us advance to running line feeder tactics as well as short poles and at Emerald Thomas caught two 4 lb carp, while Daniel was chuffed with a first cast 9 lb 8 oz common from Avalon.

The elder lads now have their own fishing boxes and angling has become part of their worlds. I'd like to think they will carry on as anglers throughout their adult lives too but I can't help thinking if they had not had the one to one help to start with, that fish would not have been caught and fishing would not appeal as a pastime.

For me it has meant giving up my own fishing sessions purely to help the lads and believe me it is exhausting as you are constantly in demand showing how to do different things like baiting up, casting, playing fish and unhooking them.......oh and untangling rigs!

At the same time it has been very rewarding to see the enjoyment on their faces when they catch, and I urge any anglers with youngsters to give them the same help. If you are not a parent how about offering to take relatives children fishing and start them on the road of discovery that we all know and love.

There are umpteen places in the westcountry suitable for novices where bites should be easy to come by especially in summer. Run through the pages of this guide and you should find plenty of venues to choose from. In my own personal experiences aside from the venues I have already mentioned the Viaduct at Somerton Somerset run by Steve Long and Ian Parsons are keen to help young anglers and have run novice matches with one to one advice from experienced anglers. At Tavistock in Devon Milemead fishery manager Harry Dickens operates help and advice sessions in summer holidays, and the venue is popular with local youngsters, but these are just the tip of the iceberg. Call a few fisheries up and enquire if they run junior sessions, they are a great way for parents who are not anglers themselves to realise their offspring can actually learn about fishing from people who know.

Of course booking a holiday at a place like White Acres near Newquay in Cornwall is a perfect way to break the kids into the sport with junior competitions and plenty of coaching advice on hand.

Wherever you visit or live in the westcountry there is a suitable venue on your doorstep you may not know it yet but studying the directory listings can reveal venues round the corner you just don't know are there!

I hope I have given you food for thought and if you follow my approach with my kids, be patient and have good luck!

Eight year old Elliot Cole with his first fish!
Elmfield

Red Letter Day

The Editor

I extracted this editorial from a fishing diary I dug out the other day. It covered 1981, a year when when I was single, no responsibilities, and lots of spare time! It details what was a great day, by our standards, on our local pond Dutson Water which has always been pretty difficult. The map, drawn at the time and with all the swims as we named them, helps set the scene. Reading it 20 years later it brought back real memories and I could almost feel the morning mist on my face. Apologies for the picture quality. Oh, and I was right about never improving on that day's catch.

My alarm did not even have to go off this morning as I woke two minutes before it went off, a very rare occurence! Martin met me at my place and we set off at 4.30am.

By the time we started fishing it was almost light, a perfect Tench fisher's dawn and what a date to go Tench fishing. The glorious 16th, the traditional start of the coarse fishing season although in Cornwall there is no close season for coarse fish.

We both started fishing in the same area using very similar tactics, float fishing with the bait on the bottom, 15-20 feet out with size 12 hook. Martin was using sweetcorn as bait and I was trying small dungworms (brandlings). After 15 minutes or so Martin started to get bites so I changed to sweetcorn as well. Before long the float slid away and I was into the first fish of the day, a nice Tench of about 1lb 8oz and a good fighter. Well, I've never known such good sport

at Dutson and the fish continued to feed fairly consistently until they 'went off' at about midday.

Our Total so far was:
Me 8 Tench
Martin 3 Tench and a 2lb Common

I was really pleased as my previous best was 5 Tench in a session and we already had about 20lb of fish in the net.

We picked up and went home for some lunch and also got some bread with a view to doing some 'crusting' in the afternoon. We returned to the pond at about 3pm to find it predictably quiet. Martin almost immediately went to sleep in the A40 (An Austin A40 was our mode of transport at the time).

A couple of hours earlier I had seen a couple of Carp under the trees in 'carp corner' so I wandered off to have a go. I first tried a small bit of crust on a size 12 for the Rudd but they were

3lb Golden Orfe for Stewart Grant.
Lower Hollacombe

as frustrating as ever, taking every bit of bread in sight, except for the bit on the hook. I changed to a bigger hook and tried to get a crust under the trees for a Carp but cocked up the first cast and put all the fish down!

I returned to my original swim and threw out a couple of crusts in the area of the pit and one of these was taken quite quickly. Straight away I took the crusting rig to the swim by the reeds just next to the pit and cast out to let the crust drift nicely through the taking area. Two crusts drifted right into the bank undisturbed but I was not paying attention when the third crust was about 4ft from the bank and I heard a loud 'cloop'.

I grabbed my rod and could still see the crust on the water so after a couple of minutes I decided the fish must have gone and reeled in to re-bait. As I started to retrieve I noticed the line entered the water nowhere near where it should have and as I tightened it became apparent the fish had hooked itself.

My first thoughts were that the fish would have already buried itself under the trees that hang in the water but, by keeping the rod tip well under the water, I managed to get the fish into the open where it put up a fine fight before Martin netted my first Carp of the season, a nice Mirror of 7lb.

That fish took at about 5.40pm and put me back in the mood so I started fishing hard once more. I had a few bites from 6 to 6.30 and as the evening drew on the fish started taking the bait more confidently, in fact by 8pm they were almost taking on the drop!

By 9pm the fish had stopped feeding after two hours of the best Tench fishing I have ever had. My brother turned up to take my photos (this was the only one I found). As I've said this was the best day's Tench fishing I've had and I am never likely to improve on it at this water.

I finished up with 15 Tench and that bonus 7lb Carp while Martin had three Tench and a 2lb common. We reckon our total weight for the day was at least 50lb which, on this difficult water of just over an acre, was really excellent.

The Editor (somewhat younger on the left) and Martin

Why the fish should feed so well today I do not know. I suppose it is early in the season and they have not been 'hammered' yet and we've had a lot of bad weather keeping the anglers away. Strangely I was the only angler catching fish consistently, in fact I caught seven fish in the evening while Martin (same bait, terminal tackle etc.) was in the next swim and hardly had a bite!

I do feel the brandlings gave me an edge as in the morning the fish went off the sweetcorn only hookbait and the sweetcorn/brandling cocktail really got them going!

Book Review

The Flyfisher's Classic Library

This is not really a book review, more a review of books!

The Flyfisher's Classic Library comprises a range of flyfishing 'bibles'. The list of authors includes F.M. Halford, A. Ransome, G.E.M. Skues, H. Falkus and F. Sawyer and, of course, Isaak Walton among many others.

Most flyfishermen will recognise many of these famous anglers and may be aware of the contributions they made to the sport.

Now you can buy these publications in a format that reflects their significance. The copies supplied were 'Rod & Line' by Arthur Ransome (the subject of a TV series) and 'Fishing - It's cause, treatment and cure', a wry look at the sport and it's 'victims' by H.T. Sheringham.

Both books were superbly bound in leather with marbled endpapers and a silk marker ribbon as well as a protective slipcase and would grace any bookcase.

The Flyfisher's Classic Library Ltd also do many limited edition volumes and titles start from as little as £25.

Much of what is written in these books holds as true today as it did when their authors first put pen to paper. We can still learn a lot!

For a catalogue and more details:
The Flyfisher's Classic Library Ltd
The Old Police Station
Moretonhampstead
Devon TQ13 8PA
Tel: 01647 441046
Or view the collection on line at: www.ffcl.com

Tackle Review

Accessories

Pike/Conger Pliers - £9.99

These pliers are available in 300mm or 200mm making them perfect for removing hooks from Conger and Pike.

The shaped grips greatly facilitate control, essential when removing hooks from fish to be returned.

Polyolefin Heatshrink Tubing - from 30p mtr

As with many pieces of modern tackle this tubing was never intended as a tackle accessory, it was originally developed for the aircraft industry.

However it has many applications. Polyolefin is warm to the touch and very strong and is commonly used on rod butts by tournament casters. It's range of colours makes it suitable for landing net handles, rod rests, tripods and as underwhipping for rod building.

Available from:
TW Tackle Direct
15 Church St
Ilfracombe **Tel: 01271 862363**
or TW International Group
TW House
Oxford Road
Calne **Tel: 01249 822100**

A very pleased Chloe Masters with a cracking Carp from Avallon Lodges.

Angling Link
- the way forward

Terry Moseley

Angling Link, a disability angling charity formed to unite disabled anglers across the world, has now become the first point of contact for anglers with disabilities worldwide.

The charity formed in 1996 by England International disabled angler Terry Moseley has firmly established it as the number one regarding information and advice concerning disability-angling issues. The charity has been able to help thousands of disabled people and advise fisheries as to what is needed regarding access to waters, special adaptations, contacts, information and much more.

Angling Link initially concentrated on the coarse fishing side of angling, following requests for help they now include activities encompassing sea, game, carp & pike fishing into their armoury of help and information. The introduction of the new web site at www.anglinglink.co.uk and the ability to offer world wide on line membership FREE of charge has seen a dramatic increase in calls for help and people wishing to join and share their information and experiences with the organisation.

Sky Sports program 'Tight Lines' has dedicated a programme each series specifically to cover the subject of disability angling, the response to the programme is phenomenal with callers and emails jamming the switchboards. The programme features Angling Link, its work and live question and answer debates. Their magazine production has also seen an increase in popularity as it covers the new subjects and a "how to" range of articles. A brochure has now been printed where members of Angling Link can order specialised angling adaptations from around the world directly through the charity.

The items now include Hi tech electric reels developed in the USA for anglers with disabilities. Fly angling adaptations for those with limited use or no use in an upper limb, right down to simple items that will allow you to thread a line through rings without the annoyance of losing the line, ideal for those with limited strength, Arthritis etc.

In essence Angling Link has bridged a gap that has been present for far too long. With the introduction of its contests funded by companies such as Tarmac Topmix and the Clos-O-Mat salmon fishing experience we have been able to offer a wider audience the opportunity to try angling or get back into angling after disability or illness. The children's days of which the charity are so proud of, still give the opportunity to youngsters of school age to try angling possibly for the first time. Hospitals, occupational therapy units, community centres, individuals have all benefited by this rapidly growing organisation.

Angling Link would like to offer all disabled people the chance to join in their success, the charity also offers FREE web site design to disabled clubs as part of their work. Membership of Angling Link includes FREE membership to the governing body; the National Federation of Anglers.

The charity is currently on a recruitment drive hoping that disabled people across the world will be made aware of and be able to enjoy the benefits of joining them in their work. They also respectfully ask that if you are interested in helping raise funds, or making donations to enable the good work to continue, please contact them at the address below.

If you are disabled and want to know more about what we do or would like to try angling without cost to yourselves, we can arrange introductions to disability angling as part of our service.

For more information please contact
Terry Moseley
Angling Link
9 Yew Tree Road
Delves
Walsall
West Midlands
WS5 4NQ

Tel 01922 860912
Web site www.anglinglink.co.uk
Email terry@anglinglink.co.uk

Beautifully proportioned Common Carp
weighing in at 20lb 3oz.
Bush Lakes

The Anglers' Conservation Association

What it is and why every angler needs it

In 1949, backed by funds of just £200, a new pollution-fighting body fought its very first case in court - and won the action.

Three years later it forced a city corporation to spend £1.8M (£20M at today's prices) on a new sewage works.

The same organisation, with just four people on its full-time staff, was the only one which dared sue British Coal over the discharge of filthy mine water from abandoned pits and to make the privatised water companies face up to their responsibility for the phosphates in sewage which destroy plant and fish life.

The organisation in question? The Anglers' Conservation Association, known to Britain's anglers simply as 'The ACA'.

In its entire history, the ACA has lost only two cases. One was solely because of technical change in the law after the case had started. The other - the prosecution of British Coal referred to above - was halted on a point of law. Undeterred, the ACA has launched a civil action on the issue.

The aca has teeth and polluters know it.

In over 50 years, the ACA has successfully fought in excess of 2,500. Such is the ACA's reputation, that most of the cases it handles are settled out of court - with awards being made to enable ruined fisheries to be cleaned up and restocked.

The ACA is presently helping anglers on the river Fowey. Works have been carried out on Bodmin Moor which have caused large quantities of sand to be washed into the river. This has raised considerable fears over the effects the deposition of sand will have on the salmon and sea trout in the river. The sand has covered the spawning gravels in the river raising concerns for the survival of fish ova and fry. It has also filled in pools in the river depriving fish migrating upstream of the cover they need. This may have severe impacts on the future viability of the migratory fish population.

In general the ACA has continued its work in fighting pollution and protecting water resources. Last year it won its largest recovery of £415,000 for anglers on the River Eden. Much of this money has been paid into a Trust to be used for habitat improvements on the river for many years to come.

Member angling clubs and riparian owners consult us all the time to help them win compensation for pollution. The ACA has also started

"You're not putting me back in that, are you?"

a new service for members in providing advice on legal matters affecting angling. At any given time, the ACA is handling approximately 40-50 cases. There is no rest in the fight against pollution.

If we're so successful, why do we need money?

The ACA is nearly always awarded costs in its court cases, on top of the damages which it passes on to its members. So why is the Association continually asking anglers for money? The answer is quite simply that under the present legal system we can never recover more than 50% to 80% of the costs: the shortfall comes out of our own resources.

Besides, the line between legal success and financial disaster is always perilously thin. For example, in 1986 an apparently straightforward case against a trout farm accused of polluting one of Yorkshires finest chalk streams became one of the most complex in our history. Only the most rigorous (and costly) scientific research enabled us to produce the evidence necessary for a successful common law prosecution.

WE NEED YOU - YOU NEED US

Nowadays, no stream, lake or river can be completely safe from pollution. The work of the ACA is conservation at its most practical and effective, it benefits not only anglers but everyone who loves the countryside.

Above all, it gives the wildlife, whose very existence depends on pure rivers - plants, insects, animals and fish - a fighting chance.

If you would be interested in joining what was once described as "the most successful war waged against pollution by any voluntary body in the world", please contact us now....

ACA,
Shalford Dairy,
Aldermaston,
Reading,
Berkshire RG7 4NB
Tel: 0118 971 4770
Email: admin@a-c-a.org

Anglers'
Conservation
Association

Six year old James Thomas is over the moon with this 10lb 10oz Mirror from a private Devon lake.
Combe Martin Sea Angling Club

69

The Angling Trades Association

Many things about the century we now find ourselves in have changed but the intent of the Angling Trades Association (ATA) remains the same: to promote the cause of angling to new and would be anglers.

It's been the mission of the ATA to promote fishing in the United Kingdom for over quarter of a century now and over the years the organisation has received considerable backing from most of the major tackle manufacturers for it's various schemes, most of which have met with considerable success. The ATA fully intends to continue that drive this year.

UK National Fishing Week

The ATA is right behind UK National Fishing Week, which has been hugely successful in introducing new faces to angling over the years. In 2000 thousands of events were organised and around 500,000 people took part in them. The week also received a substantial boost from the Government funded Sports Match scheme.

Not content to rest on their laurels the ATA has made sure that plans for UK National Fishing Week 2001 are well underway with the scheme

aiming to smash all existing records.

If you fancy getting involved, either as an organiser or a participant it's simple! Just write to National Fishing Week Headquarters, Merley House, Merley House Lane, Wimborne, Dorset BH11 3AA. Alternatively visit the Fisheries UK website at www.fisheries.co.uk

Centres of Excellence

Last year The ATA handed out two Centres of Excellence awards to fisheries they deemed had met their exacting standards. The two fisheries had each met the ATA's criteria for being suitable for families to spend time fishing and also to provide serious sport for anglers in an enjoyable atmosphere in attractive surroundings.

As a reward for achieving the ATA standards the fisheries were given ten full sets of tackle which they are now able to use for coaching prospective anglers, young and old. The ATA is very aware that if the sport is to attract newcomers it must offer an appealing environment for people to participate in.

All Centres of Excellence have full toilet and catering facilities, disabled access and plenty of car parking space.

For information on the ATA's Centres of Excellence call the ATA on (02476 414999).

Professional Anglers Association

In 1999 the ATA – not content with its existing crop of initiatives – launched another new scheme, again with the aim of attracting more people into the sport of angling. The plan was to enlist the help of tackle shops, fisheries and angling coaches across the country to work together to bring in new blood to the sport.

Tackle shops were to introduce one new angler to the sport who would then receive quality coaching from an instructor at his local fishery. To achieve this the ATA put in place for the first time ever a Professional Anglers Association (PAA) with the sole objective of promoting the sport. It worked!

1. A new coaching register was created and made available to clubs, Retailers and fisheries.
2. Coaching manuals were written.
3. A national standard tariff was set.

4. Coaches were taught to effectively sell their services through retailers and fisheries.

5. Fees were created for the PAA from coaching and joining fees.

6. Details were provided of the coaches performance.

While the scheme is in progress over 50 outlets and fisheries have been asked to examine the strengths and weaknesses of the scheme as it progressed.

ATA Conservation Project

The ATA also made a significant commitment to the environment in 2000. A conservation initiative was launched for fishing related causes. Links were formed by the ATA with the Royal Society for the Protection of Birds and the World Wildlife Fund for Nature in an effort to protect fish and their environment around the world.

The ATA signalled it's serious intent in this area by appointing former President of the National Federation of Anglers, David Bird, to head up the initiative, which has so far been a great success.

Give Angling A Go

This scheme has been successfully run by the ATA since 1996 and it continues to go from strength to strength introducing would be anglers to the sport right across the country.

The idea of the scheme is to get experienced anglers to give newcomers a taste of what fun the sport can be by showing them the skills and tricks of the trade they have acquired through their own participation in the sport.

'Give Angling a Go' was originally aimed at introducing youngsters to angling but has since been widened to target a wider age range with considerable success. In fact, during 2000 a number of fishing excursions were organised for groups of varying ages with the help of ATA sponsored teams, Commercial Coarse Fisheries Association waters and the Environment Agency.

Take a Friend Fishing

This is probably the most successful of all angling drives by the ATA. The 'Take a Friend Fishing' campaign has been successfully adding to the nation's fishing ranks for over 20 years.

The scheme works on the premise that most people are introduced to angling by a friend or a family member and centres around the provision of free information packs aimed at four target groups.

The four key groups singled out by the ATA were; new and would be anglers, returning anglers, 'takers' of anglers and organisers of group introductory sessions.

If you're interested in ordering one of these 'Take a Friend Fishing' packs containing info sheets, a fishing newspaper, stickers and guide leaflets, send a SAE to the following address:

Take a Friend Fishing
101 Springfield Road
Bury St Edmonds
Suffolk IP33 3AR
Tel: 01284 763397

Pretty 18lb 8oz Mirror Carp
Darts Farm

Wimp with a Wetfly

By JB

Editor's note: OK, so it's about fly fishing and it's in the coarse section but the message here applies to all branches of angling. The potential embarrassment of fishing with an expert and looking foolish in their company is something I'm sure we can all relate to.

My father in the 1950s wrote many serious fishing articles, one memorably for The Field entitled "Duffer with a Dryfly". My father was overly modest, however, as he was a fine fisherman, both in temperament, cunning and dexterity. Alas, these are all characteristics I lack.

Whilst my father saw travel as a means to indulge his passion for fishing and thought nothing of punctuating a business trip to New Zealand with several (highly successful) days fishing on Lake Taupo, I always felt pressured on business travel to keep my mind on the job in hand. Father would weasel a few days free salmon fishing off the Canadian Government without any qualms, or even address stony-faced Serb soldiers in schoolboy French in order to get a permit to travel - and fish - in postwar Yugoslavia. But he sadly never had the chance to enjoy retirement and died quite young.

So when I took early retirement I settled in Devon, as far as possible from the business end of England, determined to enjoy the rural life.

One of the first local friends that I made was a retired doctor. Still fishing in his nineties, the doctor is like quicksilver over a style and has the enthusiasm of a teenager. A prodigious catcher of fish, he ties most of his own flies including a hairy monstrosity he once proudly showed me, called a 'Woolly Bugger'.

"You must join our little club" he said, early in our acquaintance, when I carelessly admitted to the ownership of my father's old fly rod. Since the doctor had been the founding secretary of this fishing fraternity for the previous 35 years, it was like receiving an order from Christ to join the disciples at the High Table.

I suppose I should have immediately confessed that my casting technique with a fly rod was sadly lacking, but I was too timid to admit this. After all, it was just a matter of extending a line and whirling it around one's head like a dervish, as indeed I seemed to remember my father trying to show me on school holidays in Austria. When the fish bit, you 'struck' and just reeled in with a last-minute swoop of the net to complete the fight. Simple.

Anyway, to be on the safe side, on my first excursion with the doctor, I wore cap, glasses and a high collared jacket on a warm Summer's day.

This was because I remembered my father telling the awful story of Jock Whitney, one-time US Ambassador to Britain, who inadvertently plucked out his own eye with a mis-cast trout fly. Clearly one needed protection. I would have gladly considered chain mail if it had been light and flexible enough.

Positioned at the other side of the lake, and sandwiched between the venerable doctor and another aged angler, I rapidly realised that I was casting at right angles to the wind which was blowing in steadily from the Bristol Channel. Downwind would have been a much happier option, but this wasn't immediately available. I soon demonstrated my amateur status by snagging a bramble bush some 20 feet behind me.

Later in the morning I found that I was casting with a complete bird's nest at the end of my line. Not literally, of course, the trees weren't close enough, but the cast had become so entwined with the fly that the only remedy was to produce a pair of nail scissors from my creel (a trick learnt from my father) and cut my way out of trouble. Thus both line and cast were dramatically shortened. Still, that meant less of that finicky cast at the end of the line to get caught up on itself.

For a while there was almost total peace and quiet. The only sound was the whistle and 'thhtt' of line from my neighbours, who threw out some 30 yards of line on each long, leisurely cast. A

Fishery Owner Martin Sexton with a 5lb Mirror.
Simpson Valley

moorhen clucked, distant sheep bleated and bright blue damsel flies fornicated elegantly in front of me.

Ah, this was the life. Moments for Wordsworthian reverie. A quick glance at the sky to reassure myself that the scudding clouds did not presage rain.

Oops, oh BUGGER IT. That really was a PATHETIC cast. How could I have about 20 foot of line out and manage to drop the fly only a couple of feet in front of me?

Oh well, pull it all in by hand . . .hope the doctor isn't looking... Hello, . . .who's having me on here? It seems I have snagged the weeds at my feet. No, no it can't be. By God it is. Something silvery-gold is twisting around at the end of my line. Either I've caught a clockwork mouse or a live fish.

Reel in, reel in. Oops, too fast. It's bending the rod double. What if it snaps? Let go a bit. The reel gives an angry buzz and the weight comes off the rod, but slowly, slowly I reel in again. Hey Presto, in 5 minutes (it felt like ages) it's in my net - a glistening, thrashing 2lb rainbow trout on the end of a red Montana fly so well digested that it took almost as long again to dislodge from the back of its gullet.

"Did you catch one there?" asked my friend at lunchtime. I wondered if I detected a note of sardonic amusement at my inept bungling, or whether he was just being polite.

"Well done" he said. "Actually four is the quota, you know", and he showed me four fine trout that he had already caught without my seeing.

But I didn't need to catch anything else after lunch. I moved to a position of solitude where I could cast smoothly downwind and bask in reflected glory. A wimp perhaps, but the luckiest wimp with a wetfly on that water.

Children from Launceston College on their annual visit to Rose Park Fishery. Twelve children landed 15 Rainbow Trout

77

South West Lakes Trust Fisheries

Float tubing on Kennick

Last year proved to be an exciting one for the newly created Lakes Trust, an independent charity formed to promote and enhance sustainable recreation, access and nature conservation on and around inland waters in the South West of England for the benefit of the general public. We plan to build on last years success, and aim to offer something for all levels of competence (from complete novices through to international match anglers) in both coarse and game disciplines.

The Trust is spearheading a drive to introduce the sport to all newcomers, from children to pensioners. We plan to hold introductory and training days in various aspects of coarse angling at Upper Tamar Lake, with the help of the E.A. and N.F.A. accredited instructors. Fly fishing tuition and introductory days will be available at Wimbleball, Kennick, and sites in Cornwall, all run by qualified professional instructors, throughout the season. All aspects of the sport will be covered, as will the promotion of a responsible and healthy interest in the environment. Juniors again will be encouraged to fish for trout — the parent/child ticket allows the youngster to fish for free and share the parent's bag limit.

The 'Peninsula Classic' bank competition will be held at Kennick on the 20th May, in which there will be a special junior prizes category. The 'Wimbleball 2000' boat competition will be held on 16th September.

The fish that were moved from College to Argal have thrived in their new home, with pike of up to 34lb and carp up to 27lb being caught this season.

Brown Trout anglers at Roadford experienced their best season ever, topped by a new fishery record of 8lb 4oz — maybe 2001 will see the first double figure fish from this productive water!

Fly fishermen wishing to try out float tubing in the region need look no further — starting in May the Trust will organise float tubing days on the first Sunday in each month at Kennick, and local suppliers Snowbee and Orvis are enthusiastic to promote this aspect of the sport.

The Trust remains committed to angling and customer care, and welcomes all comments to help us provide what the angler really wants.

For further information, including instruction and competition information, please contact:

Chris Hall, Head of Fisheries on 01837 871565
Or E-mail: chall@swlakestrust.org.uk
Or visit our website:
www.swlakestrust.org.uk

sw **lakes** trust

sw lakes trust *Coarse Fishing*

COARSE FISHING PERMIT AGENTS:
A: The Post Office, Slade, Ilfracombe, Devon, EX34 8LQ
Tel: (01271) 862257
B: Variety Sports, 23 Broad Street, Ilfracombe, Devon.
Tel: (01271) 862039
C: Summerlands Tackle, 16-20 Nelson Road, Westward Ho!,
Devon, EX39 1LF. Tel: (01237) 471291
D: The Kingfisher, 22 Castle St, Barnstaple, Devon, EX1 1DR.
Tel: (01271) 344919
E: Powlers Piece Garage, Powlers Piece, East Putford,
Holsworthy, Devon EX22 7XW Tel: (01237) 451282
F: Bude Angling Supplies, 6 Queen Street, Bude, Cornwall.
Tel: (01288) 353396
G: Bideford Tourist Information Centre, The Quay, Bideford,
Devon Tel: (01237) 477676
H: Whiskers Pet Centre, 9 High Street, Torrington, Devon.
Tel: (01805) 622859
I: Exeter Angling Centre, Smythen St, Exeter, Devon EX1 1BN
Tel: (01392) 436404
J: Exmouth Tackle & Sports, 20 The Strand,
Exmouth, Devon EX8 1AF. Tel: (01395) 274918
K: Knowle Post Office, Budleigh Salterton. Tel: (01395)
442303
L: Newtown Angling Centre, Newtown, Germoe, Penzance,
Cornwall TR20 9AF. Tel: (01736) 763721
M: Sandy's Store, 7 Penryn St., Redruth, Cornwall TR15 2SP.
Tel: (01209) 214877
N: Ironmonger Market Place, St Ives, Cornwall. TR26 1RZ.
Tel: (01736) 796200
O: Heamoor Stores, Heamoor, Gulval, Nr Penzance. TR18
3EJ. Tel: (01736) 65265

LOWER SLADE - Ilfracombe, Devon
Stocked with mirror and common carp to 20lb plus
bream to 5lb plus, perch to 2.25lb, roach, rudd, gudgeon
and pike.
Fishing Times:Open all year, 24 hours per day
Permits: From agents: A,B,C,D. Tel: (01288) 321262
JENNETTS - Bideford, Devon
Best fish: Common 22lb, Mirror 23lb. Produces quality
bags of smaller carp, roach, and tench to float & pole.
Fishing Times: Open all year, 6.30am to 10pm.
Permits: From agents: C,F,G. Tel: (01288) 321262
DARRACOTT - Torrington, Devon
Roach up to 1lb. Mixed bags to 20lb plus of roach, rudd,
bream, tench, perch to 2.25lb, carp to 15lb.
Fishing Times: Open all year, 24 hours per day.
Permits: From agents: C,D,F,G,H,
Tel: (01288) 321262
Seasons Permits - (01837) 871565
MELBURY - Bideford, Devon
Best mirror 27.75lb. Good mixed bags of roach, rudd,
bream to pole, float and feeder.
Fishing Times: Open all year. 6.30am - 10pm.
Permits: From agents: C,D,E,F,G
Limited season permits from our office.
Tel: (01288) 321262

TRENCHFORD - Nr Christow, Devon
Pike weighing up to 30lbs.
Fishing Times: Open all year -
1 hour before sunrise to 1 hour after sunset.
Permits: Self service kiosk at Kennick Reservoir
Tel: (01647) 277587
UPPER TAMAR LAKE - Bude, Cornwall
Carp to 28lbs. 50lb plus bags of bream and 30lb bags
of rudd. Regular competitions.
Fishing Times: Open all year, 24 hours a day.
Permits: From agents: C,D,F Tel: (01288) 321262
SQUABMOOR - Exmouth, Devon
Good head of carp to 25lb, roach to 3lb 2oz, Tench.
Fishing Times Open all year, 24 hours a day.
Permits: From agents: I,J,K
Season Permits from our office Tel: (01837) 871565
OLD MILL - Dartmouth, Devon
Carp to over 20lbs, roach to 2lb, tench and bream.
Fishing Times: Open all year, 24 hours a day.
Permits: Season permits from our Office
Tel: (01837) 871565
PORTH - Newquay, Cornwall
Bags of 130lb plus have been caught. Best bream 9lb
2oz, tench 9lb 12oz. rudd to 3lb, roach to 1.25lb plus.
Mixed bags of roach, rudd/skimmers to 60lb.
Fishing Times: Open all year, 24 hours a day
Permits: Agent L. Self service at Porth car park.
Season permits from our Office. Great competition
water. Tel: (01637) 877959
BOSCATHNOE - Penzance, Cornwall
Common, mirror and crucian carp with fish into the low
20lb range. Roach and bream also stocked.
Fishing Times: Open all year, 1 hour before sunrise to 1
hour after sunset. Season permits from our Office.
Permits: From agents: L,M,N,O. Tel: (01579) 342366
ARGAL - Nr Falmouth, Cornwall
Carp to 20lb plus. Best fish: carp 26lb, bream 8lb 6oz,
tench 8lb 8oz and eel 7lb, Pike over 30lb.
Fishing Times: Open all year, 24 hours per day.
Permits: From agents: L,M and self service unit at Argal
Reservoir car park. Tel (01579) 342366
Season permits from our Office (01837) 871565.
BUSSOW - St Ives, Cornwall
Rudd to 1.5lb, roach bream and carp.
Fishing Times: Open all year, 24 hours a day.
Permits: From agents: L,M,N. Season permits from our
Office. Tel (01579) 342366
CRAFTHOLE - Nr. Torpoint, Devon.
Stocked with carp and tench.
Quality Carp up to 30lb.
Fishing Times: Open all year
1hr before sunrise to 1hr
after sunset.
Limited day and season
permits from our office
(01837) 871565

The Big Freeze

The Editor

I don't often attempt to fish in January but it was a nice bright day with plenty of sunshine and no real wind.

There was sweetcorn and bread in the freezer so Alf and I loaded up and headed out.

Unfortunately when we arrived the lake was completely frozen over. We are not put off easily so we set about clearing a swim.

This was new to us and throwing stones was a waste of time as they either got stuck in the ice or punched stone sized holes through it.

We got around the problem by tying a bit of branch, about a pound in weight, on the end of the carp rod and dropping that on the ice. This did work but it took us an hour to clear a passage from our bank to the nearest island. We fished with sweetcorn and then bread, feeding gently and we did get a few bites. Predictably as the fish appeared to be moving into the swim we had to go, I'm sure another hour would have seen some landed! honest.

How do you get around the problem? I reckon by the time we'd broken all that ice all the fish must have been on the other side of the pond with their fins over their ears! If you have the solution let us know.

Email: editor@gethooked.co.uk or write to the address on page one.

Alf ponders a chilly problem

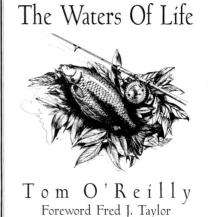

Coarse Fishing in the Bristol Avon area

by Mike Goodchild

Mike Stevens with a 12lb 8oz Barbel from the Avon at Chippenham

The Bristol Avon flows from its twin sources near Sherston and Tetbury to its confluence with the River Severn at Avonmouth and travels some 117 kilometres in total (72 miles). The river has five major tributaries, the Rivers Marden, Somerset Frome, Chew, Bristol Frome and the By Brook. All provide excellent coarse fishing although the By Brook is mostly controlled by private syndicates so it is not available to the average angler.

Most waters in the area are controlled by local angling clubs and membership must be obtained before fishing. Club membership can usually be purchased from local tackle shops. There are some sections of the river in Malmesbury, Bath, Saltford, Keynsham and Bristol that are considered "free fishing". These sections of the river are mostly owned or controlled by local authorities and not leased to angling clubs. It is important to note that a valid Environment Agency rod licence is also required when fishing any of these waters; licences can be obtained from all post offices as well as from local Environment Agency offices.

Malmesbury, a picturesque old Cotswold market town with its 12th century Abbey as its' focal point, is the uppermost point on the Avon open to the coarse angler. Although fishing is difficult when the water is clear it has produced roach and perch of over 3lb and carp of 20lb plus in the past two seasons.

From Malmesbury the river meanders its way downstream to the market town of Chippenham and has many weirs that provide impounded sections above weirs, with riffle and pool below. Barbel, chub and roach predominate in the faster water giving way to large bream shoals just upstream of Chippenham town. Notable catches include a five hour match record of 140lb of bream. Individual records include a monster pike of over 33lb and the almost unbelievable tench of 12lb 7oz caught by Rick Seal from Cardiff in the river at Christian Malford in November 1998.

Downstream of Chippenham town centre "free fishing" extends from the weir to the bypass road bridge (fishing the right hand bank) and then transfers to the left hand bank downstream to and including Mortimers Wood. This section is some 1.25 miles in length and contains good quality fish. Most notably barbel to 12lb, chub to 4½lb, bream to 7lb, tench to 4lb, perch to 2lb and pike to 18lb.

Further downstream at Lacock, the river passes by this National Trust village, best known for its Abbey and as the home of early photographer Fox-Talbot, and onto Melksham which is dominated by the Avon Tyre factory (now owned by Coopers of America). Match weights vary from 2lb to 12lb on the upper reaches to perhaps 60lb on the lower reaches near Melksham (if the bream are feeding!).

Onward to Staverton, then Bradford on Avon with its tythe barn, old church and antique shops (a must for tourists), Avoncliffe and Limpley Stoke. All have large impoundments above their weirs. Here fish can be a little more difficult to locate but large bream shoals are here to be found and caught. The liberal use of ground bait, an open ended feeder with a hook bait of red maggot, worm or caster usually does the trick. One place not to be missed after a hard day's slog on the river bank is the Cross Guns Public House at Avoncliffe — well known by the locals for its good beer and steaks at a reasonable

Four year old Josh at Spires Lakes

price. Below Avoncliffe are the Limpley Stoke and Claverton weirs, nestling within a scenic valley, where wooded sides rise in places, some 300 feet above. In these sections where the water runs faster and is quite weedy in the summer months, lie the haunts of very large barbel. The best captured so far, nearly 15½lb weight, is very close to the national rod caught record. Most other species can also be caught with good roach, dace, chub, tench, perch and bream. Also, it is not unusual for the pike angler to capture specimens of 12-20lb with the best reported fish of 26lb caught by Gary Court at Claverton in 1988.

The city of Bath with its Roman Baths and internationally renowned Georgian architecture provides a scenic backdrop to over 2.5 miles of "free fishing". Below Pulteney Weir hot water spills into the river from the Roman Baths, which provides interest for carp of over 20lb. Individual anglers have reported superb roach catches of over 30lb, just upstream of North Parade Bridge and 40lb plus nets of chub, taken on caster at Widcombe. Another hot spot near Windsor Bridge produces large quantities of bream, with individual fish weighing over 7lb in weight. It makes this particular stretch well worth consideration.

The river below Bath becomes slower and boat usage more intense. Newbridge, Saltford and Keynsham provide excellent match stretches where individual weighs vary from 2 to 20lb with roach, chub, bream and eels predominating. There are further "free" sections at the Shallows in Saltford and a small area 200 yards downstream of Keynsham weir on the far side of the roadbridge.

At Hanham the "free fishing" extends on the right hand bank through Conham Park to Netham Weir some 3.5 miles in total. Conham Park has a car park, toilets and facilities for the disabled. Fishing on this stretch is quite good with mixed nets of dace, roach, chub, perch and eels. From Netham to the river's confluence with the River Severn at Avonmouth, the river becomes an estuarine environment with one of the largest tide variations in the world. Near Netham Weir some coarse fish can still be caught together with the occasional mullet and flat fish.

Bristol has numerous attractions, few more inviting, for the angler, than the sight of a large expanse of water. The City docks, also known as the Floating Harbour, is a large area, and situated in the centre of the City. This, together with its connection to the main river, the Feeder Canal, provides a venue with numerous swims for the match and pleasure angler. Permits are available both on the bankside and from tackle shops or the Harbour Masters Office, situated near the restored SS Great Britain. The Docks have an average depth of 15 feet. Roach, dace, bream and perch can be caught in good numbers with carp or chub as a bonus. Most fish are caught using an open ended feeder with a hook bait of maggot, bread, worm or sweetcorn. In the summer months fish tend to feed off the bottom more, float fished baits presented at a depth of 3 to 6 feet can produce good catches.

Most barbel fishing is upstream of Bath, popular venues being Warleigh, Limpley Stoke, Avoncliffe, Lacock, Chippenham, Peckingell, Kellaways and Christian Malford. Any of these venues offer the realistic prospect of a double figure barbel. Legering with large bait such as meat, flavoured paste or lob worm will often bring results, though this approach generally works best when the river is coloured. In hard fished areas or in clear water conditions, try using particle baits like maggots or sweetcorn, which can be put down with a bait dropper or fished in a feeder. Hemp will usually get fish feeding, but in some areas barbel have become wary of feeding on hemp. Experimenting with different baits and techniques is often the key to catching barbel consistently. Where permitted, fishing large baits after dark is without doubt the best way to target the larger fish. It is best to return barbel to the water as soon as possible, avoiding the use of keepnets. They can become exhausted when caught, particularly in hot weather, and should be supported in the flow until they regain strength to swim away.

The Kennet and Avon Canal, a navigation built to join the rivers Thames and Bristol Avon, was opened in 1810. After years of neglect in the 1950s and 1960s, work started on its restoration. Now some 30 years later and with many millions of pounds spent, the canal is nearly restored to its former glory. In North Wessex, our area commences at Horton just east of Devizes.

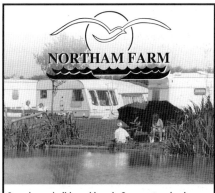
85

From Horton it winds its way through Devizes and drops down the spectacular Caen Hill flight of 29 locks to Sells Green, Semington and onwards to Bradford on Avon, Limpley Stoke and Bath where it joins with the River Avon, a distance of approximately 25 miles. The canal will provide the angler with plenty of sport, particularly during the summer months, with favoured swims for large carp in the ponds below Devizes.

Most species can be caught throughout the canal's length with roach, rudd and bream falling to float fished punched bread with small balls of liquidised bread used as an attractant. Tench, crucian carp, perch and eels can be tempted with red worm, maggot or caster used as hook bait. Small amounts of chopped worm or pinkies added to the ground bait keep their interest. Remember to stake your keepnet securely to the bank or it may be carried away by a passing boat. Also please remember that walkers and cyclists are entitled to use the tow path and you must not obstruct them with fishing tackle, rod or pole. *The Waterways Code is available from all Waterways Offices.*

There are more than 100 lakes and ponds in the North Wessex area for the angler to take advantage of. Some are managed by syndicates, others privately owned and available to fish on day tickets. Lakes such as Sevington, a small village on the outskirts of Chippenham, Erlestoke near Devizes, Longleat (a series of lakes in the grounds of Lord Bath's Estate) and Ivy House Lakes at Grittenham in the Wootton Bassett area provide good coarse fishing. Trout fishing is also catered for with large lakes like the nationally renowned Chew Valley Lake and smaller venues like Mill Farm at Great Cheverell. There are many lakes and ponds run by angling clubs such as Newton Park which are available through Bathampton AA membership. Bristol, Bath and Wiltshire AA has Shackells, Sword and Sabre lakes. Both clubs have other larger facilities, two of which are:

Tockenham Reservoir near Lyneham lies just three miles from M4 intersection 16 via the A3102. This beautiful 12.5 acre lake, surrounded by oak woodland, was created in 1836 to provide water for the Wilts and Berks Canal. Purchased by Bristol, Bath and Wiltshire AA in 1980 it has since been developed into a magnificent fishery stocked with carp to 30lb, tench to 7lb, bream to 8lb, plus roach, perch and crucian carp. All fishing is from platforms, including three purpose built for the wheelchair disabled, and there are good parking facilities.

Bathampton AA's **Hunstrete Lakes** are situated 7 miles west of Bath. They comprise a mature 5 acre lake plus two newly constructed lakes of 3.5 acres. These are set in 21 acres of landscaped grounds and provide picturesque and tranquil surroundings with provision for 120 swims. The main lake contains carp to 28lb, tench to 7lb, pike to 20lb and plenty of other fish to maintain your interest. The new lakes, Bridgepool and Withypool, have been recently stocked with over £30,000 worth of fish, with carp to 5lb, bream to 4lb, roach to 2lb, plus perch, crucian carp and chub. Car parking and toilets are provided with facilities for the disabled, including 15 purpose built platforms.

Please remember that as an angler you are an ambassador for the sport. It is important to remove all litter and discarded line from your swim and return all fish to the water with the utmost care.

Stunning 3lb 2oz Roach from the upper Avon

Coarse Fishing in South Wessex

By Matt Carter

The principal rivers in the South Wessex Area most recognised by coarse fishermen include the Avon, Stour and Frome. These rivers are widely accepted to be amongst the best coarse fisheries in the country and have over the years produced a number of rod caught records; these include the old barbel and pike records as well as the current roach record of 4lbs 3oz from the Dorset Stour.

The Hampshire Avon

This river passes through several counties including Wiltshire, Hampshire and Dorset but the name 'Hampshire Avon' commonly sets it apart from the other seven 'River Avons' found across the British Isles. The Hampshire Avon is a chalk stream which means that its water rises mostly from groundwater aquifers in the surrounding catchment. This characteristic sets it apart from many other rivers and is highly advantageous to coarse fish and fishermen alike. The water quality in this river is exceptionally high and significantly contributes to the diverse flora and fauna found in the system.

Coarse fishing mainly takes place between Salisbury in Wiltshire and Christchurch in Dorset. The principal species found in this reach include roach, dace, chub, barbel, bream, pike, perch and more recently carp. Specimens for all of these species can be found on this river, some of which are thought to be in excess of current British records; however these still need to be caught and verified!

The Avon is perhaps best known for its superb roach fishing. Many specimens of 2lbs+ are caught every year including several fish of over 3lbs. The best roach fishing can be found on the upper and middle reaches of the river, especially near Fordingbridge. Chub fishing has also been exceptionally good in recent years with several specimens of over 7lbs and up to 8lbs 14oz being reported from the middle and lower river. Barbel are also most prolific in the middle and lower reaches and are often captured at weights between 10 and 14lbs.

Fishing access to the river is controlled by a small number of angling clubs, including Christchurch AC, Ringwood & District AC and Salisbury & District AC. Guest tickets and day tickets can be obtained for these clubs from local tackle shops. There are also a number of smaller syndicates that offer limited membership and access to estate waters. Day ticket fisheries can be found at Fordingbridge, Ringwood and Bisterne.

The Dorset Stour

The Stour is quite different in character to the Hampshire Avon and is often thought to be the poorer cousin to the Avon. This is not the case. The Stour originates in the predominantly clay based Blackmoor Vale where much of the water is derived from surface run-off. This means that the river reacts more quickly to rainfall in comparison to groundwater dominated chalk streams in neighbouring catchments. Coarse fishing mainly takes place between Gillingham and Christchurch in Dorset.

The Stour is a extremely 'productive' river and is home to many species including roach, dace, chub, barbel, bream, pike, perch and tench. Roach tend to be quite numerous on this river however few specimens are recorded each year; notably the current British record of 4lbs 3oz was recorded at Corfe Mullen in 1990. Big roach can be found in the middle and upper reaches, especially near Wimborne and Blandford. Chub of over 7lbs have been captured in recent years as well as barbel of up to 14lbs 14oz from the middle and lower river. Good tench of up to 7lbs and bream over 8lbs can be found in the middle and upper sections near Sturminster Newton. Fishing for dace and small roach is best in the

*Richard Price with a 19lb Mirror
Bake Lakes*

lower river near Christchurch. Large perch of over 3lbs have also been captured from this reach.

Fishing access to the river is controlled by several angling clubs including Christchurch AC, Ringwood & District AC, Wimborne & District AC, Blandford AC, Durweston AC, Sturminster Newton AC, Stalbridge AC and Gillingham AC. Day tickets can be obtained for most of these club waters from local tackle shops.

The River Frome

This river is not dissimilar in character to the Hampshire Avon where the water predominantly rises from chalk based aquifers. This river is largely maintained for salmon and trout fishermen however some excellent coarse fishing can be found in the middle reach at Dorchester and in the lower reach at Wareham.

Local angling clubs control access to the river in these locations and details can be obtained from nearby tackle shops.

The main coarse fish species found in these locations include dace, roach, grayling and pike. Specimens for each of these can be caught from the River Frome. Perhaps most notably grayling

regularly attain weights of over 3lbs and occasionally are reported up to 4lbs.

Stillwaters and Canals

A short section of the Kennet & Avon canal passes through the South Wessex Area near Devizes. The local angling clubs at Devizes and Pewsey control the access to this water where good fishing for small roach, bream and tench can be found.

There are many stillwaters offering coarse fishing throughout the South Wessex Area, however several of these are concentrated near Ringwood. This series of gravel pits and ponds are largely controlled by Christchurch AC and Ringwood & District AC and contain many large carp of up to 40lbs, tench and bream of up to 12lbs and pike in excess of 30lbs. A typical example includes the Somerley Estate lakes which are leased to Christchurch AC.

Good fishing lakes in the north of the area include Witherington farm ponds, Peter's Finger lake and Wardour lake near Salisbury. Notable lakes to look for in West Dorset include Warmwell, Radipole and Pallington near Weymouth.

Twelve year old Michael Hawksworth with a 14lb Common.
Legge Farm

Fishing with Wessex Water

Whether you are a keen angler or enjoy an occasional day fishing, Wessex Water hopes you enjoy using the facilities at Wessex Water's beautiful reservoirs in Somerset and Dorset

The fisheries at Clatworthy, Hawkridge and Sutton Bingham reservoirs offer a friendly personal service and the chance of sport in surroundings second to none. The season is from 17 March 2001 - 14 October 2001. Durleigh reservoir, just west of Bridgwater, provides coarse anglers with a similar opportunity.

Bob Palmer with a 12lb 12oz Rainbow from Hawkridge

Sutton Bingham reservoir

Sutton Bingham reservoir is a lowland fishery set in the gently rolling hills on the Somerset and Dorset border. Situated some four miles south of Yeovil it can be approached from the A37 Dorchester Road.

The reservoir offers excellent fly fishing for rainbow and brown trout, either from the bank or a boat. Fishing boats may be hired for rowing or you may use your own motor (electric outboard only). An 'Allan' wheelie boat is available for wheelchair users.

Because Sutton Bingham is a lowland reservoir, the water is not deep and the most popular method of fishing is with a floating line and mainly small lures and nymphs. The best catches in 2000 included an 8lb 5oz rainbow trout and a 5lb 7oz brown trout.

Tuition and tackle are available by appointment from the ranger who will also point visitors to the best spot and advise on the best fishing method of the day. The fishing lodge has been designed to cater for the disabled and includes a fish cleaning room, hot drinks, a shower and a large lounge area.

For more details about Sutton Bingham, contact ranger Ivan Tinsley on 01935 872389.

Clatworthy reservoir

Clatworthy reservoir is situated in the Brendon Hills on the edge of Exmoor National Park in West Somerset. It impounds the head waters of the River Tone and the surrounding rolling hills provide a picturesque setting for walking and fishing.

Anglers can enjoy fishing for rainbow and brown trout from the banks of this 130 acre reservoir or from a boat. Fishing boats may be hired for rowing or you may use your own motor (electric outboard only).

There are seven water inlets at Clatworthy which are all described as hot spots for anglers, but generally the south bank is considered to be the best area. Clatworthy offers good top of the water fishing with nymphs or dry flies or at the deep areas with sinking lines and flashing lures. Clatworthy fished consistently well in 2000. The largest rainbow trout caught in 2000 weighed in at 7lbs, while the reservoir record is 16lbs 10oz caught in 1998. The biggest brown record being 8lbs 2oz caught in 1994.

The fishing lodge has facilities for the disabled, plus an 'Allan' wheelie boat. The local fishing club is Clatworthy Fly Fisherman's Association. For more information about the club and competitions, contact club secretary Fred Yeandle on 01823 283959. For further information about fishing at Clatworthy, contact the ranger Dave Pursey on 01984 624658.

Durleigh reservoir

The lowland reservoir is one of the oldest on the Wessex Water region and was formerly a trout fishery. It is open every day of the year except Christmas Day, Boxing Day, New Year's Eve and New Year's Day.

Durleigh reservoir is the only Wessex Water reservoir dedicated to public coarse fishing. Anglers can fish over 80 acres, from the bank.

An abundance of coarse fish means Wessex Water can offer superb coarse fishing for matches or the casual angler. The reservoir contains carp, roach, bream, perch, tench and specimen size pike.

Durleigh fished well again during the 2000 season with some of the heaviest fish taken including a 23lb carp.

For further details about fishing or matches, contact ranger Paul Martin on 01278 424786.

Hawkridge reservoir

This upland reservoir nestles in a small valley on the Quantock Hills in an Area of Outstanding Natural Beauty. The reservoir lies some seven miles west of Bridgwater, just beyond the village of Spaxton and provides fishing facilities for brown and rainbow trout from the bank or a boat - anglers are recommended to book boats.

Anglers can use the facilities at the fishing lodge which include a lounge with a drinks machine and toilets. An updated fishing report as well as information on the latest flies, tactics and catch rate can be found in the lodge.

The car parking adjacent to the lodge is restricted and reserved for disabled anglers. Other fishermen are requested to use the main car park at the entrance to the reservoir.

During 2000 Hawkridge fished well with the largest rainbow trout weighing in at 12lbs 12oz. Fishing tackle can be supplied to anglers provided they have a rod licence. Basic casting lessons are available by prior arrangement with the ranger.

Flydressing, inter-club matches and away events as well as casting tuition for beginners are available from Hawkridge Fly Fishing Club. For details, contact Mrs Sally Pizii on 01823 480710.

For further details about fishing at Hawkridge, please contact ranger Gary Howe on 01278 671840.

General Fishing Information

For general enquiries on fishing, a request for our free brochure on fishing and recreation or season tickets, please ring Wessex Water customer services on 0845 600 4 600 or contact the ranger at the reservoir.

Day or evening tickets for fishing and boat hire are available on a self-serve basis from the public fisheries at each lodge.

2001 Price Guide

TROUT

Season Ticket	£390
Season Concession	£290

(valid for one site only four days per week)

Day Ticket	£ 13
Day Concession	£ 11
Evening Ticket	£ 8

(no concessions)

Book of tickets - £70 for six available from ranger.

Book of tickets (concession) £60 for six (book of tickets valid at all Wessex Water reservoirs)

Bag limit - season tickets four, day permit five, evening permit two. For beginners, a reduced ticket and tuition are available at the discretion of the ranger.

Parent and junior concessions are available with the junior angler fishing free, but sharing the parent's bag limit. Rod and tackle may also be available for introductory sessions or for hire. Evening tickets and boats start at 4pm.

BOAT HIRE

Boat (rowing)	£10 per day per boat
Boat (evening)	£ 6

Boat anglers are requested to wear the life jackets, which are available at the reservoirs.

COARSE FISHING

Day Ticket	£5
Day Concession	£3.50
Evening Ticket	£3.50
Book of Tickets	£40 for 10

CONCESSIONS

These are available for anglers aged under 17 or over 60 or disabled. Anglers must provide proof of age or disability, such as a doctor's certificate or registered disabled card on request.

95

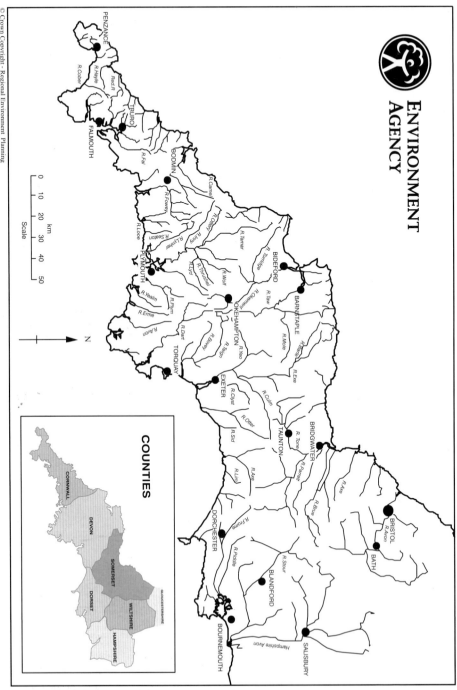

ENVIRONMENT
AGENCY

© Crown Copyright - Regional Environment Planning

Scale
Km
0
10
20
30
40
50

N

PENZANCE
R.Cober
R.Hayle
Red.R
TRURO
FALMOUTH
R.Fal
BODMIN
R.Fowey
R.Camel
R.Looe
R.Seaton
R.Lynher
R.Tamar
R.Inny
R.Fowey
R.Tiddy
PLYMOUTH
R.Lyd
R.Thrushel
R.Wolf
R.Yealm
R.Plym
OKEHAMPTON
R.Okement
R.Torridge
BIDEFORD
R.Taw
BARNSTAPLE
R.Erme
R.Avon
R.Dart
R.Bovey
R.Teign
R.Yeo
R.Mole
R.Bray
R.Exe
TORQUAY
EXETER
R.Clyst
R.Culm
R.Otter
R.Sid
TAUNTON
R.Tone
R.Parrett
BRIDGWATER
R.Axe
R.Brue
R.Lim
R.Axe
DORCHESTER
R.Frome
R.Piddle
R.Stour
BLANDFORD
BRISTOL
R.Avon
BATH
SALISBURY
BOURNEMOUTH
Hampshire Avon

COUNTIES

CORNWALL
DEVON
SOMERSET
DORSET
WILTSHIRE
HAMPSHIRE
GLOUCESTERSHIRE

96

A perfect 14lb 'Ghostie'.
Milemead

Vic Barnet on Wanda's Lake with a brace of Bream. Vic holds the record here with a bag of 13 Bream for 72lb 8oz.
Clawford

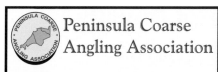

The Royalty Fishery

By Andy Sloane

Please feel free to visit one of southern England's premier chalk streams, the Hampshire Avon. The Royalty Fishery offers some of the finest game and coarse fishing in the U.K with a reputation for quality specimens, of which barbel and chub are the favourite quarry for anglers who visit our venue.

If you are after a challenge visit the Royalty, where the atmosphere is happy and friendly. The regular anglers are more than happy to give advice on the best tactics and equipment to give the best possible chance of success.

The Royalty Fishery is by no means easy, but with hard work, skill and of course a touch of luck, you will reap the rewards of quality fish, which fight like Trojans and are in tremendous condition.

John Stack with 11lb 5oz Barbel

A Quick Tour of the Fishery

The fishery has always been maintained to make it as comfortable as possible. If you come to Christchurch on holiday, our venue is perfect, as there are guesthouses, pubs, and restaurants within easy reach. On site, there are toilet facilities and access to all parts of the fishery is good, helped by a new bridge across the river at the main car park. This new bridge is wider, allowing disabled anglers to fish the East Bank of the main river for the first time. Anglers who have large amounts of tackle to carry can cross the bridge with ease.

During your walk around the fishery you will come across the famous swims like the legendary Railway Pool, Pipes, Trammels, Fiddlers, Waters-meet, Parlour Pool, Bridge Pool and the Great Weir. These swims have been in many books and conversations of angling adventures from fishermen all over the world.

Our fish species consist of barbel, chub, pike, bream, roach, dace, carp, tench, perch, salmon and sea trout.

Pointers to help at the Royalty

Use a minimum of 8lb breaking strain line to allow specimen fish to be played in the weed beds.

Mastering the art of rolling meat will definitely increase your catch rate for barbel. It will also produce for many other species - vary your bait.

Watercraft and experience are essential to achieve good results. Probably 80% of my fish are caught through observation. More time spent looking, rather than just fishing, will enable a distinct pattern of feeding times and patrol routes to become apparent.

Polaroid's are vital for stalking. They also reduce the strain on your eyes on a bright summer's day.

Showing respect for fish is so important! Take time to return a fish back to the water, nursing it until it swims away totally revived and in the best of health to fight another day.

In some swims an unhooking mat is needed to avoid any harm to the fish. If any fish are captured and harmed in any way, the use of antiseptic such as 'KLIN-IK' made by Kryston is ideal for sores and abrasions to give them a helping hand to a full recovery.

TIGHT LINES FOR THE FUTURE!

Contacts:

From 1 April 2001
Davis Tackle. Tel 01202 485169 for day tickets, bookings and information.
Christchurch Angling Club membership available.

A Royalty Fishery Web Site
www.royaltyfishery.co.uk
created by Andy Sloane.

Christchurch Angling Club website:
www.christchurchac.org.uk

101

A Golden Pleasure

Taken from 'The Waters of Life' by Tom O'Reilly, see advertisement on page 80.

My float has been bobbing up and down, showing signs of movement from rudd and roach. I've caught, in the hour or so I've been here, about twenty small fish, and one large, and very beautiful, golden rudd, the first I've ever caught. I was surprised at how golden it was, it's back was almost orange fading to a brilliant gold leaf colour on its body. I felt so happy holding it, as if I'd caught my first salmon or carp. It brought a new and bright enthusiasm to me, reminding me of my old feelings of why I fish, which sometimes, after spending weeks after uncatchable carp, fades and disappears.

The enjoyment of catching fish is overwhelming as my float sinks and I'm reeling in another. A rudd, its silver scales glisten and sparkle in the sunshine and its blood red fins move in time with its mouth and gills. The hook is easily removed with a disgorger and the fish happily swims away.

I caught my largest roach to date from this pool, it must be a little over a year ago now. I'd spied three well rounded tench skulking close in to the bank but hidden by an overhanging hazel. I'd managed to crawl through a labyrinth of bamboo, under the fence that surrounds the water, and slithered my way close to the tree. There, in full technicolour, were the tench but to my surprise four very large roach nudged the water's surface. They looked lazy and arrogant, as though no one knew that roach that size inhabited the pond. How big? The largest looked to be close to three pounds and the others very nearly the same.

I then fished in earnest for them. Stooped in a very awkward position I managed to thread my rod's tip through the undergrowth and out to where they basked. I tried all manner of baits, even artificial flies, but they seemed to know all about the threats from above, perhaps this was why they had grown so big? I eventually made the mistake of leaning too hard on the branch of the hazel tree and promptly fell in!

Golden Rudd

103

It took three weeks of being scratched and torn to find their new hiding place, again they were with the tench, but under the roots of a fallen tree. I tried to lure them out. I did proudly catch two of the tench, one of which weighed over four pounds. The weeks turned to months and I found out that they had a routine of moving with the sun. The water was incredibly clear and as the light moved around the pond, so did the shadows from the surrounding trees. They'd drift slowly, staying well away from the large shoals of dead-bait sized roach and rudd, who were content to bask in full sunlight.

When the sea trout were running in good numbers and the carp season was at its height, they took up a lot of my time. I slowly started to see sense and realise that I could never catch them, and with the greatest of respect left them alone. The autumn rains came and stirred up the water making it into a thick stew of run-off and silt.

On my last outing of the year for the carp I had pre-baited with sweetcorn; and was happily float fishing for them around the groundbait, when the float sunk to my surprise and I reeled in, after a small scale tussle, the largest of the roach! It was entirely luck and not due to the skill or the amount of time I'd spent, that finally caught the emperor of roach!

But I don't hold out any hope of catching him or his brethren today. I cast out again and manage to curve my float as it sails through the air. It lands very close to the reeds which stretch out to my right. Almost immediately it ducks under again but I miss the bite. I'm using bread as bait and if I fail to hook a fish when I strike then it falls off, and I have to reel in, re-bait and re-cast.

Two black silhouettes drift under the water's surface near the reeds. They look to be carp about the size of my fore-arm. I fling my float and bait out near to where they are but they sink down and swim out into deeper water. A wind whispers in the trees and wrinkles the surface which moves my line and float closer to the reeds.

It's hard to see my float tip when the ripples from the wind swallow it, and it also rides up and down on the swell. My eyes lower and look at my rod point, then I follow the curve of the rod down to my reel. My line jerks out quickly and becomes taught. I raise my head quickly and try to find my float, which has gone. I lift my rod and am instantly amazed as the fish on the other end is hardly a small rudd and my light float rod hoops over under the force.

The fish on the other end bends it as if it's a car aerial. I sharply stand up to apply more pressure. My heart begins to pound once more. The fish dives towards an overhanging holly tree by my left hand side. I lean out and lever the fish around in my direction. It rises to the surface and I have a pleasant surprise to see a small carp. I bring it closer to me and lift it out of the water with my hands, It looks to weigh three or so pounds. A mirror carp and its small scales along the ridge of its back are silver and grey.

I should really fish more often like this, casting in hope for anything that swims really! My line is four pounds breaking strain, so it's fine and light for the smaller fish yet man enough to handle any surprises, the same as my rod I suppose. 'Pleasure angling' is the term used, but surely all fishing is pleasurable? I do feel particularly satisfied when I fish in this way though and I never feel that frustrated emptiness that fishing for salmon and carp can often bring.

However you can't have the pleasure without pain - can you?

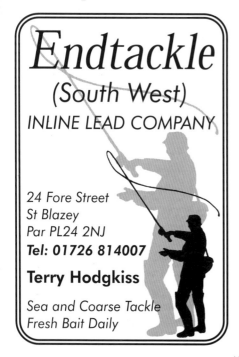

106

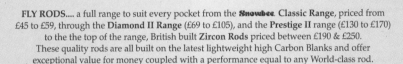

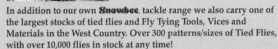

TACKLE

Dave Reed with a 'golden' haul of Carp and Rudd from the Island Lake at Millaton

Keith Ratcliffe with an 8lb 4oz Rainbow caught on a Red Buzzer in Oak Lake.
Watercress Fishery

112

Ashley Clarke with a superb shore caught
Tope weighing 50lb 2oz. Landed while night
fishing at Lynmouth.
Combe Martin Sea Angling Club

Golden Tench - picture by Brian Gay

Where to Stay

The following section details some of the increasing number of locations throughout the westcountry offering holidays with a fishing theme. Most have their own lakes, many with residents only fishing. Don't forget to mention us when you phone them!

Crap weather, nice Perch!
Josh and Alf at Elmfield

118

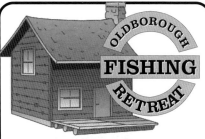
119

A 17lb Mirror for Ann Bennet from Valley Lake. Penvose

Rainbow from Wimbleball Lake
Picture - Mike Weaver

John Clark with a 13lb Ghost Carp and (top left) Colin Delaney and Michael Green with Carp of 18lb 8oz and 17lb 4oz. New Barn

Nick Phillips, Combe Martin Sea Angling Club Chairman, with a nice Plaice from the Skerries off Dartmouth.

The Core Issues

by Malcolm Gilbert

Fisheries Liaison Representative for The
National Federation of Sea Anglers &
European Liaison Officer of The Bass Anglers
Sportfishing Society.

In the last issue of "Get Hooked", I outlined the problems facing the recreational sport fishing industry because of the traditional mindset that fish stock resources are exclusively for commercial exploitation, and as such the entire management process both nationally and at European level has sought to manage from a commercial exploitation perspective only. The appalling degradation of the commonly owned fish stocks (described by the United Nations as one of 'humanities natural heritage') shows clearly and unequivocally how this approach has failed. The resources themselves have been sacrificed for the short term benefit of the commercial fishing industry who are now suffering the consequences.

Unfortunately, the recreational sector who also support thousands of livelihoods are also suffering the consequences. The resources should have been and must become the priority. This is the only way that the long term harvesting of resources will be achieved.

I pointed out that in other parts of the globe the sport angling industry was perceived as being socially and economically important enough for some fish stock species to be managed either primarily or in some cases exclusively as 'sport fish'. During the spring of 1999, MAFF civil servants clearly stated that they had no responsibility for sport angling. Now, in late September 2000, MAFF is singing an entirely different tune and claims to have responsibility for recreational sea angling matters!

Why the change of heart? Clearly, political pressure from MPs, MEPs, the Recreational Angling Conference at Aston, are all beginning to focus the need for some serious and innovative alterations to traditional mindsets.

However, being a sceptic I believe there is one single factor that is concentrating the minds of senior MAFF civil servants more than any other, and that is the assertion that the management of some fish stocks should be contributed to, by other government departments such as Tourism and Sport. The notion that specific fish stocks can generate significant socio-economic benefits as sport fish is overwhelmingly supported by some of MAFF's own research, and many examples around the globe. By far the biggest beneficiary to a healthy, robust sport angling industry is tourism, which is a seriously large industry with immense political clout. The suggestion that both the Minister for Tourism and the Minister for Sport should become more involved in the decision making process about what happens to fish stocks is, I believe, bringing about abject panic amongst senior MAFF civil servants, and in an attempt to protect their territory, their response to the growing suggestion that they will no longer have exclusive control over fish stocks, they have now accepted responsibility for sea angling matters.

The National Assembly for Wales commissioned Nautilus Consultants Limited to produce a study into inland and sea fisheries in Wales. Nautilus Consultants Limited are well respected and regularly used by the European Union for similar work. Their findings are wholly supportive of the arguments that the proponents of sport angling have been proffering for many years. Nautilus concluded, amongst other things, that the gross economic impact of salt water sport angling was £28 million in Wales, dwarfing the impact of commercial fishing. Bearing in mind that salt water sport anglers have no direct interest in a great many species (including shellfish), then those specific resources that are being targeted by sport anglers are clearly generating far more economic value, utilised as sport fish. Nautilus identifies the degradation of fish stock resources from commercial overfishing as being one of the serious threats to the potential to develop the sport angling industry and most pointedly points out that the beneficiaries for development of the recreational sector are tourism, tourism, and yes tourism. The pace of change is for me painfully slow, but undeniably traditional cultural mindsets are in the process of being altered, and they must be altered very much more if saltwater

sport angling is to achieve the status that it needs in order to develop. There is much work to be done by anglers.

Sea anglers should identify any organisation which is seen to be active in the political field lobbying for angling and support them by joining. At the very least, all sea anglers should subscribe to the governing body (National Federation of Sea Anglers) as personal members and when sending in their membership, write a letter outlining their main concerns so that the federation can respond to member's wishes. Better still, if an angler feels they would like to contribute some of their time to sea angling in areas such as Education, Conservation, Political Lobbying etc, write to the federation.

National Federation of Sea Anglers, 51A Queen Street, Newton Abbot, Devon, TQ12 2QJ

Bass Anglers Sportfishing Society, 18 Highfields Close, Stoke Gifford, Bristol, BS34 6YA

Visit: www.ukbass.com

Charlie (left) and Lee with a 14lb 7oz Ghostie and a 16lb 2oz Common from Simpson Valley

The
Directory *and how to use it.*

The directory has been divided up into counties
The counties are sub-divided into river fishing, stillwater coarse fishing and stillwater trout fishing.

Many associations offer both game and coarse fishing on many different rivers and lakes. Each association entry gives brief details of the fishing on offer.

Each section starts with river fishing and includes a short description of the rivers, canals etc. within the county. This section is sorted alphabetically by river catchment area so all fishing on, say, the Dorset Stour will be in the same section of the guide.

Stillwater coarse and stillwater trout fisheries are sorted alphabetically under their nearest town. Where coarse and game fishing is offered by the same association or fishery the entry will be cross referenced to a main entry.

There is a map depicting river locations and county areas on page 96.

www.gethooked.co.uk

Every entry in this directory also appears on our web site - **www.gethooked.co.uk** (unless we have been requested not to do so by the owner).

The 'Fish Finder' on the web site enables you to do a text based search of all the records. You can search by species, town, county, name, post code or any combination. You can also search by weight but this will exclude records where the owners have not supplied this information.

ADD YOUR FISHERY!
If you wish to add your fishery to the directory you can use the 'Submit your Fishery or Club' option on the web site, Email info@gethooked.co.uk, fax the information to 01271 860064 or post to Diamond Publications, PO Box 59, Bideford, Devon EX39 4YN.
THERE IS NO CHARGE FOR INCLUSION IN THIS DIRECTORY OR AN ENTRY ON THE WEB SITE.

CORNWALL
River Fishing

CAMEL

The Camel rises on the north west edge of Bodmin Moor and flows past Camelford to its estuary at Wadebridge. The run of Salmon tends to be late with some of the best fishing in November and December. Sea Trout in summer. Also moorland Brown Trout fishing.

River Camel Fisheries Association
Contact: E.D.T. Jackson, Butterwell, Nr Nanstallon, Bodmin, PL30 5LQ, 01208 831515, *Water:* The association represents all major riparian owners and fishing clubs on the River Camel and agrees fish limits, conservation policy and enhancement projects in co-operation with the Environment Agency

Bodmin Anglers Association (Camel)
Contact: R. Burrows, 26 Meadow Place, Bodmin, 01208 75513, *Water:* 11.5 Miles on River Camel, 0.25 miles on River Fowey, *Species:* Salmon, Sea Trout, *Permits:* Roger Lashbrook at Stan Mays Store, Bodmin. D.Odgers, Gwendreath, Dunmere, Bodmin, *Charges:* 1st May - end November £15 per day or £40 per week. Juniors half price. Membership details from Secretary, *Methods:* Fly, Worm, Spinner.

Butterwell
Contact: Tyson & Janet Jackson, Butterwell, Nr Nanstallon, Bodmin, PL30 5LQ, 01208 831515, tyson@butterwell.u-net.com, *Water:* 1.5 miles River Camel, *Species:* Sea Trout (to 10lb 2oz) & Salmon (to 18lb), *Permits:* On site, *Charges:* £18/day, Max. 5 rods/day, *Season:* 1st May - 30th August, night fly fishing only for Sea Trout. 1st September - 15th December for Salmon, *Methods:* Any method for Salmon

Fenwick Trout Fishery (River Camel)
Contact: David & Shirley Thomas, Old Coach Road, Dunmere, Bodmin, PL31 2RD, 01208 78296, *Water:* 570 yards on the River Camel. See also entry under stillwater Trout, *Species:* Sea Trout and Salmon, *Permits:* On site. EA licence required, *Charges:* Please phone for details, *Season:* As current EA Byelaws, *Methods:* Fly fishing from bank only

Lifton Hall Hotel (Camel)
Contact: 01566 784863, *Water:* See entry under Devon River Fishing - Teign

Wadebridge & Dist. Angling Association
Contact: Mr Stan Spry, 101 Egloshayle Road, Wadebridge, 01208 813494, *Water:* 10 miles River Camel, 1 mile River Allen, *Species:* Salmon to 27lb, Sea Trout to 10.25lb, *Permits:* Day / Week permits, Bait Bunker, Polmorla Road, Wadebridge 01208 816403, *Charges:* Day £25, Week £100, *Season:* Visitor permits end 31st September, *Methods:* No maggots permitted. Fly and spinning, natural baits on some beats

FAL

Fal River Association
Contact: Mr. Tom Mutton, 01872-273858, *Water:* Association protecting the interests of the River Fal

FOWEY

Rises near the highest point of Bodmin Moor from which it flows south, then turns to the west, and finally south again through Lostwithiel to its long estuary. A late Salmon river. Also good Sea Trout fishing and some Trout fishing.

Fowey River Association
Contact: Chris Marwood (sec), Withy Cottage, Huish Champflower, Taunton, TA4 2EN, Tel/Fax 01398 371384, *Water:* An association of representatives of angling clubs and riparian owners on the Fowey whose aim is to secure and maintain the well being of the river and its ecology. It exists largely as a pressure group and negotiating body on behalf of its members, *Permits:* No fishing permits sold through the Association. For membership details please contact the secretary at the above address, *Methods:* E.A. Byelaws apply; catch restrictions: Salmon 1/day, 2/week, 5/season; Sea Trout 4/day, all Sea Trout to be returned in September

Bodmin Anglers Association (Fowey)
Water: See entry under Camel. 0.25 miles River Fowey

Lanhydrock Angling Association
Contact: Brian Muelaner, The National Trust, Regional Office, Lanhydrock, Bodmin, PL30 4DE, 01208 265211, *Water:* 2 miles on River Fowey, *Species:* Sea Trout, Salmon, *Permits:* Available from the above telephone number, *Charges:* £10 Daily, £25 Weekly (maximum 6 tickets daily), *Season:* 1st April - 30th September, Sea Trout 31st August, *Methods:* Artificial bait only

Lifton Hall Hotel (Fowey)
Contact: 01566 784863, *Water:* See entry under Devon River Fishing - Teign

Liskeard & District Angling Club (Fowey)
Contact: Bill Eliot (Hon Sec), 64 Portbyhan Road, West Looe, PL13 2QN, 01503 264173, *Water:* 23 Miles of Rivers Fowey, Lynher, Inny, Seaton River, West Looe River; Map of waters with day/week tickets, *Species:* Salmon to 20lb (typically 7-12.5lb) & Sea Trout to 10lb (typically 2.5-4lb), *Permits:* Tremar Tropicals shop, Liskeard. Lashbrooks Tackle Shop, Bodmin. East Looe Chandlers, The Quay, East Looe. Shillamill Lakes, Lanreath. Homeleigh Garden Centre, Dutson Village, Launceston, *Charges:* Adult: £15/day, £50/week, Membership £55. Joining fee £8. Membership limited to 250 adults, *Season:* River Fowey 1st April - 15th December; Sea Trout season closes end September, *Methods:* Spinning, Fly Fishing or Bait. Artificials only on some beats

Lostwithiel Fishing Association
Contact: Roger Lashbrook, Rogers Tackle Shop, 1st Floor, Stan Mays Store, Higher Bore Street, Bodmin, PL31 1JZ, 01208 78006, *Water:* 2 miles water, Both banks, River Fowey, *Species:* Salmon, Sea Trout, Brown Trout, *Permits:* Rogers Tackle Shop, Bodmin. *Charges:* Season tickets only: £55, *Season:* 1st April - 15th December, *Methods:* All baits

Newbridge Angling Association
Contact: Mr. D Maskell, Jefferys, 5 Fore Street, Lostwithiel, PL22 0BP, 01208-872245, *Water:* 1.5 miles single bank on River Fowey, *Species:* Trout + Salmon, *Permits:* Members only - no day tickets. For membership details please contact Mr. Maskell

THE DIRECTORY

LOOE

The twin rivers, East and West Looe, have their sources near Liskeard and join shortly before reaching the sea at Looe. Although small, there is a run of Sea Trout, and Brown Trout throughout.

LYNHER

Rises on Bodmin Moor and joins the Tamar estuary opposite Plymouth. Brown Trout and runs of Salmon and Sea Trout.

River Lynher Fisheries Association
Contact: Arthur White (hon. secretary), River Lynher Fisheries Association, 14 Wadham Road, Liskeard, PL14 3BD, Tel/Fax 01579 345428, efsa@talk21.com, *Water:* Consultative body for the River Lynher. Membership comprises riparian owners, angling clubs, lessees of fishing rights, individual anglers and others interested in the Lynher valley environment, *Species:* Salmon, Sea Trout, Trout, *Charges:* £5 annual membership
Liskeard & District Angling Club (Lynher)
Contact: Bill Eliot, 64 Portbyhan Rd, West Looe, PL13 2QN, 01503-264173, *Water:* 23 miles of Rivers Fowey, Lynher, Inny, Seaton, West Looe; Map of waters with day/week tickets, *Species:* Salmon to 16lb & Sea Trout to 6lb (some very big ones April/May), *Permits:* Tremar Tropicals Shop, Liskeard; Lashbrooks Tackle Shop, Bodmin; East Looe Chandlers, the Quay, East Looe; Shillamill lakes, Lanreath; Homeleigh Garden Centre, Launceston, *Charges:* Adult: £15/day, £50/week, Membership £55. Joining fee £8. Membership limited to 250 adults, *Season:* River Lynher & Inny; 1st March - 14th October; Sea Trout season closes end September, *Methods:* Spinning, Fly Fishing or Bait
Woodcocks Club
Contact: Michael Charleston, The Gift House, Buckland Monachorum, Yelverton, PL20 7NA, 01822 853293, mwcharl@aol.com, *Water:* Two miles of the lower and middle Lynher, *Species:* Salmon, Sea Trout and Brown Trout, *Permits:* Very limited number of annual permits for which there is a waiting list. No short term permits, *Season:* March 1st to October 14th, *Methods:* Fly only for Sea Trout and Brown Trout except in spates. Return of Salmon (catch and release) is encouraged

MENALHYL

Small stream starting near St. Columb Major and entering the sea north of Newquay. Brown Trout fishing.

St. Mawgan Angling Association
Contact: Mr. T. Trevenna, Lanvean House, St. Mawgan, Newquay, TR8 4EY, 01637-860316, *Water:* Stretch around Mawgan Porth, *Species:* Trout, Brown Trout, *Charges:* Limited day tickets from The Merrymoor, Mawgan Porth. Club membership restricted to those in parish of St. Mawgan, *Season:* April 1st - end September, *Methods:* See details on site

SEATON

Short stream to the east of Looe with fishing for Brown Trout.

TAMAR

The Tamar rises near the north coast, and for most of its course forms the boundary between Devon and Cornwall. It is always a lowland stream flowing through farmland and this fact is reflected in the size of its Trout which have a larger average size than the acid moorland streams. Around Launceston, the Tamar is joined by five tributaries - Ottery, Carey, Wolf, Thrushel and Lyd - which offer good Trout fishing, as does the Inny which enters a few miles downstream. There is a good run of Salmon and Sea Trout, the latter being particularly numerous on the Lyd. There are also Grayling in places.

Angling 2000 (Tamar)
Contact: 01566 784488, wrt@wrt.org.uk, *Water:* More than 20 beats on the Tamar, Taw & Torridge. Flexible permits fishing for Trout, Salmon, Sea Trout, Grayling and Dace
Bude Angling Association
Contact: Mr L.Bannister, 2 Creathorn Road, Bude, EX23 8NT, 01288 352476, *Water:* 3 miles upper reach of the River Tamar, *Species:* Brown Trout (Wild), *Permits:* Bude Angling Supplies, Queen Street, Bude, *Charges:* £3 day, week tickets available, *Season:* March 15th - Sept 30th, *Methods:* Fly only

Dutson Tamar Fishery
Contact: Mr Broad, Lower Dutson Farm, Launceston, PL15 9SP, 01566 773147 or 01566 776456, *Water:* Half a mile on the River Tamar at Launceston, *Species:* Brown Trout, Salmon and occasional Sea Trout, *Permits:* Homeleigh Angling and Garden Centre, Dutson, Launceston. Tel: 01566 773147, *Charges:* £5 per day, *Season:* 1st March - 14th October, Salmon as current EA Byelaws, *Methods:* See current EA Byelaws.
Lifton Hall Hotel (Tamar)
Contact: 01566 784863, *Water:* See entry under Devon River Fishing - Teign

CORNWALL Stillwater Coarse

Bodmin
East Rose Farm
Contact: Veronica Stansfield, East Rose Farm, St. Breward, Bodmin Moor, PL30 4NL, 01208-850674, eastrose@globalnet.co.uk, *Water:* Complex of four lakes with 22 permanent pegs (two specially constructed for disabled). 3 acres of water, *Species:* Mixed fishing in two largest lakes: Tench / Roach / Rudd and Crucian. Lower lake has Carp to 8lb. Carp to 20lb & Tench to 3lb in deep pool, *Permits:* Day tickets available from Farmhouse at East Rose, *Charges:* Day tickets: £4 adults, £3 under 16s. Reduced rate evening tickets, *Season:* No closed season, No night fishing, *Methods:* No keepnets unless by prior arrangement. No barbless hooks. No boilies
Lakeview Coarse Fishery
Contact: Don, Old Coach Road, Lanivet, Bodmin, PL30 5JJ, 01208 831808, admin@lakeview-country-club.co.uk, *Water:* 2 lakes, 4 acres in total, *Species:* 13 in total inc. Carp, Tench, Bream & Roach, *Permits:* On site Tackle Shop & Main Reception, *Charges:* £4.50/day/ Adult, £2.50 Junior-O.A.P-Disabled. Season ticket available, *Season:* Open all year, *Methods:* No boilies or night fishing

133

CORNWALL - STILLWATER COARSE

Bude

Bude Canal Angling Association
Contact: Mr Dick Turner, 2 Pathfields, Bude, EX23 8DW, 01288 353162, *Water:* Bude Canal (1.25 miles), *Species:* Mirror, Common, Crucian Carp, Bream, Tench, Roach, Rudd, Perch, Eels, Gudgeon, Dace, *Permits:* On the bank, *Charges:* Seniors day £4, Seniors week £18, Juniors & O.A.Ps day £2, Juniors & O.A.Ps week £10, *Season:* Closed season April 1st May 31st inc, *Methods:* Micro barb or barbless hooks only, Strictly one rod only, No camping or any equipment deemed to be associated with camping.

Peninsula Coarse Angling Association
Contact: Roy Retallick, 21 Alstone Road, Tiverton, EX16 4LH, 01884 256721, r.retallick@btinternet.com, *Water:* All 14 South West Lakes Trust fisheries plus 1 exclusive member only water at Lower Tamar, *Species:* All coarse fish - Carp 35lb, Pike +20lb, Bream +8lb, Tench +7lb, Roach 2lb, Perch 3lb 7oz, Eel 4lb, *Permits:* Please contact Roy Retallick, *Charges:* £5 per year membership entitles 10% discount on day and season tickets to fish any South West Lakes Trust Coarse Waters, *Season:* Open all year, *Methods:* As South West Lakes Trust rules displayed on site

Upper Tamar Lake
Contact: South West Lakes Trust, 01837 871565, info@swlakestrust.org.uk, *Water:* Ranger Tel 01288 321262, *Species:* Carp to 28lb. 50lb plus bags of Bream and 30lb plus bags of Rudd. Regular competitions, *Permits:* See South West Lakes Trust coarse advert. Self service permit hut on site, *Charges:* Full day £4.50, Concession £3.50, 24 Hour £8.50, Season Day £80, Season Concession £60, Season Child (under 16) £35, Season Day & Night £120, Additional Fisheries £20 each, *Season:* Open all year 24 hours a day, *Methods:* No child under 14 years may fish unless accompanied by an adult over 18 years. No child under 16 may fish overnight unless accompanied by an adult over 18 years, and then only with permission of parent or legal guardian (letter to this effect must be produced)

Water Front Fishing Lake

Contact: Water Front Fishing, The Lower Wharf Centre, Bude, EX23 8LG, 01288 359606, Fax: 01288 356448, simon@waterfrontfishing.freeserve.co.uk, *Water:* One acre lake, *Species:* Carp (mixed species), Rudd, Roach and Eels, *Permits:* Day tickets from the above, *Charges:* £4.50 per day, *Season:* Open all year, dawn to dusk, *Methods:* Barbless hooks only. No keepnets, Groundbait restrictions on request.

Delabole

Ferndale
Contact: Steve Davey, Rockhead, Delabole, PL33 9BU, 01840 212091, *Water:* Three half acre lakes set in a sheltered valley 3 miles off the North Cornwall coast, *Species:* Roach, Rudd, Bream and Carp, *Charges:* Adults £3.50 per day. OAP's and juniors £2.50 per day. After 5pm £2. Extra rod £1 per day, *Season:* Open all year from dawn to dusk

Falmouth

Argal
Contact: South West Lakes Trust, 01837 871565, info@swlakestrust.org.uk, *Water:* Ranger 01579 342366, *Species:* Carp to 20lb plus, Bream,Tench, Pike to over 30lb, and Eels, *Permits:* Self service unit at Argal Car Park. See South West Lakes Trust coarse advert, *Charges:* Full day £4.50, Concession £3.50, 24 Hour £8.50, Season Day £80, Season Concession £60, Season Child (under 16) £35, Season Day & Night £120, Additional Fisheries £20 each, *Season:* Open all year 24 hours a day, *Methods:* No child under 14 years may fish unless accompanied by an adult over 18 years. No child under 16 may fish overnight unless accompanied by an adult over 18 years, and then only with permission of parent or legal guardian (letter to this effect must be produced)

Hayle

Marazion Angling Club
Contact: Mr Andrew Bradford, 7 Chy Kensa Close, Hayle, 01736 757330, *Water:* St. Erth Fishery (3 acres), Bills Pool (2.5 acres), Wheal Grey (4 acres), River Hayle (600yd upstream from St. Erth Church), *Species:* Carp, Bream, Tench, Roach, Rudd, Perch, Golden Orfe, Golden Rudd, Gudgeon, Trout, Flounders & Eels; Wheal Grey reputed to hold Cornwall's biggest Carp (+30lb), *Permits:* Available in local shops: Newtown Angling Centre, Praa Sands. Tims Tackle, St. Ives. Atlantic Tackle, Helston. County Angler, Camborne. Post Office, St. Erth plus many more outlets (Please phone for more details) - Permits MUST be obtained prior to fishing, *Charges:* Day £4.50, Conc. £3.50, Week £18, Full membership £40, Assoc. membership £28 (must reside outside Cornwall), Night fishing £60, *Season:* Open all year dawn till dusk; Night fishing by appointment only; Matches held regularly throughout the year, *Methods:* Barbless hooks, full rules + byelaws displayed at lake side (best baits: maggot, worm, pellet, sweetcorn, meat, boilies, nuts)

Sharkey's Pit
Contact: Dave Burn, Strawberry Lane, Joppa, Hayle, 01736 753386, *Water:* 2 lakes approx 2.5 acres, *Species:* Common, Crucian, Mirror + Ghost Carp, Tench, Golden Orfe, Roach, Rudd, Gudgeon + Eels, *Season:* Open all year

Helston

Middle Boswin Farm
Contact: Jonno, Middle Boswin Farm, Porkellis, Helston, TR13 0HR, 01209 860420, *Water:* 1 acre lake; New Carp Lake and match lake proposed for 2001, *Species:* Roach 2lb, Rudd 1.5lb, Bream 4lb, Tench 3lb, Perch 2lb, Hybrid (Roach/ Bream) 2.5lb, *Permits:* Day tickets available at farm, *Charges:* Adult £4, concessions £3, Second rod £1 extra, *Season:* Winter; Dawn to Dusk, Summer 7am - 9 pm, *Methods:* Barbless hooks only, No fixed legers, No cereal groundbait, hemp or nuts, No keepnets or Carp sacks

Launceston

Dutson Water
Contact: Mr Broad, Lower Dutson Farm, Launceston, PL15 9SP, 01566 773147 or 01566 776456, *Water:* 0.75 acre lake, *Species:* Carp, Tench to 6lb 2oz, Bream to 5lb 2oz, Rudd, Perch to 3lb 4oz etc, *Permits:* Available on farm and Homeleigh Garden and Angling Centre, Dutson. Tel: 01566 773147, *Charges:* Day ticket £5. Night fishing by arrangment, *Season:* Open all year, *Methods:* No Groundbait, Barbless hooks only.

Elmfield Farm Coarse Fishery
Contact: Mr J Elmer, Elmfield Farm, Canworthy Water, Launceston, PL15 8UD, 01566 781243, *Water:* 2 acre & 1.25 acre lake, *Species:* Carp to 24lb, Tench to 6lb, Roach to 3lb, Perch to 3.5lb, Bream, Orfe to 1lb, Chub to 3lb & Koi; also new stock of Barbel, *Charges:* £5 - 2 Rods, £4 Children/OAP's, *Season:* Open all year, *Methods:* No keepnets, ground bait in feeders only, barbless hooks, no boilies

Hidden Valley Coarse Fishing Lakes
Contact: Mr. P. Jones, Tredidon, Nr Kennards House, Launceston, PL15 8SJ, 01566 86463, hiddenvalley@tredidon.freeserve.co.uk, *Water:* 2 acre + 0.75 acre lake, *Species:* Common, Mirror, Crucian & Ghost Carp, Tench, Roach, Bream & Rudd, *Charges:* Adults £4.50 for 2 rods, Child/OAP £3.50 for 2 rods, *Season:* Open all year, 7am - 9pm

St. Leonards Coarse Fishing Lake
Contact: Andy Reeve, St. Leonards Equitation Centre, Polson, Launceston, PL15 9QR, 01566 775543, paintballpolson@totaleyes.co.uk, *Water:* 2 Acre lake, *Species:* Carp, Rudd, Bream, Perch, Tench, *Permits:* From House, *Charges:* £3.50 per rod per day, *Season:* Open all year. Please phone before arrival, *Methods:* Barbless hooks, No ground bait

Stowford Grange Fisheries
Contact: Ken Ashworth, Bude Angling Supplies, 6 Queen Street, Bude, 01288 353396, *Water:* 2.5 acre, 1 acre and 1.25 acre lakes, *Species:* Roach, Rudd, Carp 20lb, Bream 10lb 2oz, Tench 6lb 4oz, Perch 4lb 14oz, Gudgeon, Golden Tench, *Permits:* Bude Angling Supplies 01288 353396, evenings 01566 773963, Club membership Mikens Angling Club £25 per year, *Season:* Open all year, *Methods:* Barbless or whisker barbs, no boilies in bottom lake, no nuts, no large Carp in nets

Liskeard

Badham Farm
Contact: Joyce and Robert Brown, St Keyne, Liskeard, PL14 4RW, 01579 343572, *Water:* 0.75 acre lake, *Species:* Carp 15lb, Roach 2.5lb, Tench 3lb and Rudd 2lb, *Permits:* On site, *Charges:* £4/rod/day, *Season:* Open all year dawn to dusk, *Methods:* Barbless hooks only; No boilies; No keepnets; Landing nets to be used at all times; No groundbait

Looe

Shillamill Lakes & Lodges
Contact: Shillamill Lakes, Lanreath, Looe, PL13 2PE, 01503 220886, *Water:* 3 Lakes totalling approx 5 acres, *Species:* Main specimen lake: Common, Mirror and leather Carp. Second lake: Common, Mirror and Ghost, Roach, Perch. Third: Common and Mirror, Golden Rudd, Golden Orfe, Perch, Tench + Roach + Crucian, *Charges:* Private fishing for residents and season ticket holders only, *Methods:* Fishery requirements on applications.

Newquay

Gwinear Pools
Contact: Simon & Jo Waterhouse, Gwinear Farm, Cubert, Newquay, TR8 5JX, 01637 830165, *Water:* 3 acre mixed lake, 60 peg match lake, *Species:* Carp, Roach, Bream, Perch, Rudd, Tench, *Charges:* Day tickets from farm and self service kiosk: £5 adult. £3 OAP's & Juniors. Evening £3 & £2, *Season:* No Close season, *Methods:* Barbless hooks. No keepnets

Oakside Fishery
Contact: Brian & Sandra Hiscock, 89 Pydar Close, Newquay, TR7 3BT, 01637 871275, *Water:* 3 Acre Lake, *Species:* Carp to 20lb, Tench 6lb, Rudd, Bream 5lb, Perch, Roach 2lb, Crucians 2lb, *Permits:* Pay Kiosk, or from bailiff, *Charges:* Adult £3.50 (Two rods), Junior, O.A.P's, Disabled £2.50 (Two Rods), *Season:* All year round, *Methods:* Barbless hooks, No tiger nuts or peanuts and no Carp in keepnets.

Penvose Farm Holidays
Contact: Jonathan Bennett, St. Mawgan, Nr. Newquay, TR8 4AE, 01637-860277 or -860432, *Water:* 2.5 acres of water set in a beautiful valley; this year extending to 3.5 acres in total, *Species:* Carp (Common 15-16lb, Mirror 16-17lb, Ghost 19.5-20lb), Tench (Green 3-4lb, Golden 1/2lb) Bream 4-5lb, Crucians 1.5lb, Rudd 1.5lb, Roach 1lb, *Charges:* Using 2 rods - Static Caravan Residents: free; Tourers & Camping Residents: adults £2, u.14 £1.5; Non-residents: adults £4, u.14 £3, *Season:* No closed season, fishing dawn till dusk, *Methods:* Anglers must hold a valid licence; All nets to be dipped in solution tanks, no keepnets except for matches, landing nets must be used; Ground bait up to 2kg max.; Barbless hooks only

Porth
Contact: South West Lakes Trust, 01837 871565, info@swlakestrust.org.uk, *Water:* Ranger Tel 01637 877959, *Species:* Bags of 130lb plus have been caught. Best Bream 9lb 2oz, Tench 9lb 12oz. Rudd to 3lb. Roach to 1lb 4oz plus. Mixed bags of Roach, Rudd, Skimmers to 60lb, *Permits:* Self service at Porth car park .See South West Lakes Trust coarse advert, *Charges:* Full day £4.50, Concession £3.50, 24 Hour £8.50, Season Day £80, Season Concession £60, Season Child (under 16) £35, Season Day & Night £120, Additional Fisheries £20 each, *Season:* Open all year 24 hours a day, *Methods:* No child under 14 years may fish unless accompanied by an adult over 18 years. No child under 16 may fish overnight unless accompanied by an adult over 18 years, and then only with permission of parent or legal guardian (letter to this effect must be produced)

Trebellan Park
Contact: Trebellan Park, Cubert, Newquay, TR8 5PY, 01637 830522, *Water:* 3 Lakes totalling 2.5 acres, *Species:* Carp, Roach, Rudd, Tench, *Charges:* Day tickets £3.50 /1 rod, £5 /2 rods, *Season:* No close season, 7am to dusk, *Methods:* Barbless hooks only, No keepnets, No ground bait, no boilies

Trethiggey Farm Pond

Contact: Mr Eustice, Trethiggey Farm, Quintral Downs, Newquay, 01637 874665, *Water:* Small quarter acre farm pond, *Species:* Carp, Rudd, Tench, Roach, Bream, *Permits:* On site, *Charges:* £3 per person, max two rods per person. £1.50 juniors and OAP, *Season:* Open all year dawn to dusk. Please telephone before travelling in the winter months, *Methods:* Barbless hooks, no Carp in keepnets, no boilies.

White Acres Country Park

Contact: White Cross, Newquay, TR8 4LW, 01726-862113, *Water:* 8 Lakes totalling approx 20 acres, *Species:* Wide range of almost all species (no Pike or Zander), *Permits:* Available from fishing Lodge, *Charges:* please call for info, *Season:* Fishery open all year round, *Methods:* 'The Method' is banned, Barbless hooks prefered, Some keepnet restrictions, No peas, nuts, or beans

Penzance

Boscathnoe

Contact: South West Lakes Trust, 01837 871565, info@swlakestrust.org.uk, *Water:* Ranger 01579 342366, *Species:* Common Mirror and Crucian Carp with fish into the 20lb range. Roach, Tench, Rudd and Bream also stocked, *Permits:* See South West Lakes Trust coarse advert, *Charges:* Full day £4.50, Concession £3.50, 24 Hour £8.50, Season Day £80, Season Concession £60, Season Child (under 16) £35, Season Day & Night £120, Additional Fisheries £20 each, *Season:* Open all year 1 hour before sunset to 1 hour after sunset, *Methods:* No child under 14 years may fish unless accompanied by an adult over 18 years. No child under 16 may fish overnight unless accompanied by an adult over 18 years, and then only with permission of parent or legal guardian (letter to this effect must be produced)

Choone Farm Fishery

Contact: Mr V.B. Care, Choone Farm, St. Buryan, Penzance, 01736 810220, *Water:* 2 lakes, *Species:* Carp, Tench, Perch, Rudd, *Charges:* 1 rod - £3.50/ person, 2 rods - £4.50, *Season:* Please telephone before travelling, *Methods:* Barbless hooks only, no Carp in keepnets.

Tindeen Fishery

Contact: J. Laity, Bostrase, Millpool, Goldsithney, Penzance, TR20 9JG, 01736 763486, *Water:* 3 lakes approx 1 acre each, *Species:* Carp, Roach, Rudd, Gudgeon, Perch, Tench, Trout, *Charges:* Adults £3, Juniors under 14 £2, Extra rod £1 each, *Season:* All year, night fishing by arrangement, *Methods:* Barbless hooks to be used.

Saltash

Bake Fishing Lakes (Coarse)

Contact: Tony Lister, Bake, Trerule Foot, Saltash, 01752 849027, tony.lister@bakelakes.co.uk, *Water:* 7 lakes adding up to 15+ acres, Coarse and Trout, *Species:* Mirror 21lb, Common 21lb, Ghost 18lb, Crucian Carp, Tench 4lb 2oz, Bream 8lb, Roach, Rudd, *Permits:* At Bake Lakes, *Charges:* £6 per day Specimen Lake, £4.50 per day Small fish lakes. 2 rods per person, reduced rates for pensioners and juniors, *Season:* 8am - Dusk. Earlier by appointment, open all year, *Methods:* Barbless hooks, No nuts or Trout pellets. No keepnets specimen fish. Landing mats. All nets to be dipped before fishing

Bush Lakes

Contact: J Renfree, Bush Farm, Saltash, PL12 6QY, 01752 842148, *Water:* 4 Lakes from half to 1 acre, *Species:* Carp to 30lb, Tench to 3.5lb, Rudd to 1.5lb, Roach to 1.5lb, Bream, Perch to 4.5lb, *Charges:* £5 per person, two rods max, *Season:* Open all year, *Methods:* Barbless hooks, landing mat, no nets for big Carp.

St Austell

Glenleigh Farm Fishery

Contact: Mr & Mrs A Tregunna, Glenleigh Farm, Sticker, St Austell, PL26 7JB, 01726 73154, *Water:* One acre lake, *Species:* Carp (Common, Ghost, Mirror, Leather), Tench, Rudd, Roach, Eels, Gudgeon, Perch, *Permits:* Tickets from lakeside, permits from Sticker post office, *Charges:* £4.50 day, £3.50 child / OAP. £2.50 evening, £1.50 child /OAP. 12 month membership available, *Season:* Open all year dawn to dusk. Night fishing by prior arrangement, *Methods:* Barbless hooks. No keepnets for Carp or any fish over 6lb. No nuts, peas or beans. Max 2 rods per person. Mats to be used

Roche (St Austell) Angling Club

Contact: Mr K. Pyke - Membership Secretary, 41 Roman Drive, Bodmin, PL31 1EN, 01208-79578, *Water:* 6 fresh water lakes in St Austell area, *Species:* Roach, Perch, Rudd, Tench, Eels, Carp, Pike & Bream, *Permits:* Fishing restricted to Members and their guests only. Membership applications available from membership secretary direct, *Charges:* Full Annual membership £30, concessionary £10 plus initial joining fee. Membership to Game and Sea sections only at reduced rates, *Season:* Open all year, *Methods:* As specified in club byelaws

Sunnyview Lake

Contact: Philip Gale, 01726 890715, *Water:* Half acre lake, *Species:* Roach, Rudd, Tench, Perch & Carp, *Permits:* Limited day tickets available by prior booking only - please phone number above, *Charges:* £4 /day /person (maximum 4) Sole hire £16 per day, *Season:* All year, dawn to dusk

St Columb

Meadowside Fishery

Contact: Mr. Terry Price, Meadowside Farm, Winnards Perch, St. Columb, TR9 6DH, 01637 880544, *Water:* 2 lakes mixed coarse fishery, 1 Carp lake, *Species:* Carp, Roach, Perch, Rudd, Tench, Bream, *Charges:* £3.50/1rod, concessions £2.50/1 rod, £1/extra rod, max. 2 rods, *Season:* No close season, 7am to dusk, *Methods:* Barbless hooks, fisheries keepnets, unhooking mats

Retallack Waters

Contact: Retallack Waters, Winnards Perch, Nr St Columb Major, 07971-795907, *Water:* 6.5 acre main lake, separate match canal, *Species:* Common, Mirror and Ghost Carp, Pike, Bream, Tench, Roach and Rudd, *Charges:* Canal £4 adults, £3 children/ OAPs. Main specimen lake £5 adult, £4 children/OAP's, *Season:* Open all year, *Methods:* Barbless hooks only. Unhooking mats required on specimen lake. Dogs allowed by prior arrangement, please phone first.

St Ives

Bussow

Contact: South West Lakes Trust, 01837 871565, info@swlakestrust.org.uk, *Water:* Ranger Tel 01579 342366, *Species:* Rudd to 1.5lb. Roach, Bream and Carp, *Permits:* See South West

Lakes Trust coarse advert, *Charges:* Full day £4.50, Concession £3.50, 24 Hour £8.50, Season Day £80, Season Concession £60, Season Child (under 16) £35, Season Day & Night £120, Additional Fisheries £20 each, *Season:* Open all year 24 hours a day, *Methods:* No child under 14 years may fish unless accompanied by an adult over 18 years. No child under 16 may fish overnight unless accompanied by an adult over 18 years, and then only with permission of parent or legal guardian (letter to this effect must be produced)

Nance Lakes
Contact: Mr or Mrs Ellis, Nance Lakes, Trevarrack, Lelant, St Ives, TR26 3EZ, 01736 740348, *Water:* Three lakes, various sizes, *Species:* Carp, Roach and Bream, *Permits:* No EA Licence required. Permits at site, *Charges:* £5 per day (evening tickets available), *Season:* Open all year 8am to 5pm, *Methods:* Barbless hooks, no keepnets unless competition.

St. Ives Freshwater Angling Society
Contact: Dr. Charles Franklin, Chy-An-Meor, Westward Road, St. Ives, TR26 1JX, 01736-798251, *Water:* 1.5 acre spring-fed lake with depths from 6 to 24 feet, situated in farmland, 5 miles from St.Ives, *Species:* Bream, Carp, Tench, Roach, Rudd, Perch, Gudgeon, and Eels, *Permits:* 1) Tims Tackle, Ayr, St.Ives. 2) Mr. K. Roberts, Woonsmith Farm, Nancledra, Nr. Penzance. 3) Newtown Angling Centre, Newtown, Germoe, Penzance. Location maps available with permits, *Charges:* Adults: Day £4, Weekly £12. Juniors (under 16): Day £2.50, Weekly £8, *Season:* Open all year. No night Fishing, *Methods:* Barbless hooks only. No fish over 3 lb to be retained in a keepnet. All nets to be dipped in disinfectant tank before use. Good baits are maggots, casters, sweetcorn and Trout pellets

Torpoint
Crafthole
Contact: South West Lakes Trust, 01837 871565, info@swlakestrust.org.uk, *Species:* Carp and Tench. Quality Carp up to 30lb, *Permits:* See South West Lakes Trust coarse advert, *Charges:* Full day £5 (limited availability from Trust Headquarters), Season Day £150, Concession £135.Family £250 (Husband, wife and up to 2 children under 16). Additional Fisheries £20

each, *Season:* Open all year 1hr before sunrise to 1hr after sunset, *Methods:* No child under 14 years may fish unless accompanied by an adult over 18 years. No child under 16 may fish overnight unless accompanied by an adult over 18 years, and then only with permission of parent or legal guardian (letter to this effect must be produced)

Millbrook
Contact: Mark or Rebecca Blake, Treganhawke Cottage, Millbrook, PL10 1JH, 01752 823210, *Water:* 1 Acre water in sheltered, wooded valley, *Species:* Perch, Tench, Carp, Crucians, Roach, Rudd, Bream, *Permits:* Self service at water in old phone box, correct money needed, *Charges:* £5 per day, £3 after 5 p.m.-evening, *Season:* Open all year, *Methods:* Barbless hooks, Landing net. Night fishing by arrangement.

Truro
Mellonwatts Mill Coarse Fishery
Contact: Pensagillas Farm, Grampound, Truro, 01872 530232, *Water:* 2 Acre lake, *Species:* Carp to 25lb, Common & Mirror 14lb, Roach, Tench, Golden Rudd, *Charges:* Day ticket £5, Evening £3, *Season:* Open all year. Night fishing by arrangement only

Rosewater Lakes
Contact: Mike & Andy Waters, Hendravossan Farm, Rose, Truro, 01872 571598, 07977 666025, *Water:* 1.5 Acre lake, *Species:* Carp, Tench, Roach, Chubb, Bream, *Permits:* At hut on lakeside, *Charges:* Day £4, u16/OAP £3, Evening from 5pm £2, *Season:* Open all year from dawn till dusk, *Methods:* Barbless hooks only

Threemilestone Angling Club
Contact: Mrs T. Bailey, 9 Sampson Way, Threemilestone, Truro, TR3 6DR, 01872 272578, khaux@aol.com, *Water:* 2 Pools, *Species:* Carp, Tench, Roach, Rudd, Bream, Perch, Goldfish, *Permits:* At lakeside, *Charges:* Seniors £4, Juniors £3, *Season:* All season, No night fishing, *Methods:* Barbless hooks only, No Peanuts etc.

CORNWALL Stillwater Trout

Bodmin
Colliford Lake
Contact: South West Lakes Trust, 01837 871565, info@swlakestrust.org.uk, *Water:* Ranger Tel 01579 342366, *Species:* Brown Trout, *Permits:* Colliford Tavern, *Charges:* Full day £9, Season £120, Reduced day £7, Season £90, Child/Wheelchair £2, Season £30, *Season:* Opens 15 March 2001 - 12th October, *Methods:* Catch & Release operates. Barbless hooks only

Fenwick Trout Fishery
Contact: David & Shirley Thomas, Old Coach Road, Dunmere, Bodmin, PL31 2RD, 01208 78296, *Water:* 2 acre lake plus river fishing. See also entry under Camel, *Species:* Rainbow 1.5lb - 12lb, Browns to 10lb+, *Charges:* £20/Full day (4 fish, 8hrs), £13/Half day (2 fish, 4hrs), *Season:* All year, *Methods:* Fly fishing only

Temple Trout Fishery
Contact: Mr Julian Jones, Temple Trout Fishery, Temple Road, Temple, Bodmin, PL30 4HW, 01208 821730 or 07787 704966, julian@fish43.freeserve.uk, *Water:* 2.7 Acre lake. Plus new 4.5 acre 'any method' lake, *Species:* Rainbows (15lb 5oz) & Brown Trout (16lb 6oz), *Permits:* Available at fishery Tel: 01208-821730, *Charges:* Club membership £6 (2000 price) entitles members to 10% discount on tickets, to fish club events and to purchase a season ticket at £108.75 for 25 Trout - Full day £20.50, 5 fish - 3/4 day £18, 4 fish - 1/2 day £14.50, 3 fish - evening £10.50, 2 fish - child under 16 & disabled £10.50, 2 fish all day, extra fish £5.75. New lake - half price fishing, prices on request, *Season:* Open all year round from 9 a.m to dusk, in winter open 3 days a week Wednesday, Thursday and Sundays or by appointment, *Methods:* Fly fishing on 2,7 acre lake. Any legal method on one bank of new 4.5 acre lake

Boscastle

Venn Down Lakes

Contact: Ted & Sue Bowen, Trebowen, Trevalga, Boscastle, 01840 250018, *Water:* 2 pools, 3 acres, *Species:* Rainbow Trout, *Charges:* Ticket to fish £5, plus fish at £1.85/lb. Junior ticket £3 - 1 fish, *Season:* Open all year except Xmas day, *Methods:* Max hook size 10, single fly only

Camelford

Crowdy

Contact: South West Lakes Trust, 01837 871565, info@swlakestrust.org.uk, *Species:* Brown Trout, *Charges:* Free to holders of a valid Environment Agency Licence, *Season:* 15 March - 12 October, *Methods:* Angling by spinning, fly or bait

Hayle

Tree Meadow Trout Fishery

Contact: John Hodge, Tree Meadow, Deveral Road, Fraddam, Hayle, 01736 850899/850583, *Water:* Two lakes, 2.75 and 1 acre, *Species:* Rainbow and Brown Trout, *Permits:* From fishery. Also contact on mobile: 07971 107156, *Charges:* Day ticket £7 plus £1.85/lb (first four fish killed then catch and release). Sporting ticket £15 all fish returned. Other tickets from £15 - £35, *Season:* Open all year 9 a.m. to dusk, *Methods:* Fly fishing, barbless or debarbed hooks, no droppers, Hook size 10 max.

Launceston

Braggs Wood Water

Contact: Braggs Wood Water, Braggs Hill, Boyton, Nr Launceston, *Water:* 1 Acre lake, *Species:* Rainbow & Brown Trout, *Charges:* 2 Fish ticket £11, 4 Fish ticket £19, Sporting ticket £5 + £1.60 per lb, *Season:* All year round 8am-9pm, *Methods:* Max hook size 8

Rose Park Fishery

Contact: Rose Park Fishery, Trezibbett, Altarnun, Nr Launceston, PL15 7RF, 01566 86278, *Water:* Two lakes, *Species:* Rainbow 13lb, Wild Browns 2.5lb. Stocked Brown Trout 9lb 5oz, *Permits:* From the fishery, *Charges:* 1st fish £4 + £1.65/lb. Thereafter each fish £1.65/lb.Please note £4 charge applies only to first fish. All browns £2.05/lb, *Season:* Open all year, *Methods:* Fly fishing. No catch and release.

Liskeard

Siblyback

Contact: South West Lakes Trust, 01837 871565, info@swlakestrust.org.uk, *Water:* Ranger Tel 01579 342366, *Species:* Premier Rainbow Fishery - Boat & Bank (boats may be booked in advance: 01579-342366). Rod average 2000: 3 fish/rod/day, *Permits:* Self Service Kiosk at Watersports Centre, *Charges:* Full day £15.75, Season £385. Reduced day £12.50, Season £290, Child/Wheelchair £3, Season £90. Evening Monday - Friday £12.50. Season Permits can be used on any Premier Fishery only. Boats £9.50 per day inc. 2 fish extra to bag limits, *Season:* Opens 24 March 2001 - 31st October, *Methods:* Fly fishing. No child under 14 years may fish unless accompanied by an adult over 18 years

Padstow

Pig Trough Fisheries

Contact: Padstow, 01841-520623, *Water:* 3 acre lake, *Species:* Rainbow + Brown Trout: 2 - 10lb approx, *Permits:* From Pig Trough Restaurant, *Charges:* Day: £20/4-fish, half day (5 hrs): £10/2-fish, *Methods:* Barbless Hooks. No Boobies

St. Merryn Fly Fishing Club

Contact: Hon. Sec. Bill Newcombe, 8 Coastguard Station, Hawkers Cove, Padstow, PL28 8HW, 01841 533090, bill@wr-newcombe.fsbusiness.co.uk, *Water:* 3 Acre Lake, *Species:* Rainbow Trout, *Permits:* Pig Trough Restaraunt, St. Merryn, *Charges:* £10 Half day, £20 Full day, *Season:* 1st April - 28th February, *Methods:* Barbless Hooks. No Boobies.

Penzance

Drift Reservoir

Contact: T.B.Shorland (Bailiff), Drift Ways, Drift Reservoir, Penzance, TR19 6AB, 01736 363869, *Water:* 65 acre reservoir, *Species:* Stock Rainbows (3 per day 10 weekly) Wild Browns (No limits on Brown's), *Permits:* At Bailiff's house on reservoir (also Environment Agency licences available), *Charges:* £120 season, £20 weekly, £7 day, £5 evening (at time of printing), *Season:* 1st April - 12th October Brown Trout, 1st April - 31st October Rainbows, *Methods:* No static with boobies, any other traditional fly or lures

Redruth

Stithians

Contact: South West Lakes Trust, 01837 871565, info@swlakestrust.org.uk, *Water:* Ranger Tel 01579 342366, *Species:* Intermediate Rainbow & Brown Trout Fishery. Trout to 6lb, *Permits:* Stithians Watersports Centre (01209 860301), Londis Supply Store, Stithians (01209 860409), *Charges:* Full day £10.50, Season £190, Reduced day £9.50, Season £170, Child/Wheelchair £2, Season £40. Boats £8/day, *Season:* Opens 15 March 2001 - 12th October, *Methods:* Fly fishing only. Catch and release - barbless hooks

Saltash

Bake Fishing Lakes (Trout)

Contact: Tony Lister, Bake, Trerule Foot, Saltash, 01752 849027, tony.lister@bakelakes.co.uk, *Water:* 5 Lakes adding up to 14+ acres, Coarse and Trout. Troutmaster Water, *Species:* Rainbow 12lb 7oz, Brown Trout 10lb, *Permits:* At Bake lakes, *Charges:* Sporting ticket £10 per day. Catch only £5 + £5 - 1 fish, £14 - 2 fish, £18 - 3 fish, £22 - 4 fish, specimen to 15lb or £12 - 2 fish to £20 - 5 fish, Dunes and Flamingo to 8lbs, *Season:* 8am - Dusk, earlier by appointment, *Methods:* Catch and release on 2 lakes. Barbless or debarbed hooks when releasing

St Austell

Orvis Innis Fly Fishery

Contact: Mrs Pam Winch, Orvis Innis Fly Fishery Clubhouse, Innis Moor, Penwithick, St. Austell, PL26 8YH, 01726 851162, innis@butterwell.u-net.com, *Water:* 15 Acres (3 Lakes), Stream fed enclosed water, *Species:* Rainbow Trout, *Permits:* As above, *Charges:* Full day £20 (5 Fish), half day £10.50 (2 Fish), Catch and release £12, *Season:* All year, 8.00 a.m. to dusk, *Methods:* Barbless hooks when catch & release, no static fishing.

Truro

Gwarnick Mill Fishery

Contact: Sue Dawkins, Gwarnick Mill, St. Allen, Truro, TR4 9QU, 01872 540487, *Water:* 1.5 Acre spring and river fed lake, *Species:* Rainbow Trout to 10lb, *Charges:* 4 Fish £18, 3 Fish £14.50, 2 Fish £10, *Season:* Open all year, *Methods:* Barbless Hook preferred.

Ventontrissick Trout Farm
Contact: Gerald Wright, St. Allen, Truro, TR4 9DG, 01872 540497, *Water:* Half acre, *Species:* Rainbow Trout 1.25lb - 10lb, *Charges:* £4.50 per day rod ticket, £1.50 per lb fish killed, First two fish to be killed, thereafter release optional, *Season:* 8.00am till 1hr after sunset 10 p.m, *Methods:* Fly only, Barbless if releasing.

DEVON
River Fishing

South West Rivers Association
Contact: Michael Charleston (secretary), The Gift House, Buckland Monachorum, Yelverton, PL20 7NA, 01822 853293, mwcharl@aol.com, *Water:* South West Rivers Association is the regional organisation of the river associations of Devon and Cornwall and is a consultative and campaigning body for the protection and improvement of south west rivers, their fish stocks and ecology

AVON
South Devon stream not to be confused with Hampshire Avon or Bristol Avon. Rises on Dartmoor and enters sea at Bigbury. Brown Trout, Sea Trout and Salmon.

Avon Fishing Association
Contact: Mr J.E. Coombes, 19 Stella Road, Preston, Paignton, TQ3 1BH, 01803 523139, *Water:* 14.5 miles on the River Avon, *Species:* Salmon, Sea Trout, Brown Trout, *Permits:* From the above. No day tickets, *Charges:* £40 weekly, £65 fortnightly, £70 monthly. Plus a £2 donation to the N.A.S.T, *Season:* 15th March to 30th Sept. 30th Nov for Salmon only, *Methods:* Fly only except spinning below Silveridge Weir 1st October - 30th November

Newhouse Fishery (River Avon)
Contact: Adrian Cook, Newhouse Farm, Moreleigh, Totnes, 01548 821426, *Water:* 0.25 mile on the River Avon, *Species:* Brown Trout, Sea Trout and Salmon, *Permits:* On site, *Charges:* £10 Brown Trout, £25 Salmon, *Season:* As current EA byelaws, *Methods:* As current EA byelaws

AXE & TRIBUTARIES
This quiet meandering stream rises in the hills of west Dorset, runs along the boundary with Somerset before flowing past Axminster to the sea at Seaton. The Axe is a fertile river with good Trout fishing and a run of Salmon and Sea Trout. The two main tributaries, the Coly and Yarty, are also Trout streams and the Yarty has a good run of Sea Trout.

Axmouth
Contact: Harbour Services, Harbour Road, Seaton, 01297 22727, *Water:* Axmouth from lower end Pool below Coly-Axe confluence to Axmouth Bridge, *Species:* Mullet, Bass, Sea Trout, *Permits:* Harbour Services. Seaton, *Charges:* £2.50 Day Adult, £1 Child. £12.50 week Adult, £5 Child, *Methods:* Fishing from East Bank of Estuary Only
Stillwaters (Axe)
Contact: info@land-own.demon.co.uk, *Water:* See under stillwater Trout, Honiton. One Sea Trout rod on River Axe

CLAW
Tetcott Angling Club
Contact: Mr & Mrs J Miller, The Old Coach House, Tetcott, Holsworthy, EX22 6QZ, 01409 271300, *Water:* Approx. half a mile of the River Claw, *Species:* Brown Trout, *Permits:* No day tickets - private club, *Season:* 16th March to 30th September. Daylight hours only, *Methods:* Artificial lures, fly, spinning, worm.

COLY
Higher Cownhayne Farm
Contact: Mrs Pady, Higher Cownhayne Farm, Cownhayne Lane, Colyton, EX24 6HD, 01297 552267, *Water:* Fishing on River Coly, *Species:* Brown & Sea Trout, *Charges:* On application, *Methods:* Fly fishing, no netting

DART & TRIBUTARIES
Deep in the vastnesses of lonely Dartmoor rise the East and West Dart. Between their separate sources and Dartmeet, where they join, these two streams and their tributaries are mainly owned by the Duchy of Cornwall and provide many miles of Salmon, Sea Trout and Trout fishing for visitors. The scenery is on the grand scale and the sense of freedom enjoyed when you know that you can fish away over miles and miles of river is seldom realised on this crowded island. This is a moorland fishery - swift flowing, boulder strewn, usually crystal clear.
Below Dartmeet the river rushes through a spectacular wooded valley before breaking out of the moor near Buckfastleigh and flowing on to its estuary at Totnes. Although there are Brown Trout throughout the river, these middle and lower reaches are primarily Salmon and Sea Trout waters.

Buckfastleigh
Contact: South West Lakes Trust, Higher Coombepark, Lewdown, Okehampton, EX20 4QT, 01837 871565, info@swlakestrust.org.uk, *Water:* 1/4 mile on River Dart. Austins Bridge to Nursery Pool, *Species:* Salmon & Sea Trout, *Permits:* From South West Lakes Trust at above address, *Charges:* Season - £80. Limit of 16 rods, *Season:* 1st February - 30th September
Dart Angling Association
Contact: D.H. Pakes, Holly How, Plymouth Road, South Brent, TQ10 9HA, 01364 73640, *Water:* 9 miles on River Dart. (3.9 miles open to visitors), *Species:* Salmon, Sea Trout, Brown Trout, *Permits:* All permits - Sea Trout Inn, Staverton Tel: 01803 762274, *Charges:* Membership details from secretary. Totnes weir pool £20 per day (only 1 day Salmon, 1 night Sea Trout ticket available). Buckfast (Austin's Bridge) - Littlehempston (left bank) only 2 per day (unless resident at the Sea Trout Inn), *Season:* Salmon 1st February - 30th September. Sea/Brown Trout 15th March - 30th September, *Methods:* Fly (some stretches fly only), spinning, prawn (below Staverton) see club regulations

THE DIRECTORY

DEVON - RIVER FISHING

Duchy Of Cornwall

Contact: Duchy Of Cornwall Office, Duchy Hotel, Princetown, Yelverton, PL20 6QF, 01822-890205, csturmer@duchyofcornwall.gov.uk, *Water:* East & West Dart Rivers and its tributaries down to Dartmeet, *Species:* Salmon and Trout, *Permits:* Charles Bingham Fishing Ltd, West Down, Warrens Cross, Whitchurch, Tavistock. Braileys Field Sport Centre, Market Street, Exeter. The Old Post Office, Poundsgate, Newton Abbot. Two Bridges Hotel, Two Bridges, Princetown, Yelverton. The Post Office, Postbridge, Yelverton. Princetown Post Office, Princetown, Yelverton. Prince Hall Hotel, Two Bridges, Princetown, Yelverton. The Arundell Arms, Lifton. James Bowden & Sons, The Square, Chagford. Badger's Holt Ltd, Dartmeet, Princetown. Exeter Angling Centre, Smythen Street, Exeter. The Forest Inn Hexworthy, Poundsgate, Yelverton. Peter Collings, Huccaby's News, 33 Fore St, Buckfastleigh, *Charges:* Salmon Season: £125, Week £70, Day £20. Trout Season: £55, Week £15, Day £4, *Season:* Salmon: 1st February to 30th September. Trout: 15th March to 30th September, *Methods:* Fly only. Additional information on permit

Hatchlands Trout Farm

Contact: Malcolm Davies, Greyshoot Lane, South Brent, TQ10 9LL, 01364 73500, *Water:* 600 yards, both banks of the River Harbourne (tributary of the Dart), *Species:* Brown Trout, *Charges:* On application, *Season:* See current EA byelaws, *Methods:* Barbless hooks only

Prince Hall Hotel

Contact: Mr Adam Southwell, Nr. Two Bridges, Dartmoor, PL20 6SA, 01822-890403, game@princehall.co.uk, *Water:* Access to all Duchy water, *Species:* Wild Brown Trout 1.5lb, Sea Trout 6lb, Salmon 11lb, *Permits:* Duchy, *Charges:* Trout £4 per day / Salmon £20. Trout week £15. Salmon week £70, *Season:* March - September, *Methods:* Fly only

Two Bridges Hotel

Contact: Two Bridges Hotel, Two Bridges, Rattery, South Brent, 01822 890581, twobridges@warm-welcome-hotels.co.uk, *Water:* Stretch of 600yds double bank fishing, *Species:* Trout & Salmon, *Permits:* At hotel reception, *Charges:* See Duchy permit, *Season:* E.A. Byelaws apply

DEER

Tetcott Angling Club
Contact: Mr & Mrs J Miller, The Old Coach House, Tetcott, Holsworthy, EX22 6QZ, 01409 271300, *Water:* Approx.one mile of the River Deer, *Species:* Brown Trout, *Permits:* No day tickets - private club, *Season:* 16th March to 30th September. Daylight hours only, *Methods:* Artificial lures, fly, spinning, worm.

ERME

A small Devon stream rising on Dartmoor and flowing south through Ivybridge to the sea. The Erme is probably best known for its Sea Trout, but there is also a run of Salmon and Brown Trout are present throughout its length.

EXE & TRIBUTARIES

The Exe rises high on Exmoor and flows through open moorland until it plunges into a steep wooded valley near Winsford. By the time Tiverton is reached the valley has widened and from here to the sea the Exe meanders through a broad pastoral vale until it flows into the estuary near Exeter and finally into the sea between Exmouth and Dawlish Warren. It is the longest river in the south west.

Throughout most of its length the Exe is a good Trout stream, the fast flowing, rocky upper reaches abounding in fish of modest average size, which increases as the river becomes larger and slower in its middle and lower reaches, where fish approaching a pound feature regularly in the daily catch. The Exe has a good run of Salmon and some fishing can be obtained on hotel waters in the middle reaches. In the deep slow waters around Exeter there is a variety of coarse fish, as there is in the Exeter Ship Canal which parallels the river from Exeter to the estuary at Topsham. In an area noted for its Sea Trout streams, the Exe is unusual in that it has no appreciable run of Sea Trout, but it does have some Grayling, a species not often found in the south west. The two main tributaries - the Barle and the Culm - could not be more different in character. The Barle is a swift upland stream which rises high on Exmoor not far from the

source of the Exe, and runs a parallel course, first through open moor and then through a picturesque wooded valley, before joining the parent river near Dulverton. It has good Trout fishing throughout and Salmon fishing on the lower reaches.

The Culm issues from the Blackdown Hills and in its upper reaches is a typical dry fly Trout stream, with good hatches of fly and free-rising fish. From Cullompton until it joins the Exe, the Culm becomes a coarse fishery, with the Dace in particular of good average size.

River Exe & Tributaries Association
Contact: Ian Cook, 01392-254573, *Water:* Association to protect and enhance the natural Trout + Salmon fisheries of the River Exe, *Permits:* No day tickets to fish available

Bellbrook Valley Trout Fishery (River)
Contact: Mike Pusey, Bellbrook Farm, Oakford, Tiverton, EX16 9EX, 01398 351292, mike_pusey@notes.interliant.com, *Water:* Approx 1 mile on Iron Mill Stream, *Species:* Wild Brown Trout, *Charges:* £10 per day (members only), *Season:* March 15th to September 30th, *Methods:* Fly only

Bridge House Hotel
Contact: Brian Smith, Bridge House Hotel, Bampton, EX16 9NF, 01398 331298, *Water:* 1 Mile on River Exe, *Species:* Salmon & Trout; (2000 Season: 12lb Salmon, 3lb Brown Trout), *Permits:* As above, *Charges:* Salmon £20 per day, Trout £10 per day, *Season:* March 15th - Sept 30th, *Methods:* Fly, occasional spinner

Environment Agency - Exe and Creedy
Contact: 01392 444000, *Water:* 3 Miles; 4 sections between Cowley Bridge and Countess Wear Bridge, *Species:* Salmon, *Permits:* Season and Day permits - Exeter Angling Centre, Smythen Street, Off City Arcade, Fore Street, Exeter. (Tel: 01392 436404). Day permits - Topp Tackle, 63 Station Road, Taunton; The Environment Agency, Manley House, Exeter, *Charges:* Season (Limited) £40, Day £4, *Season:* 1st June - 30th September, *Methods:* No worm or maggot. No bait fishing before June 16th. Catch and release of all Salmon prior to June 16th.

140

Exe Duck's Marsh
Contact: Exeter City Council, River & Canal Manager, Civic Centre, Exeter, EX1 1RP, 01392-274306 Fax:01392 265265, *Water:* River Exe, left bank 1 mile downstream Salmon pool weir, *Species:* Salmon (Trout), *Permits:* River & Canal Office, Canal Basin, Haven Rd, Exeter, EX2 8DU, *Charges:* Day tickets only: £5.50, *Season:* 14/2 - 30/9; no night fishing, *Methods:* Voluntary restrictions + E.A.byelaw controls; only artificial fly & lures and all fish returned before June 16

Half Stone Sporting Agency
Contact: Mr Roddy Rae, 6 Hescane Park, Cheriton Bishop, EX6 6SP, 01647 24643, roddy.rae@virgin.net, *Water:* 3.5 miles of prime fishing on the River Exe divided into 3 beats, 4 rods per beat per day. Also 1 mile of River Taw and access to Rivers Yeo, Creedy and Mole, *Species:* Salmon, Brown Trout & Grayling on the Exe. Salmon, Sea Trout & Brown Trout on River Teign, *Permits:* Daily weekly and occasional season lets, *Charges:* Exe - £35 day, Taw - £30 per day, *Season:* Exe: 14th February - 30th September for Salmon. Brown Trout 15th March - 30th September, *Methods:* Fly & Spinner on Exe. All other waters fly only.

Lifton Hall Hotel (Exe)
Contact: 01566 784863, *Water:* See entry under Devon River Fishing - Teign

River Exe (Exeter)
Contact: Exeter City Council, River & Canal Manager, Civic Centre, Exeter, EX1 1RP, 01392-274306 Fax: 01392 265265, *Water:* River Exe, 10 beats between Head Wear & Countess Wear, *Species:* Salmon, *Permits:* Annual, available by post with payment and photograph, *Charges:* £54.60, limited permits, *Season:* 14th Febuary - 30th September, *Methods:* Voluntary restrictions apply, only artificial fly & lures and all fish returned before June 16th

Tiverton Fly Fishing Association
Contact: Exe Valley Angling, 19 Westexe South, Tiverton, EX16 5DQ, 01884 242275, *Water:* 3.5 Miles on River Exe, *Species:* Trout & Grayling, *Permits:* Exe Valley Angling 01884-242275, *Charges:* Senior £13, Conc. £4, Guests £5, *Season:* 15th March - 30th September, *Methods:* Fly only

LYN
Chalk Water, Weir Water, Oare Water, Badgeworthy Water - these are the streams that tumble down from the romantic Doone Country of Exmoor and join to form the East Lyn, which cascades through the spectacular wooded ravine of the National Trust's Watersmeet Estate. The main river has good runs of Salmon and Sea Trout, and wild Brown Trout teem on the Lyn and the tributary streams.

Environment Agency - Watersmeet and Glenthorne
Contact: 01392 444000, *Water:* The fishery is in two parts: The Watersmeet Fishery, leased by the E.A. from the National Trust - Tors Road, Lynmouth to Woodside Bridge, right bank only; Woodside Bridge to Watersmeet both banks; upstream of the Watersmeet right bank only to Rockford. The Glenthorne Fishery - right bank only upstream of Rockford to 300 yards downstream of Brendon Road Bridge. Half a mile of Trout fishing is available on the Hoaroak Water between Hillsford Bridge and Watersmeet; this is specifically for children, who only require a Trout rod licence when fishing this particular stretch if they are aged 12 years or over. Care should be taken as the rocks are slippery. River Lyn information line - 01398 371119, *Species:* Salmon, Sea Trout, Brown Trout, *Permits:* Mr & Mrs Hillier, Brendon House Hotel, Brendon. Tourist Information Centre, Town Hall, Lynton; Mrs J. Fennell, Variety Sports, 23 Broad Street, Ilfracombe; Mrs Topp, Topp Tackle, 63 Station Road, Taunton. Ms Turner, Porlock Visitor Centre, West End, High Street, Porlock. Rockford Inn, Brendon, Lynmouth, N.Devon, *Charges:* Salmon & Sea Trout, season withdrawn for conservation reasons, week £35, day £13.50, evening (8 pm to 2 am) £4; Brown Trout, season £27.50, week £10, day £3. Bag Limits: 2 Salmon, 6 Sea Trout, 8 Brown Trout, *Season:* Salmon 1st March - 30th September; Sea Trout & Trout 15th March - 30th September. Fishing permitted 8 am to sunset, except from 1st June - 30th September when fishing by traditional fly fishing methods is permitted until 2 am between Tors Road & Rockford, *Methods:* Brown Trout, fly only. Salmon, no shrimp or prawn. Artificial fly or lure only before 16th June. Catch and release of all

Salmon prior to 16th June. No weight may be used whilst fly fishing. The weight used for worm fishing and spinning must be lead free and not weigh more than 0.5 ounce and must be attached at least 18 inches from the hook.

OTTER
The Otter springs to life in the Blackdown Hills and flows through a broad fertile valley to join the sea near the little resort of Budleigh Salterton. This is primarily a Brown Trout stream noted for its dry fly fishing for Trout of good average weight. There is also some Sea Trout fishing in the lower reaches.

River Otter Association
Contact: Alan Knight (sec), 01404 42318, *Water:* Comprises riparian owners, anglers and conservationists concerned with the preservation of the total ecology of the River Otter

Clinton Devon Estates
Water: 1.5 miles on the River Otter from Clamour Bridge (footpath below Otterton) to White Bridge near Budleigh Salterton, *Species:* Brown Trout, *Charges:* Free to EA rod licence holders, *Season:* 1st April to 30th September

Deer Park Hotel
Contact: Reception, Deer Park Hotel, Weston, Nr Honiton, EX14 OPG, 01404 41266, *Water:* 6 miles on River Otter, 1 mile on Coly, *Species:* Brown Trout, Occasional Sea Trout & Salmon, *Charges:* Day or season permits available. Prices on application, *Season:* 15th March - 30th September, *Methods:* Dry Fly only.

PLYM
A short stream rising on Dartmoor and running into Plymouth Sound. Trout fishing on the Plym and its tributary the Meavy, with some Sea Trout on the lower reaches and a late run of Salmon.

Plymouth & Dist Freshwater Angling Assoc. (Plym)

Contact: Mr D.L.Owen, 39 Burnett Road, Crownhill, Plymouth, PL6 5BH, 01752 705033, douglas@burnettrd.freeserve.co.uk, *Water:* 1 Mile on River Plym, 1.5 miles on River Tavy, *Species:* Salmon, Sea Trout, Brown Trout, *Permits:* Snowbee, Drakes Court, Langage Business Park, Plymouth. D.K.Sports/Osborne and Cragg, 37 Bretonside, Plymouth, *Charges:* £10 a day Monday to Friday up to 30th September incl.; £15 a day Monday to Friday from 1st October. To join the association, contact secretary. Annual subscription is about £95, *Season:* Plym: April - 15th December; Tavy: March - 14th October, *Methods:* Artificial baits only

Plymouth Command Angling Association (River)

Contact: Mr Vic Barnett Hon.Sec, 5 Weir Close, Mainstone, Plymouth, PL6 8SD, 01752 708206, victor.barnett@talk21.com, *Water:* Fishing rights on the Plym, Tavy and Walkham plus a small private pond near Ivybridge, *Species:* Salmon, Sea Trout and Trout, *Permits:* Membership is open to all serving members of the Royal Navy and Royal Marines with associate membership for serving members of the Army and Air Force. Associate membership is also open to ex-serving members of the Armed Forces, no matter when the time was served, *Charges:* Costs for full membership or associate membership are available on application or enquiry at the above contact, *Season:* Plym, Tavy and Walkham as per Environment Agency Byelaws

Tavy, Walkham & Plym Fishing Club (Plym)

Contact: John Soul, Trevenevow, Crapstone Road, Yelverton, PL20 6BT, 01822 854923, johnsoul@globalnet.co.uk, *Water:* See entry under Tavy, *Species:* Salmon, Sea Trout and Brown Trout, *Permits:* From: DK Sports, Barbican, Plymouth. Moorland Garage, Yelverton. Tavistock Trout Fishery, Mount Tavy, Tavistock, *Charges:* Season Tickets: Salmon £110. Sea Trout £110. Brown Trout £45. Day Tickets available, *Season:* As E.A. byelaws. No day tickets after 30 September, *Methods:* No worm, prawn or shrimp fishing. Complete rules are issued with permit. Full returns must be made to the club secretary as a condition of purchase

TAMAR

The Tamar rises near the north coast, and for most of its course forms the boundary between Devon and Cornwall. It is always a lowland stream flowing through farmland and this fact is reflected in the size of its Trout which have a larger average size than the acid moorland streams. Around Launceston, the Tamar is joined by five tributaries - Ottery, Carey, Wolf, Thrushel and Lyd - which offer good Trout fishing, as does the Inny which enters a few miles downstream. There is a good run of Salmon and Sea Trout, the latter being particularly numerous on the Lyd. There are also Grayling in places.

Arundell Arms

Contact: Mrs Anne Voss-Bark, Lifton, Devon, PL16 0AA, 01566 784666, arundellarms@btinternet.com, *Water:* 20 miles of private fishing on Rivers Tamar, Lyd, Carey, Thrushel, Wolf. Also 3 acre private lake stocked with Rainbow and Brown Trout, *Species:* Rivers: Salmon, Sea Trout and Brown Trout. Lake: Rainbow & Brown Trout, *Charges:* Trout £16/18. Salmon & Sea Trout £16 to £25, *Season:* Salmon March 1st to October 14th. Trout and Sea Trout March 15th to September 30th, *Methods:* Fly and spinner for Salmon (1 fish limit then catch and release). Fly only for Trout and Sea Trout

Endsleigh Fishing Club

Contact: Mr D.Bradbury, Endsleigh House Hotel, Milton Abbot, Tavistock, PL19 0PQ, 01822 870248, medd@crownoffice.chambers.com, *Water:* River Tamar, *Species:* Salmon & Sea Trout, *Charges:* Per rod per full day, £20 March - April; £25 May to June 15th inclusive; £34 June16th to August 31st; £54 September - October; £12 5pm-midnight April-August, *Season:* Endsleigh House Hotel opens March 29th, fishing ends October 10th, *Methods:* Fly

Launceston Anglers Association

Contact: Colin Hookway, 7 Grenville Park, Yelverton, PL20 6DQ, 01822 855053, *Water:* 6 miles on River Tamar and Carey, 7 miles River Inny, *Species:* Brown Trout, Sea Trout, Salmon, *Permits:* The Fishmonger, 16 Southgate Place, Launceston, *Charges:* Salmon & Sea Trout; Day £15, Week £40. Brown Trout: Day £7.50, Week £25, Juniors £2 a day. Day tickets valid for 24 hours from time of purchase, *Season:* From 1st March to 14th October, *Methods:* Brown Trout - fly only, Salmon & Sea Trout - any method subject to byelaws

TAVY

This noted Salmon and Sea Trout river rises deep in Dartmoor and flows its swift rocky course through Tavistock to its estuary, which joins that of the Tamar to the north of Plymouth. The main tributary is the Walkham, which also rises on Dartmoor and provides good moorland Trout fishing.

Plymouth & Dist Freshwater Angling Assoc (Tavy)

Contact: Mr D.L. Owen, 39 Burnett Road, Crownhill, Plymouth, PL6 5BH, 01752 705033, douglas@burnettrd.freeserve.co.uk, *Water:* River Tavy above Tavistock, *Species:* Salmon, Sea Trout and Brown Trout, *Charges:* Tavy fishing is available to members of the association. Contact the secretary for membership details. See entry under River Plym, *Season:* 1st March to 14th October, *Methods:* Artificial baits only

Tavy, Walkham & Plym Fishing Club (Tavy)

Contact: John Soul, Trevenevow, Crapstone Road, Yelverton, PL20 6BT, 01822 854923, johnsoul@globalnet.co.uk, *Water:* Rivers Tavy, Walkham, Plym, Meavy, *Species:* Brown Trout, Salmon, Sea Trout, *Permits:* Only through D.K.Sports, Barbican, Plymouth. Moorland Garage, Yelverton. Tavistock Trout Fishery, Tavistock, *Charges:* Season Trout £45, Season Salmon / Sea Trout £110, plus other permits. Please phone above No. for details, *Season:* See Environment Agency season dates. Please note, no day tickets after 30th September, *Methods:* No worm, prawn, shrimp on Club permit waters. Please note club rules on back of permit including the dates by which accurate returns must be made as a condition of taking a permit

TAW

Like the neighbouring Torridge, the Taw is a Salmon and Sea Trout stream with several hotel waters, offering the visiting angler the opportunities to fish on many miles of river. The Taw quickly leaves Dartmoor after rising close to Okehampton and flows through the rolling farmland of north Devon to its estuary at Barnstaple. Its main tributary, the Mole, also has good Salmon and Sea Trout fishing, and the Mole's own main tributary, the Bray, is a good little Trout stream.

Angling 2000 (Taw)
Contact: 01566 784488, wrt@wrt.org.uk, *Water:* More than 20 beats on the Tamar, Taw & Torridge. Flexible permits fishing for Trout, Salmon, Sea Trout, Grayling and Dace

Barnstaple & District Angling Association (River)
Contact: S.R. Tomms (Secretary), Barnstaple & District Angling Association, Upcott Farm, Brayford, EX32 7QA, 01598 710857, *Water:* Approx 3 miles on the River Taw plus a stretch on the River Yeo, *Species:* Salmon, Sea Trout, Brown Trout, Rainbows, *Permits:* Limited day tickets from: Kingfisher, Barnstaple. Summerlands, Westward Ho!. Variety Sports, Ilfracombe, *Charges:* Membership details from the Secretary. Day tickets from tackle shops, *Season:* Current EA byelaws apply, *Methods:* Current EA byelaws apply.

Crediton Fly Fishing Club (Taw)
Water: See entry under Yeo. 1.5 miles River Taw

Eggesford Country Hotel
Contact: Mr J Pitts, Eggesford, Chulmleigh, EX18 7JZ, 01769 580345, relax@eggesfordhotel.co.uk, *Water:* Fishing on Rivers Taw & Little Dart, *Species:* Prime Salmon, Sea Trout & Brown Trout, *Charges:* Prime Salmon & Sea Trout £20/day (24 hrs), Brown Trout £12.00/day. Salmon, Trout and Sea Trout full week permit (7 days) £100, *Season:* 1st March - 30th September, *Methods:* Spinning March only. Rest of season fly only

Highbullen Hotel
Contact: Chris Taylor, Chittlehamholt, Umberleigh, EX37 9HD, 01769 540561, info@highbullen.co.uk, *Water:* 3 miles River Mole & +2 miles River Taw, *Species:* Salmon 24.5lb (2000), Sea Trout 12lb (1998) & Brown Trout 2lb (1998), *Permits:* From Higbullen Hotel, *Charges:* Brown Trout £15/rod/day. Salmon and Sea Trout from £25/rod to £40/day, *Season:* Salmon 1st March - 30th September, Brown/Sea Trout 15th March - 30th September, *Methods:* Spinner March. Fly March - September. Local byelaw, August and September all Salmon over 70cm have to be returned

Lifton Hall Hotel (Taw)
Contact: 01566 784863, *Water:* See entry under Devon River Fishing - Teign

Nick Hart Fly Fishing (Taw)
Contact: Nick Hart, Exford View, 1 Chapel Street, Exford, Minehead, TA24 7PY, 01643 831101 or 0797 1198559, nick@hartflyfishing.demon.co.uk, *Water:* 1 mile on Taw (Please see entry under Torridge), *Species:* Salmon (to double figures), Sea Trout (excellent numbers), *Permits:* From Nick Hart Fly Fishing, *Charges:* £20/day, 2 rods available, *Season:* 1 March - 31 September, *Methods:* Fly only

Rising Sun Inn
Contact: Heather Manktelow, Rising Sun Inn, Umberleigh, near Barnstaple, EX37 9DU, 01769 560447 Fax:01769 560764, risingsuninn@btinternet.com, *Water:* Access arranged (for residents only) to approx 6 miles of Taw fishing, *Species:* Sea Trout 11.5lb, Brown Trout, Salmon 23lb (18lb Salmon Aug. 2000), *Permits:* Post Office, Umberleigh for licence, *Charges:* £30.00 - £41.13, *Season:* Salmon 1st March - 30th Sept, Sea/Brown Trout 15th March - 30th Sept, *Methods:* As per E.A. rules

Tremayne Water
Contact: J.G. Smith, 020 89958109, gilbert.smith@virgin.net, *Water:* 1.5 miles single + double bank fishing on the upper Taw and Little Dart, *Species:* Salmon, Sea Trout, *Charges:* Limited season rods only, *Season:* FA Byelaws apply, *Methods:* EA Byelaws apply

TEIGN

The Teign has two sources high up on Dartmoor which form the North and South Teign but the two branches of the Teign quickly leave the moor to join west of Chagford while still very small streams. Between Chagford and Steps Bridge the river runs through a dramatic wooded gorge which is at its most spectacular at Fingle Bridge, a popular beauty spot. All along the Teign the Spring fisherman is greeted by myriads of daffodils, which are at their most numerous around Clifford Bridge. The upper Teign offers good fishing for wild Trout and Sea Trout, with Salmon fishing in suitable conditions from April to the end of the season. Much of the upper river is controlled by the Upper Teign Fishing Association. From just south of the Moretonhampstead - Exeter road to the estuary at Newton Abbot. the Teign is mostly controlled by the Lower Teign Fishing Association. This water has plenty of Brown Trout but is essentially a Sea Trout and Salmon fishery.

River Teign Riparian Owners Association
Contact: Mr. W.J.C. Watts, Park House, 18 Courtenhay Park, Newton Abbot, TQ12 4PS, 01626-332345, cwatts@wbb.co.uk, *Water:* Riparian Owners Association representing interest of owners of fishing waters on River Teign, *Permits:* No day tickets available through the association

Lifton Hall Hotel (Teign)
Contact: Lifton Hall Country House Hotel, New Road, Lifton, PL16 0DR, 01566 784863, *Water:* Private beats on - Tamar, Fowey, Teign, Camel, Exe, Taw, *Species:* Salmon, Brown Trout, Sea Trout, *Charges:* Please enquire at hotel

Lower Teign Fishing Association
Contact: Mr R Waters, 121 Topsham Road, Exeter, EX20 4RE, 01392-251928, *Water:* 14 miles River Teign, *Species:* Salmon, Sea Trout, *Permits:* 3 Beats with 3 tickets on each (beat 3 not available until 1st May), *Charges:* £15 por day (24 hour period - night-time Sea Trout fishing). Beat 3 - September £25 per day, *Season:* 1st Febuary - 30th September, *Methods:* Spinning, fly (fly only at night), No worming or maggots.

DEVON - RIVER FISHING

Mill End Hotel
Contact: Sandy Park, Chagford, TQ13 8JN, 01647 433106, millendhotel@talk21.com, *Water:* 3 miles plus access to a further 8 miles, *Species:* Brown Trout, Salmon and Sea Trout, *Charges:* £15 per day, Free to residents

Upper Teign Fishing Association
Contact: Roddy Rae, 6 Hescane Park, Cheriton Bishop, EX6 6SP, 01647 24643, roddy.rae@virgin.net, *Water:* Approx 8 miles on upper Teign, *Species:* Brown Trout to 1lb 4oz, Sea Trout to 8lb & Salmon to 18lb, *Permits:* From: The Anglers Rest, Drewsteignton. Drewsteignton Post Office. Bowdens, Chagford. Drum Sports, Newton Abbot. Mill End Hotel, Sandy Park, Chagford. Clifford Bridge Caravan Park. Braileys Field Centre, Exeter. Exeter Angling Centre. Orvis, Exeter tel: 01392 272599. All anglers must be in possession of a current Environment Agency licence, *Charges:* Ordinary Member - Annual Subscription £145 Full season for Salmon, Sea Trout & Brown Trout. Trout Member - Annual subscription £52.50 Full season for Brown Trout. Temporary Members' Tickets - Salmon & Sea Trout £15 per day (6 ticket limit per day from Anglers Rest plus 4 ticket limit -Salmon and Sea Trout from Drewsteignton Post Office). Sea Trout £7 per day (4 ticket limit per day from Bowdens, Chagford). Membership Enquiries to Secretary. Brown Trout Adult season £40, juvenile (under 16) £15. Week £17.50. juvenile £7. Day £5. juvenile £2.50, *Season:* Brown Trout: March 15th - September 30th. Sea Trout: March 15th - September 30th. Salmon: February 1st - September 30th

TORRIDGE
Throughout its length the Torridge flows through the rolling farmland of north Devon. It rises close to the coast near the Cornish border and swings in a great arc before flowing into the estuary that it shares with the Taw. The middle and lower reaches are best known for their Salmon and Sea Trout, but can offer surprisingly good Trout fishing. The upper reaches offer good small-stream Trout fishing, as does the main tributary, the Okement, which is formed by two branches that rise on Dartmoor to the south of Okehampton.

Torridge Fishery Association
Contact: Charles Innis, 01409-231237, Fax: 231237, *Water:* An association of riparian owners on the Torridge whose aim is to secure and maintain the well being of the river and its ecology.Several day permits available, please phone for details

Angling 2000 (Torridge)
Contact: 01566 784488, wrt@wrt.org.uk, *Water:* More than 20 beats on the Tamar, Taw & Torridge. Flexible permits fishing for Trout, Salmon, Sea Trout, Grayling and Dace

Clinton Arms
Contact: Wendy, 01805 623279, *Water:* Approx half mile of double bank on River Torridge (left hand bank only last 200yds), *Species:* Brown Trout, Sea Trout, Salmon, *Permits:* The Clinton Arms on 01805 623279, *Charges:* £15/day/rod

Half Moon Fishery
Contact: Charles Inniss, Half Moon Inn, Sheepwash, Nr Hatherleigh, EX21 5NE, (01409) 231376, Fax: 231673, lee@halfmoon.demon.co.uk, *Water:* 12 Miles on R.Torridge + 6 Acre Trout lake. See entry under stillwater Trout, *Species:* River: Salmon, Sea Trout, Brown + Wild Brown Trout. Lake: Rainbows only (2-3lb), *Permits:* Day tickets available to residents and non-residents, *Charges:* Salmon & Sea Trout £17.50, Brown Trout £10, *Season:* Mid March - September 30th, *Methods:* Dry or Wet fly only, Spinning in March

Little Warham Fishery
Contact: Group Captain P. Norton-Smith, Little Warham House, Beaford, Winkleigh, EX19 8AB, 01805 603317, *Water:* 2 Miles of River Torridge, *Species:* Salmon, Sea Trout, Brown Trout, *Permits:* As above, *Charges:* £20/day/rod, all species, *Season:* March 1st - September 30th, *Methods:* Fly only

Nick Hart Fly Fishing (Torridge)
Contact: Nick Hart, Exford View, 1 Chapel Street, Exford, Minehead, TA24 7PY, 01643 831101 or 0797 1198559, nick@hartflyfishing.demon.co.uk, *Water:* 2.25 miles on Torridge, *Species:* Salmon, Sea Trout, Brown Trout, *Permits:* From Nick Hart Fly Fishing, *Charges:* Brown Trout: £8, Sea Trout: £12 - £15, Salmon: £15 - £20, 2 rods/day available, *Season:* 15 March - 31 Sptember, *Methods:* Fly only after 30th April (Salmon & Sea Trout), Fly only all season (Brown Trout - Catch & release prefered)

Riversdale
Contact: Mr & Mrs E. Ellison, Riversdale, Weare Giffard, Bideford, EX39 4QR, 01237 423676, riversdale@connectfree.co.uk, *Water:* 0.75 mile of right bank fishing on the River Torridge every day. 2.5 miles on Mon/Tue/Wed, *Species:* Salmon, Sea Trout and Brown Trout, *Permits:* Priority to residents, see www.riversdale-devon.com, *Charges:* Daily permit £15 per rod per day, all species, *Season:* Salmon: 1st March - 30th Sept, Sea Trout: 15th March - 30th Sept, *Methods:* Spinning to 31st March, otherwise fly only.

South Hay Fishery (Torridge)
Water: See entry under stillwater Trout, Beaworthy. 2 miles on Torridge

The Half Moon Inn
Contact: Charles Innis, Half Moon Inn, Sheepwash, Beaworthy, EX21 5NE, (01409)231376, Fax: 231673, lee@halfmoon.demon.co.uk, *Water:* 12 miles River Torridge, 3x 2 acre lake, *Species:* River: Sea, Brown & Wild Brown Trout, Salmon; Lakes: Rainbow Trout 2-3lb, *Permits:* Day tickets for residents & non-residents, *Charges:* Sea Trout & Salmon: £17.50, Brown Trout: 3-fish £10, Laices: 2-fish £10, 4-fish £15, *Season:* Mid-march - 30th September, *Methods:* Dry & Wet Fly only, Spinning in March

The Haytown Beat
Contact: Fred Cogdell, Bulkworthy, Holsworthy, 01288-381669, fred@ftcogdell.co.uk, *Water:* Secluded half a mile of single bank, comprising series of pools and stickles, *Species:* Brown Trout, Salmon and Sea Trout, *Permits:* Please contact Fred Cogdell, *Charges:* £40/day, 2 rods, 4 fish limit per rod - also possible: fixed days throughout season, prices on application, *Season:* Dawn to dusk, Brown Trout: 31/3 - 30/9; Sea Trout: 15/3 -30/9; Salmon:1/3 - 30/9, *Methods:* Fly only

YEALM

Upper Yealm Fishery
Contact: Snowbee U.K. Ltd, 01752 334933, flyfish@snowbee.co.uk, *Water:* 1 Mile both banks River Yealm, *Species:* Sea Trout, Brown Trout (Stocked), Salmon, *Permits:* Snowbee U.K. Ltd, Drake's Court, Langage Business Park, Plymouth, *Charges:* Full membership £100, Half rod £50, Day ticket (All species) £10, *Season:* Brown Trout & Sea Trout 15th March - 30th Sept, Salmon 1st April - 15th December, *Methods:* Fly Fishing & Spinning

YEO

Crediton Fly Fishing Club (Yeo)
Contact: David Pope, 21 Creedy Road, Crediton, EX17 1EW, 01363 773557, *Water:* 5 miles Rivers Yeo & Creedy, 1.5 miles River Taw, *Species:* Brown Trout, Sea Trout & Salmon, *Permits:* Contact on the internet: http://freespace.virgin.net/howard.thresher/cffcl.html or 01363-773557, *Charges:* Weekly (5 days) £20, Season £65, Juniors £5. Two day weekend (Sat-Sun) £20, *Season:* Environment Agency Season, *Methods:* Fly only.

DEVON Stillwater Coarse

Bampton

Four Ponds
Contact: Mr Valentine, Bowdens Lane, Shillingford, Bampton, EX16 9BU, 01398 331169, *Water:* 2 ponds totalling approx 1.5 acres, *Species:* Carp to 20lb, Roach, Rudd, Tench to 5lb, Perch to 4lb, *Permits:* At pond, *Charges:* £4/day, *Season:* Open all year, 6am to dusk, *Methods:* Barbless hooks only, all children under 12 must be accompanied by an adult, no keepnets

Barnstaple

Barnstaple & District A. A. (Coarse Ponds)
Contact: S.R. Tomms (Secretary), Barnstaple & District Angling Association, Upcott Farm, Brayford, EX32 7QA, 01598 710857, *Water:* 5 mixed coarse fishing ponds in the Barnstaple area ranging from 0.5 acres to 2 acres, *Species:* Roach, Rudd, Carp, Perch, Bream, Tench and Eels, *Permits:* Members only. Details from the secretary, *Charges:* £27.50 per year adult. Children (18 and under) £10 per year, *Season:* All year, dawn to dusk, *Methods:* Full rules in the membership book. Barbless hooks only.

Little Comfort Farm
Contact: Little Comfort Farm, Braunton, EX33 2NJ, 01271 812414, jackie.milson@btclick.com, *Water:* 1 acre approx, *Species:* Carp, Rudd, Roach, Tench, Orfe, *Charges:* £5 all day, £4 half day, £3 evening, *Methods:* Barbless hooks, no keepnets

Riverton House & Lakes
Contact: Dave Shepherd or Sue Bryant, Riverton House & Lakes, Swimbridge, Barnstaple, EX32 0QX, 01271 830009, fishing@riverton.fsnet.co.uk, *Water:* Two 2 acre lakes, *Species:* Carp to 25lb, Bream, Tench, Roach, Perch, Chub, Rudd & Eels, *Permits:* Agent for Environment Agency rod licences, *Charges:* Adult day £5, Junior £3, Match bookings £4 (min 10 pegs). Specials: 'Dads and Lads' (one adult & one junior) £7. Family ticket (2 adults and 2 juniors) £12. Half day ticket available. Night fishing by appointment, *Season:* Open all year, *Methods:* Barbless hooks, care and consideration

Beaworthy

Anglers Eldorado
Contact: Zyg or Bailiff Don Parsons, The Gables, Winsford, Halwill,, Beaworthy, EX21 5XT, 01409 221559, *Water:* Four lakes from 1 acre to 4 acres, *Species:* Carp to 25lb, Grass Carp to 18lb, Wels Catfish to 20lb, Golden Tench to 5lb, Golden Orfe to 6lb, Blue orfe to 2lb, Golden Rudd to 2lb, Koi to 10lb, *Permits:* Also from Halwill Newsagents, *Charges:* £4 per day per rod, £3 Juniors & O.A.Ps, *Season:* All year, 8am-9pm or dusk (Which ever is earlier), *Methods:* Barbless hooks, No keepnets or sacks

Anglers Shangrila
Contact: Mr Zyg Gregorek, The Gables, Winsford, Halwill, Beaworthy, EX21 5XT, 01409 221559, *Water:* Three match only lakes, 240 pegs, *Species:* Carp, Golden Tench, Golden Orfe. Top weights of 100lbs possible, *Permits:* From Zyg only, *Charges:* You book the whole lake charges depend on how many people, *Season:* All year. Open matches on Wednesdays, *Methods:* Barbless hooks

Bideford

Bideford & District Angling Club
Contact: A.J. Kelly, Honestone Street, Bideford, 01237-476665, *Water:* Bideford based club with coarse, game & sea sections; fishing throughout South West, *Permits:* Membership form from club, open 7pm-11pm, *Charges:* £5 per annum, concessions for juniors/OAPs

Fosfelle Country House Hotel (Coarse)
Contact: Hartland, Bideford, 01237 441273, *Water:* Approx half acre pond, *Species:* Carp, Tench, Roach, Rudd, *Charges:* £5 per day, *Season:* Open all year, *Methods:* Displayed on site.

Hartland Forest
Contact: E.Y.E. Bookings Office, East Yagland Estate, Hartland Golf & Leisure Parc, Nr Clovelly, Bideford, EX39 5RA, 01237 431001, *Water:* 2 lakes covering just over 3 acres (surroundings are valuable wildlife habitat), *Species:* Carp to 30lb. Tench, Roach and Rudd, *Charges:* £5/day, £25/week, yearly membership available, *Season:* Open all year, *Methods:* No keepnets, No Boilies. Barbless hooks only, No night fishing, Full details on request

Jennetts
Contact: South West Lakes Trust, 01837 871565, info@swlakestrust.org.uk, *Water:* Ranger Tel 01288 321262, *Species:* Commons to 22lb, Mirrors to 23lb. Quality bags of smaller Carp, Roach and Tench to pole and float, *Permits:* See South West Lakes Trust coarse advert, *Charges:* Full day £4.50, Concession £3.50, 24 Hour £8.50, Season Day £80, Season Concession £60, Season Child (under 16) £35, Season Day & Night £120, Additional Fisheries £20 each, *Season:* Open all year 6.30am to 10pm. Please note that there is no access to the car park outside these times, *Methods:* No child under 14 years may fish unless

accompanied by an adult over 18 years. No child under 16 may fish overnight unless accompanied by an adult over 18 years, and then only with permission of parent or legal guardian (letter to this effect must be produced)

Knights Country Club

Contact: Freshwaters UK Ltd., Woolsery, Bideford, EX39 5RG, Tel/Fax 01409-211643, freshwaters@supanet.com, *Water:* 1½ acre, *Species:* Carp, Tench, Perch, Bream & Roach, *Permits:* Day account, *Charges:* £5/day, *Season:* All year, *Methods:* See day ticket.

Little Weach Fishery

Contact: 1 Weach Cottage, Westleigh, Bideford, 01237 479303, *Water:* 2 Lakes totalling approx 1 acre, *Species:* Crucian, Common, Mirror and Koi Carp to 16lb, Tench 7lb, Roach 1.5lb, Rudd, Bream, Goldfish 1lb, *Charges:* £4 per day, £2 Children. Under 12's must be accompanied by an adult, *Season:* Open all year dawn to dusk, *Methods:* No keepnets or boilies.

Melbury

Contact: South West Lakes Trust, 01837 871565, info@swlakestrust.org.uk, *Water:* Ranger Tel 01288 321262, *Species:* Best Mirror 27.5lb. Good mixed bags of Roach, Rudd and Bream to pole, float and feeder, *Permits:* See South West Lakes Trust coarse advert. Limited season permits from South West Lakes Trust, *Charges:* Full day £4.50, Concession £3.50, Season Child (u.16) £35, Season Day & Night £120, Additional Fisheries £20 each, *Season:* Open all year from 6.30am to 10pm, *Methods:* No child under 14 years may fish unless accompanied by an adult over 18 years. No child under 16 may fish overnight unless accompanied by an adult over 18 years, and then only with permission of parent or legal guardian (letter to this effect must be produced).

Buckfastleigh

Nurston Farm Fishery

Contact: Mabin Family, Nurston Farm, Dean Prior, Buckfastleigh, TQ11 0NA, 01364-642285, *Water:* 2.5 acre lake + 3 miles River Dart, *Species:* Roach to 2.5lb, Tench to 5lb, Rudd to 1lb, Bream to 4lb, Carp (different species) to 15lb, *Charges:* Dawn till dusk £5 / u14s £3 / 4pm till dusk £3, *Methods:* Barbless hooks, no keepnets, no boilies / match bookings

Chudleigh

Trenchford

Contact: South West Lakes Trust, 01837 871565, info@swlakestrust.org.uk, *Water:* Ranger Tel 01647 277587, *Species:* Pike up to 30lb, *Permits:* Self service kiosk at Kennick Reservoir, *Charges:* Full day £4.50, Concession £3.50, 24 Hour £8.50, Season Day £80, Season Concession £60, Season Child (under 16) £35, Season Day & Night £120, Additional Fisheries £20 each. Full day boat + fishing £8.50 (boats must be booked 48 hrs in advance), *Season:* Open all year 24 hrs/day, *Methods:* No child under 14 years may fish unless accompanied by an adult over 18 years. No child under 16 may fish overnight unless accompanied by an adult over 18 years, and then only with permission of parent or legal guardian (letter to this effect must be produced)

Combe Martin

Newberry Farm Coarse Fishing

Contact: Mr.& Mrs. Greenaway, Newberry Farm, Woodlands, Combe Martin, EX34 0AT, (01271) 882334, Fax:882880, *Water:* 2 acre lake, *Species:* Newly formed lake stocked Autumn 1999 with over 300kg (600lb) of fish; Carp & Green Tench to 4kg (8lb), Roach, Rudd & Perch, *Permits:* From above address, *Charges:* £5/day, max 2 rods; evening or half day tickets also available, half price to camping site residents, *Season:* Open Easter till end October (please book in advance to fish Nov.-March), *Methods:* Barbless hooks, no leaded weights, ground bait or keepnets

Crediton

Creedy Lakes

Contact: Sandra Turner, Longbarn, Crediton, EX17 4AB, 01363 772684, *Water:* 4.5 acre & 1/2 acre spring fed lakes, *Species:* Common, Mirror & Koi Carp plus Tench, *Charges:* Day ticket £5 (up to 2 rods). £6 (3 rods), Evening ticket £2.50 (up to 2 rods). £3 (3 rods), *Season:* March through to end December, *Methods:* Barbless Hooks, Minimum line 8lbs, No keepnets or nut baits. No poles or beachcasters. Unhooking mats and 'Klinik' antiseptic compulsory.

Lower Hollacombe Fishery

Contact: Mr. C. Guppy, Lower Hollacombe, Crediton, EX17 5BW, 01363-84331, *Water:* Approximately 1 acre, *Species:* Common Carp, Koi Carp, Rudd, Tench, Mirror Carp, Crucian Carp, Roach, Perch, *Permits:* At bank side, *Charges:* £4/day, £3/day under 14, £2.50 evenings, under 16 must be accompanied by adult, *Season:* All year round, *Methods:* Barbless hooks, no boilies or nut baits

Oldborough Fishing Retreat

Contact: Wendy Wilshaw, Oldborough Fishing Retreat, Morchard Bishop, Crediton, EX17 6SQ, 01363 877437, wendywilshaw@eclipse.co.uk, *Water:* 2 acres of lakes, *Species:* Mirror, Leather and Common Carp, Tench, Roach, Rudd, Perch and Eels, *Permits:* By prior arrangement, *Charges:* £4 per day. £3 juniors, *Season:* Open all year, *Methods:* Barbless hooks only. No keepnets. No Boilies. No night fishing.

Salmonhutch Coarse Fishery

Contact: Mr Mortimer, Uton, Crediton, EX17 3QL, 01363 772749, *Water:* Three 1 acre spring fed lakes, *Species:* Mirror to 26lb 1oz and Common Carp to 20lb 12oz, Tench to 5lb, Rudd, Perch, *Permits:* On Site, *Charges:* Day fishing 7am to 10pm, from £4 for Adults. Night fishing 9pm to 7am, from £4 (prior booking required) Evening fishing from £2.50, *Season:* All Year, *Methods:* Barbless hooks, no long shank bent hooks, no permanently fixed lead rigs. Minimum 8lb line for Carp, 4lb for general fishing. No Carp in keepnets. Full rules from the fishery

Shobrooke Lake

Contact: Clare Shelley, Shobrooke Park, Crediton, EX17 1DG, Tel/Fax: 01363 775153, *Water:* 9 acre lake in superb parkland setting, *Species:* Tench, Carp, Mirror, Rudd, Perch, Roach, *Permits:* Not from above address - Ladd's Sport Shop, Exeter Rd, Crediton 01363-772666 or Crediton Angling Centre, 109 High Street, Crediton 01363-772775, *Charges:* Adult: £5/day, £10/week, £50/year; u.16-Student-Pensioner: £2.50/day, £5/week, £25/year, *Methods:* Fishing by rod or line from bank only; no night fishing; no keepnets

Cullompton

Coombelands & Stout Fisheries

Contact: Mr & Mrs Berry, Higher Coombelands, Knowle, Cullompton, EX15 1PT, 01884 855248, rosemary@billingsmoor.fsnet.co.uk, *Water:* 4 Lakes totalling approx 3 acres + 3 lakes in 1 acre, *Species:* 1 Carp lake, Mixed coarse fishing ponds, *Charges:* From £3.50 - £5.50 /day, Evening and season tickets available, *Season:* Open all year, *Methods:* Barbless hooks only

Millhayes Fishery

Contact: Mr Tony Howe, Millhayes, Kentisbeare, Cullompton, EX15 2AF, 01884 266412, *Water:* 2 Acre spring fed lake, 0.5 acre Tench lake, *Species:* Carp 20lb, Tench, Roach, Rudd, *Charges:* £5 Adults, £2.50 Under 16, £3 Evenings, *Season:* 1st March - 31st December, *Methods:* Barbless hooks only, No boilies, No night fishing, No Carp over 1lb in nets, Nets to be dipped, No dogs

Newcourt Ponds

Contact: Andy Hitt, Newcourt Barton, Langford, Cullompton, EX15 1SE, 01884 277326, *Water:* Four lakes totalling 1.5 acres, *Species:* Carp, Tench, Bream, Golden Orfe, Rudd, Golden Tench, *Permits:* Collected on bank, *Charges:* Adults £3 two rods. under 16 £2 one rod. Extra rods £1, *Season:* Open all year dawn to dusk. No night fishing, *Methods:* No Boilies. Barbless Hooks. No Carp over 2lb in nets

Padbrook Park

Contact: Richard Chard, Padbrook Park, Cullompton, EX15 1RU, 01884 38286, *Water:* 3 acre lake, *Species:* Many Carp up to 20lb, *Charges:* £4 Day. £2.50 half day, *Methods:* No keepnets.

Pound Pond Farm

Contact: Mr A.R.Davey, Butterleigh, Cullompton, 01884 855208, *Water:* Small spring fed pond, *Species:* Mirror, Common Carp, Roach, Tench, Perch, Rudd, *Charges:* £3 per rod per day, £1.50 children, *Season:* All year, *Methods:* Barbless hooks only. No Boilies.

South Farm

Contact: Mrs. Susan Chapman, Blackborough, Blackdown Hills, Cullompton, EX15 2JE, (01823)681078, Fax: 680483, chapmans@southfarm.co.uk, *Water:* 4 lakes (1/3-2/3 acre each), *Species:* Carp, Roach, Chub, *Charges:* £5/day, *Season:* All year, *Methods:* Barbless hooks, restricted use of keepnets, no boilies, net dip

Upton Lakes

Contact: Richard Down, Upton Farm, Cullompton, EX15 1RA, Tel/Fax:01884 33097, 07968029022, richdown11@hotmail.com, *Water:* 1.5 acres + 1.25 acres new match lake (day tickets available), opening April 2001, *Species:* Carp 23lb 3oz, Bream 9lb 12oz, Tench 6lb, Perch 3lb, Roach & Rudd +/- 1lb + Crucian Carp, *Charges:* £3.50 adults, £2.50 juniors, up to 3 rods; season tickets (from April/April) £80 adults, £50 juniors, *Season:* Dawn until dusk, No night fishing, *Methods:* Barbless hooks, No boilies, No peanuts

Verbeer Manor Lakes

Contact: Jamie Snow, Verbeer Manor, Willand, Cullompton, EX15 2PE, 01884 33312 Fax:01884 32903, verb@cwcom.net, *Water:* 3 Lakes consisting of: Old lake - 1 acre, Match lake - 4 acre, Swan lake - 1 acre with islands, *Species:* Carp 20lb, Bream 8lb, Tench 5lb, Roach 1lb, Rudd 1lb, Perch 1.8lb, Eels 2lb, Hybrids 3lb, Pike 10lb, *Permits:* Tickets available on the bank, *Charges:* £2.50 per rod. Two rod limit, *Season:* No close season, *Methods:* No method fishing, barbless hooks, no Carp sacks, no pets; A full list of rules on day ticket

Dartmouth

Old Mill

Contact: South West Lakes Trust, 01837 871565, info@swlakestrust.org.uk, *Species:* Carp to over 20lb, Roach to 2lb. Tench and Bream, *Permits:* See South West Lakes Trust coarse advert, *Charges:* Season Child (u.16) £35, Season Day & Night £150, Concession £135. Family (husband, wife & up to 2 children u.16) £250. Additional Fisheries £20 each, *Season:* Open all year 24 hours a day, *Methods:* No child under 14 years may fish unless accompanied by an adult over 18 years. No child under 16 may fish overnight unless accompanied by an adult over 18 years, and then only with permission of parent or legal guardian (letter to this effect must be produced).

Dawlish

Ashcombe Fishery

Contact: Ashcombe Adventure Centre Ltd, Ashcombe, Near Dawlish, EX7 0QD, 01626 866766, *Water:* 3 Lakes approx 3 acres, *Species:* Carp 18lb, Tench 4lb, Roach 2lb, *Permits:* Day tickets/permits available from lakes (fishing inspector), *Charges:* Adults £4.50, Juniors / OAP's £3.50, *Season:* Open all Year, *Methods:* Barbless Hooks, No large Carp to be kept in keepnets, No boilies

Exeter

Darts Farm Fishing Lakes

Contact: James Dart, Darts Farm, Clyst St George, Topsham, Nr Exeter, EX3 0QH, 01392 878200 Fax:01392 878205, dartsfarm@ukgateway.net, *Water:* 3 acres lakes, *Species:* Carp max 27lb, Bream max 8-10lb, Roach, *Permits:* Available from Darts farm shop. E.A. licence required, *Charges:* Adult: 1 rod - £3.50, 2 or more rods £4.50. O.A.P/Child (under 16): 1 rod - £2.50, 2 or more rods £3.50, *Season:* All year round; Night Fishing by arrangement, *Methods:* Barbless hooks, do not encourage keep nets, disinfectant tanks for dipping tackle

Exeter & Dist. Angling Assoc
Contact: Barry Lucas, Mayfield, Gorwyn Lane, Cheriton Bishop, Exeter, EX6 6JL, 01647 24566, family@blucas.freeserve.co.uk, *Water:* 26 miles of River, Canal, Lakes, Ponds in Exeter area, *Species:* Bream, Carp (30+), Roach, Rudd, Chub, Pike (25+), Perch, *Permits:* Exeter Angling Centre, Smythen Street (Off Market Street). Bridge Cafe, Countess Weir. Braileys Field Sports, Market Street. County Sports, Station Road, Cullompton. Exmouth Tackle & Sport, The Strand, Exmouth. Tackle Trader, Wharf Road, Newton Abbot. Exe Valley Angling, West Exe South, Tiverton, *Charges:* £25/adult, £6 for Juniors 12 & over, Senior £12.50/week, Junior £3.50/week, Senior £3.50/day, Junior £1.25/day, Senior Citizens/disabled annual permit only £12.50, *Season:* Various - details from association, *Methods:* Live bait permitted up to max. 6/day from the water to be fished, no larger than 6" long.

Exeter Ship Canal
Contact: Exeter City Council, River & Canal Manager, Civic Centre, Exeter, EX1 1RP, 01392-274306 Fax:01392 265265, *Water:* 5 1/4 miles of canal, both banks; upper 2 miles free permits, *Species:* Roach, Bream, Tench, Carp, Pike & Eels, *Permits:* River & Canal Office, Canal Basin, Haven Rd, Exeter, EX2 8DU, *Charges:* Free permits with proof of identity or E.A. licence; lower level 3 1/4 miles on Exeter & DAA permit, *Season:* Open, *Methods:* No live or dead bait coarse fish

Hogsbrook Lakes
Contact: Desmond & Maureen Pearson, Russett Cottage, Greendale Barton, Woodbury Salterton, Exeter, EX5 1EW, 01395 233340, *Water:* One 1.5 acre, One 2 acre lake, *Species:* Bream, Tench, Roach, Rudd, Golden Rudd, Carp, *Permits:* At lakeside from bailiff, Night fishing by prior arrangement, *Charges:* Day ticket £3.50 per day (One Rod) £1 extra per rod, Junior £2. Night £5.50 (One Rod) £1 extra per rod, *Season:* Open all year, *Methods:* Barbless hooks, keepnets by arrangement, No Carp in nets or sacks, All Carp anglers must have unhooking mats.

Home Farm Fishery
Contact: Mr F Williams, Home Farm, Mamhead, Kenton, Exeter, EX6 8HP, 01626 866259, *Water:* 1 lake approx one acre, *Species:* Carp, Roach, Tench, Rudd, *Permits:* From the cabin by the lake, *Charges:* £4.50 per day one rod, £5 two rods, weekly ticket £25 max two rods, concessions for children. Night fishing by arrangement, *Season:* Open all year, *Methods:* No groundbaiting with boilies, no tiger nuts.

Luccombes Coarse Fishery
Contact: Amelia Keen, Towsington Lane, Exminster, EX6 8AY, 01392 832858, amelia.keen@tesco.net, *Water:* Five medium sized ponds set in 9 acres, *Species:* Carp to 21lb. Tench to 6.5lb, Skimmer Bream, Rudd and Roach, *Permits:* Season tickets available from the above, *Charges:* £5 day tickets on the bank. £3 after 4.30pm. £3 junior (under 16 accompanied). £100 season ticket (12 months), *Season:* Open all year from 6am to half hour before dark, *Methods:* No keepnets (except in matches) Barbless hooks ONLY, No nuts or seeds with the exception of hemp and sweetcorn.

Pengellies Carp Ponds
Contact: Mr Carr, Shillingford Abbot, Exeter, EX2 9QH, 01392-832286, *Water:* Two small ponds totalling 1/4 acre, *Species:* Carp to 15lb, Roach, *Charges:* Tickets from office, £10 per day up to 3 rods; lake can be prebooked for exclusive fishing, *Season:* Open all year dawn to dusk; night fishing by arrangement only, *Methods:* Barbless hooks only, no boilies

South View Farm
Contact: Mr R.K.Gorton, South View Farm, Shillingford Saint George, Exeter, EX2 9UP, Tel/Fax: 01392 832278, southviewfarmfishery@btinternet.com, *Water:* 3 Lakes totalling 3 acres, *Species:* Mirror, Common up to 28lb & Ghost Carp 15lb, Roach 2.5lb, Rudd 2.5lb, Perch 3.5lb, Bream, Green & Gold Tench to 3.5lb, *Permits:* Tickets on the bank, *Charges:* £5 for two rods, Juniors (under 16, must be accompanied) £4. Evening ticket after 5pm £3 adult, £2 junior, *Season:* Open all year round, *Methods:* Barbless hooks, No boilies, No keepnets

Upham Farm Ponds
Contact: S.J.Willcocks, Upham Farm, Farringdon, Exeter, EX5 2HZ, 01395 232247, cjjj@uphamfarm.freeserve.co.uk, *Water:* 6 Well stocked ponds, *Species:* Carp 26lb, Tench 8lb 8oz, *Permits:* Day tickets on bank, *Charges:* £5/day (concessions for O.A.P's, Junior), *Methods:* Barbless hooks, No keepnets

Exmouth

Squabmoor
Contact: South West Lakes Trust, 01837 871565, info@swlakestrust.org.uk, *Water:* Ranger Tel 01647 277587, *Species:* Good head of Carp to 25lb. Roach to 3lb 2oz, Tench, *Permits:* See South West Lakes Trust coarse advert, *Charges:* Full day £4.50, Concession £3.50, 24 Hour £8.50, Season Day £80, Season Concession £60, Season Child (under 16) £35, Season Day & Night £120, Additional Fisheries £20 each, *Season:* Open all year 24 hours a day, *Methods:* No child under 14 years may fish unless accompanied by an adult over 18 years. No child under 16 may fish overnight unless accompanied by an adult over 18 years, and then only with permission of parent or legal guardian (letter to this effect must be produced)

Hatherleigh

Legge Farm Coarse Fishery
Contact: Graham Hall, Church Road, Highampton, Beaworthy, EX21 5LF, 01409 231464, *Water:* 1.25 Acre lake & two other ponds, *Species:* Carp, Tench, Perch, Roach, Rudd, Crucians, Grass Carp, Bream, *Permits:* EA licences sold on site, *Charges:* Adults £5, O.A.Ps & Juniors & evenings after 4pm £3.50, *Season:* All year 7am - Dusk. Night fishing by prior arrangement, *Methods:* Barbless hooks, Landing nets, No radios and keepnets

Holsworthy

Clawford Vineyard (Coarse)
Contact: Clawton, EX22 6PN, 01409 254177, *Water:* 8 lakes totalling over 21 acres of water, *Species:* Common, Mirror, Crucian, Ghost & Grass Carp, Tench, Roach, Rudd, Orfe, Barbel, Golden Tench, Blue Tench, Golden/Pink Orfe, Green Rudd, Gold Carp, Goldfish, Catfish, Ide, Chub, *Charges:* On application, *Season:* Open all year, *Methods:* No live or deadbait. No particles or nuts except hemp or sweetcorn. Barbless hooks only. No Carp whatsoever in keepnets. Full rules at the fishery

Eastcott Farm & Lodges
Contact: Mrs C. Whitmill, Eastcott Farm, North Tamerton, Nr Holsworthy, EX22 6SB, 01409 271172, *Water:* 1 Lake approx 0.75 acres, *Species:* Carp & Rudd, *Charges:* Day ticket £2.50, Under 16 & OAP £1.50, Residents free, *Season:* Open all year, *Methods:* Barbless hooks, No keepnets.

Exemoor Farm
Contact: Mr A R Mills, Week St. Mary, Holsworthy, EX22 6UX, 01566 781366, *Water:* Half acre lake, *Species:* Tench 4/5lb, Golden Orfe, Rudd, Crucian, Common 13lb & Mirror Carp, *Charges:* £3 Per rod per day, cheaper rates after 5pm, *Season:* Open all year, *Methods:* No boilies or hemp

Simpson Valley Fishery
Contact: Simpson Farm, Holsworthy, EX22 6JW, 01409 253593, *Water:* 4 lakes. Two new lakes planned for 2001, *Species:* Carp to 23lb, Tench 8lb, Roach 2lb, Rudd 1lb, Gudgeon near to British record, Chub 8oz, *Charges:* £4 per day - 2 rods, £2 Juniors and O.A.P's (2000 prices), *Methods:* Barbless hooks only. No Carp in keepnets

Wooda Fisheries
Contact: Freshwaters UK Ltd., Pancrasweek, Holsworthy, EX22 6DJ, Tel/Fax 01409-211643, freshwaters@supanet.com, *Water:* 3 lakes, 1 general, 1 intermediate, 1 specimen, *Species:* Carp, Tench, Perch, Bream & Roach, *Permits:* From Turner Tackle, Holsworthy, *Charges* To be arranged, *Season:* All year, *Methods:* See day ticket.

Woodacott Arms
Contact: Len Sanders, Woodacott Cross, Thornbury, Holsworthy, EX22 7BT, 01409 261358, *Water:* 2 Lakes, 1.25 Acre, 1 Acre, *Species:* Carp, Tench, Bream, Rudd, Roach, *Charges:* Adults: Day Tickets 2 Rods £5, Juniors: 2 Rods £3, *Methods:* Barbless Hooks, No keepnets, No Boilies or Peanuts.

Honiton

Fishponds House
Contact: Anne Marie Spalding, Fishponds House, Dunkeswell, Honiton, EX14 0SH, 01404 891358, fishpondshouse@aol.com, *Water:* 2 Lakes each over 1 acre, *Species:* Carp to 20lb, Rudd, Roach and Tench, *Charges:* £6.00 per day, Children under 11yrs £3.00 per day, *Season:* Open all year dawn to dusk, *Methods:* Barbless hooks, No boilies, No keepnets

Hartsmoor Fisheries
Contact: John Griss, Bolham Water, Clayhidon, Cullompton, EX15 3QB, 01823 680460, *Water:* Two day ticket lakes - 2 acres and 1.25 acres, One syndicate lake -3.5 acres, plus one 5 acre lake being developed, *Species:* Roach and Rudd to 2lb, Tench 6lb, Bream 7lb, Barbel 4.5lb, Perch 3lb, Crucians 3.5lb (not hybrids!), Blue Orfe 2.5lb, Chub 5lb, Carp 26.5lb (syndicate 33.5lb) Gudgeon 4oz, *Permits:* Day tickets on the bank, Syndicate - get your name on the waiting list , *Charges:* £4 per day. £4 per night by arrangement, *Season:* Day tickets dawn to dusk all year round, *Methods:* Barbless hooks. No nuts of any kind. No Carp over 2lb in keepnets. Loose feed and groundbait is permitted

Milton Farm Ponds
Contact: Brian Cook, Milton Farm, Payhembury, Honiton, EX14 0HE, 01404 850236, *Water:* 5 Lakes approx 2 acres, *Species:* Carp to 22lb, Tench 7lb, Roach, Bream, *Permits:* Collected on bank, *Charges:* £3.50/person/day - no charge for extra rods, £2.50 children 14 or under, *Season:* Open all year round, *Methods:* No groundbaiting with boilies

Ilfracombe

Ilfracombe & District Anglers Association (Coarse)
Contact: Daniel Welch (Coarse Sec.), 18 Broad Park Avenue, Ilfracombe, *Water:* No Club waters. Use Slade reservoir and Mill Park at Berrynarbor, *Species:* Carp, Bream, Perch, Roach, Rudd, Gudgeon and Pike, *Permits:* From Agents' Variety Sports, 23 Broad street, Ilfracombe and The Post Office, Slade, Ilfracombe, Devon, EX34 8LQ, *Charges:* Annual fee combines Sea & Coarse plus licence and permits, *Season:* January to December. Open charity competition in June, *Methods:* Barbless hooks. No Carp in keepnets

Lower Slade
Contact: South West Lakes Trust, 01837 871565, info@swlakestrust.org.uk, *Water:* Ranger Tel 01288 321262, *Species:* Mirror & Common Carp to 20lb plus. Bream to 5lb plus. Perch to 2lb 4oz, Roach, Rudd, Gudgeon and Pike, *Permits:* See South West Lakes Trust coarse advert, *Charges:* Full day £4.50, Concession £3.50, 24 Hour £8.50, Season Day £80, Season Concession £60, Season Child (under 16) £35, Season Day & Night £120, Additional Fisheries £20 each, *Season:* Open all year, 24 hours a day, *Methods:* No child under 14 years may fish unless accompanied by an adult over 18 years. No child under 16 may fish overnight unless accompanied by an adult over 18 years, and then only with permission of parent or legal guardian. (letter to this effect must be produced)

Mill Park Coarse Fishing Lake
Contact: Brian & Mary Malin, Mill Park, Mill Lane, Berrynarbor, Ilfracombe, EX34 9SH, 01271 882647, millpark@globalnet.co.uk, *Water:* 1.5 acre lake between Ilfracombe and Combe Martin, *Species:* Bream, Carp, Perch, Roach, Rudd, Tench, Golden Orfe, Golden Tench, Crucian Carp, *Charges:* Adult £4.50, Junior £2.50, Adult+Junior £6, Reduced rates for residents of touring and camping site; All juniors (-16) must be accompanied by adult, *Season:* Lake open all year; day ticket 8am-9pm or dusk (whichever is earlier), *Methods:* Barbless hooks only, Dip all nets, No night fishing

Kingsbridge

Bickerton Farm Fishery
Contact: Mr Graham Tolchard, Bickerton Farm, Hallsands, Kingsbridge, TQ7 2EU, 01548 511220, *Water:* 1/3 acre & 3/4 acre ponds, *Species:* Carp 15lb, Roach, Rudd, Perch, Tench, Bream, *Charges:* £3 Under 16's, £4 per rod Adults, Two rods £5 & £7, *Methods:* Barbless hooks, No keepnets unless fishing match

Coombe Water Fisheries
Contact: J.W. Robinson, Coombe Farm, Kingsbridge, TQ7 4AB, 01548 852038, *Water:* 3 Lakes, *Species:* Carp to 25lb, Bream to 4lb, Tench to 3lb, Roach to 2.5lb, *Permits:* No E.A. licence required. Lakes are covered by general E.A. licence, *Charges:* £5 day-ticket, £2.50 Under 16. 1/2 day ticket £3, *Season:* All year dawn to dusk. Night fishing by arrangement only, *Methods:* Barbless hooks, No ground bait, no Carp over 1lb in keepnets.

Slapton Ley National Nature Reserve
Contact: Chris Riley, Slapton Ley Field Centre, Slapton, Kingsbridge, TQ7 2QP, 01548 580685, *Water:* 180 acre Freshwater Lagoon, *Species:* Pike, Perch, Roach, Rudd, *Permits:* Hired rowing boats only, *Charges:* Dependent on number in boat e.g. £16 for 2 anglers, *Season:* No close season, *Methods:* No bank fishing

Valley Springs (Coarse)
Contact: J. Bishop, Sherford, Nr Kingsbridge, TQ7 2BG, 01548 531574, *Water:* 2 Lakes totalling approx 3 acres, Trout & Coarse, *Species:* Coarse Fish - Carp to 33lb, Tench to 4.5lb, Roach/ Rudd to 2lb - some Catfish, *Charges:* £7/day (incl. Environment Rod Licence) + £2 per lb, *Season:* Open all year, *Methods:* Barbless hooks, Traditional fly fishing methods only

Lyme Regis

Summerleaze Pond
Contact: Summerleaze Farm, Kilmington, Axminster, EX13 7RA, 01297-32390, *Water:* 1 coarse fishing lake, *Species:* Carp, Roach, Perch. Best Carp 15lb, *Charges:* On site, £3 adults, £1.50 children (u.16), *Season:* Open all year, dawn to dusk, *Methods:* Please ask at fishery

Newton Abbot

Finlake Holiday Park
Contact: Tony Irving (Bailiff) Ext 230, Nr Chudleigh, TQ13 0EJ, 01626 853833, *Water:* 1 Acre - 30 Peg, *Species:* Crucians 1-4lb, Bream to 4lb, Tench 2-4lb, Skimmers, Roach to 2.75lb, Golden Orfe 12 inches, Rudd 1.5lb, Golden Rudd 8 inches, No Carp, *Permits:* On entry at security, *Charges:* £3 Adult, £2.50 to 14yrs, *Season:* All year round, Winter opening times: 8am - Dusk, Summer opening times: 8am-4pm (Mon-Thurs) Other days 8am-6pm, *Methods:* Barbless hooks. No keep nets. No boilies, nuts, floating baits, pellets or paste. Strictly no ground bait, landing nets essential

Newton Abbot Fishing Association (Coarse Ponds)
Contact: David Horder (secretary), 'Mistlemead', Woodlands, Higher Sandygate, TQ12 3QN, 01626 364173, *Water:* 19 coarse ponds in the Newton Abbot Area. Also a 1 mile stretch of the River Isle at Hambridge, *Species:* All coarse species including Carp to 35lb, Tench to 12lb, Bream to 8lb, Roach to 2lb and Rudd to 1.5lb, *Permits:* Full membership is restricted to a 20 mile residency radius of Newton Abbot. Available from the membership secretary, PO Box 1, Bovey Tracey. All other membership available from local tackle shops, *Charges:* Senior full members £44. Senior Associate members £39. Junior full member £12. Senior Citizen £22. Disabled and concessionary £22. Senior Day Ticket £5. Junior day ticket £2. Please ask for a rule book, *Season:* Ponds and lakes are open 24 hours a day, 365 days a year. Rivers are controlled by the national close season for coarse fish; Rocombe Ponds and Wapperwell Ponds open from dawn to dusk, *Methods:* No Carp to be retained in keepnets. Only Carp sacks allowed. Only 2 rods per angler between 1st April and 30th September. 3 rods allowed between 1 October and 31 March. No lead shot. No camping, tents or fires. No dogs. Only barbless hooks or crushed barbs allowed, all types of nuts are banned

North Tawton

North Tawton Angling Specimen Group
Contact: Mr. J.D. Mansfield, 4 Taw Vale Close, North Tawton, EX20 2EH, 01837-82122, *Water:* Any Lake or River, Sea fishing from shore only, *Species:* Any species listed in the British records, *Charges:* Membership £8/year, *Season:* June 1st - May 31st, *Methods:* Abide by regulations laid out on lake or river the group are fishing

Spires Lakes
Contact: Barry Ware, Riverside, Fore Street, North Tawton, EX20 2ED, 01837 82499, *Water:* Two lakes, 40 peg match lake and 2 acre lake, *Species:* Carp 30lb, Tench 5lb, Roach 1lb 8oz, Rudd 1lb, Bream 3.5lb, Perch 1.5lb, Orfe 1.5lb, Ghost Carp 1lb, *Permits:* On site kiosk, self service, *Charges:* £4.50 Day ticket, £3 Evening, £2.50 Junior & O.A.P.s, *Season:* Dawn to dusk, *Methods:* Barbless hooks, No boilies, No tiger or peanuts

Okehampton

Alder Farm Lake
Contact: Mr Bob Westlake, Alder Farm, Lewdown, Okehampton, 01566 783397, bobwestlake@aldersportswear.com, *Water:* 4 Acre Lake, *Species:* Perch, Carp to 25lb, Bream to 8.25lb, Specimen Roach and Tench. Plus natural stock of Trout, *Charges:* £3/rod/day, *Season:* No closed season / Night fishing allowed, *Methods:* No restrictions

Millaton Farm Coarse Fishery
Contact: Gareth or Jessica Charles-Jones, Millaton Farm, Bridestowe, Okehampton, EX20 4QG, 01837 861100, *Water:* 3 large lakes, 2 small (from 0.75 to 2 acres), *Species:* Carp - Koi 9lb, Ghost 10.5lb, Mirror 15lb, Common 14lb, Crucian 2.5lb, Leather. Tench, Bream 4lb, Perch 1lb, Roach, Rudd, American Sun Bass 2oz, *Permits:* Up to 5 day tickets allowed. You MUST RING day before to book space before setting out, *Charges:* £5 per day - 2 rods. £4 per day - 1 rod. £2.50 per day senior citizens and under 16. After 4pm £3 up to 2 rods. £1.50 senior citizens and under 16, *Season:* Dawn to dusk all year round, *Methods:* Barbless hooks only. No boilies, hemp, peanuts. Groundbait in moderation. No keepnets, dogs, radios.

Millaton-Wrigley Fishing Syndicate
Contact: Mr Vic Barnett (Syndicate Sec.), 5 Weir Close, Mainstone, Plymouth, PL6 8SD, 01752 708206, victor.barnett@talk21.com, *Water:* 3 small ponds, each cannot be seen from the other. A very private and secluded fishery. Potential to increase the water to five ponds in the near future as they are already there but need to be worked on, *Species:* Carp, Tench, Golden Tench, Bream, Perch, Gudgeon, Roach, Rudd, Large Brown Goldfish (2.5lb), Gold Carp, *Permits:* To join the syndicate costs in the first year are: £10 joining fee, £50 for year. After the first year cost is £50 p.a. 5 day tickets - price on booking (around £4.50 per day). More details from the above contact or phone 01837 861100, allowing for a long ring please, *Charges:* As above, *Season:* No close season, *Methods:* Barbless hooks only. No Carp over 2lb to be retained in keepnets. Knotless nets only. No boilies. All spawning fish to be returned to the water immediately after photographing or weighing. Syndicate members may camp overnight and generally come and go as they wish

Week Farm
Contact: John & Grenville Hockridge, Bridestowe, Okehampton, EX20 4HZ, Tel/Fax 01837-861221, *Water:* 2x 0.5 acre lakes, 0.25 acre lake, *Species:* Mixed Carp (Common, Mirror, Crucian), Bream; in 0.25 acre Roach, Rudd, Green Tench, *Charges:* £4/day + £1 extra rod, £2/evening, children + OAP half price, *Season:* Open from mid May 2001, *Methods:* Barbless hooks only, all nets to be dipped, night fishing by arrangement, no dogs

Paignton

New Barn Angling Centre
Contact: Andrew & Callie Buchanan, Newbarn Farm, Totnes Road, Paignton, TQ4 7PT, 01803 553602, *Water:* 6 ponds up to 1 acre suitable for juniors (parent supervision), beginners, pleasure and specimen angling, *Species:* Carp to 27lb, Ghost Carp to 17lb, Tench to 6.5lb, Roach to 2lb 12oz, Bream to 5lb, Perch to 4lb, *Charges:* £5 for 1 rod, 2nd rod /£1, juniors (u.14) £3, *Season:* Open all year 7am to dusk; no night fishing; 8 fishing shelters around main lake, first come first served, *Methods:* Barbless hooks only; no keepnets; no nuts; all baits effective: maggots, luncheon meat, sweetcorn,

boilies, bread & pellets; sensible ground baiting allowed; float fishing and ledgering; summertime good for floating dog biscuits

Town Parks Coarse Fishing Centre
Contact: Mr Paul Gammin, Town Park Farm, Totnes Road, Paignton, 01803 523133, *Water:* 2 acre lake + 2.5 acre lake 30 pegs + 25 peg lake available to clubs / associations / block bookings, phone for details, *Species:* Common 19lb, Crucian 2.5lb, Mirror Carp 31lb, Bream 6lb 4oz, Tench 8lb 12oz, Roach 2lb 7oz, Perch 4lb 2oz, Rudd 2lb 7oz, Eel 6lb 2oz, *Permits:* No EA Rod licence required, *Charges:* Full day £5, 5 hours £4, Summer evening £3, Night fishing £7, 24 hrs £10, *Season:* All year, Dawn - Dusk. Night fishing by appointment, *Methods:* Barbless hooks, Ground bait, Boilies etc in moderation. No tiger nuts or peanuts

Plymouth

Plymouth & District Angling Club
Contact: Mr Carl Bovey, 39 Hilton Avenue, Manadon, Plymouth, PL5 3HS, 01752 709339, carl@cbovey.freeserve.co.uk, *Water:* 3 ponds at Cadover Bridge, 2 at St. Germans and 1 at Avonwick - ranging in size from 0.5 to 2 acres, *Species:* Carp to 29lb 8oz, Tench 6lb, Bream 8lb 8oz, Rudd 11lb 6oz Roach 2lb 8oz and Crucians, *Permits:* Clive's Tackle and Bait, 182 Exeter St, Plymouth. Tel: 01752 228940, *Charges:* Seniors £30. juniors and OAP's £15, *Season:* Open all year. St Germans and Cadover 24 hours. The Mill at Avonwick dawn to dusk, *Methods:* Barbless hooks. No Carp in keepnets. Unhooking mats for all Carp.

Plymouth Command Angling Association (Ponds)
Contact: Mr Vic Barnett Hon.Sec, 5 Weir Close, Mainstone, Plymouth, PL6 8SD, 01752 708206, victor.barnett@talk21.com, *Water:* Two lakes of .5 and .9 of an acre for coarse fishing within ten minutes of Plymouth, plus several other accesses to associated waters in the Southwest open to members, *Species:* Carp, Tench, Bream, Perch, Roach, Rudd, Crucians, Goldfish, Eels, Gold Carp and some Koi, *Permits:* Membership is open to all serving members of the Royal Navy and Royal Marines with associate membership for serving members of the Army and Air Force. Associate

membership is also open to ex-serving members of the Armed Forces, no matter when the time was served, *Charges:* Costs for full membership or associate membership are available on application or enquiry at the above contact, *Season:* No close season for coarse fish, *Methods:* Barbless hooks only at the coarse fishery. Knotless keepnets to be used as per EA guidelines on minimum 3 metres length. No Trout pellets in any form allowed. Only Carp friendly and proven pellets are to be used. All spawning fish are to be returned to the water immediately. No Carp over 2lb to be kept in keepnets

Sunridge Fishery
Contact: RM and M Hammett, Sunridge Nurseries, Worston, Yealmpton, Plymouth, PL8 2LN, 01752 880438, *Water:* Approx. half acre lake, *Species:* Mirror and Common Carp up to 22lb, *Permits:* From above at the Nurseries, *Charges:* £4 adult day, £3 child/OAP, *Season:* Open all year dawn to dusk, Night fishing by arrangement only, *Methods:* Barbless hooks only, No keepnets (except by prior arrangement)

Seaton

Horriford Fishing
Contact: Mr Pady, Horriford Farm, Colyford, Colyton, EX24 6HW, 01297-552316, horriford@aol.com, *Water:* 2 ponds totalling 1 acre, *Species:* Bream (5lb), Roach (1lb), Tench (5lb), Carp (8-10lb), Perch (2lb), Rudd (1.5lb), *Permits:* From farmhouse, *Charges:* Day ticket £3.50, 1/2-day ticket £2, *Season:* Open all year dawn to dusk, *Methods:* Barbless hooks only

Wiscombe Park Fishery
Contact: Mike Raynor, Wiscombe Park Fishery, Colyton, EX24 6JE, 01404 871474, michael@wiscombe.globalnet.co.uk, *Water:* Half acre lake, *Species:* Carp, Tench, Bream, *Permits:* Self-service (No booking), *Charges:* £3.50/day, Reduced rates for O.A.Ps & Children, Children (u.15) free if accompanied by permit holding adult, *Season:* All year, *Methods:* Single rod

DEVON - STILLWATER COARSE

South Brent

Hatchlands Coarse Fishery
Contact: Malcolm Davies, Greyshoot Lane, Rattery, South Brent, TQ10 9LL, 01364 73500, *Water:* Two acre lake, *Species:* Carp, Tench, Roach, Bream, Rudd and Gudgeon, *Permits:* No EA licence required. Block EA licence held by fishery, *Charges:* £5 per person per day, *Season:* Open all year, *Methods:* Barbless hooks only; No large Carp in keepnets

Little Allers Coarse Fishery
Contact: M & J Wakeham, Little Allers Farm, Avonwick, South Brent, 01364 72563, *Water:* 2 Acre lake, *Species:* Carp, Bream, Tench, Roach, Rudd, *Permits:* On the bank, *Charges:* £4 per day adults, £2.50 under 16, £2.50 evening ticket after 5 pm, *Season:* Open all year dawn to dusk, *Methods:* Barbless hooks only, No Carp in keepnets, No boilies.

South Molton

Oaktree Fishery
Contact: George Andrews, East Anstey, Yeo Mill, South Molton, EX36 3PU, 01398 341568 Fax:01398 341511, *Water:* Three 2 Acre lakes, *Species:* All Carp, Tench, Bream, Roach, Perch, Koi Carp, Catfish, *Permits:* On site only, *Charges:* Day tickets: Adults from £5, Specimen lake £6, Junior/OAP from £4, Specimen lake £5, Eve tickets: Adult £3.50, Specimen lake £5, Junior/OAP £3.50 Specimen lake £4, *Season:* all year 24hrs, *Methods:* Barbless hooks only. No nut type baits. See board at fishery.

Tavistock

Milemead Fisheries
Contact: Mr Harry Dickens, Mill Hill, Tavistock, PL19 8NP, 01822 610888, *Water:* Two Lakes of 2 acres each. Match Lake available for bookings, please phone for details, *Species:* Carp to 15lb, Tench to 4lb, Bream to 4lb, Roach to 2lb, Rudd to1.5lb, *Permits:* Available from lakeside tackle + bait shop, *Charges:* Adult £5, Concession £4, Evening tickets available, *Season:* All year, 7am to Dusk, *Methods:* Barbless Hooks, All nets to be dipped prior to fishing, Please read the rule boards

Tiverton

Coombe Farm Fishponds
Contact: Mrs Curtis, Coombe Farm, Cadleigh, Tiverton, 01884 855337, *Water:* 3 lakes totalling 0.5 acre, *Species:* Carp to 20lb, Roach, Tench to 4lb, Bream to 1.5lb, *Charges:* £3 per day, *Season:* Open all year, *Methods:* No boilies.

Devonshire Centre
Contact: Bickleigh Mill, Bickleigh, Nr Tiverton, EX16 8RG, 01884 855419 - Fax 855416, general@bickleighmill.freeserve.co.uk, *Water:* Bickleigh Mill fishing ponds, *Species:* Rainbow Trout with occasional Rudd, Roach, Tench, *Permits:* Only at above, *Charges:* On request, *Season:* Easter to end of September, *Methods:* Rod supplied

Tiverton & District Angling Club
Contact: John Smallwood, Exe Valley Angling, 19 Westexe South, Tiverton, EX16 5DQ, 01884 242275, *Water:* 11.5 Miles on Grand Western Canal, 1.25 acre mixed fishery lake at Exebridge, *Species:* Canal: Carp, Bream, Tench, Roach, Perch, Pike, Eels. Lakeside: Carp, Bream, Roach, Tench, Eels, Crucian Carp, *Permits:* Please ring Exe Valley for details. Also available from: Exeter Angling Centre, Enterprise Angling Taunton, Topp Tackle Taunton, Country Sports - Cullompton & Minnows Caravan Park - beside Grand Western Canal, *Charges:* Senior: Day £4, Annual £18. Conc: Day £2.50, Annual £8, *Season:* Canal: Closed March 1st - May 31st inc, except one 5 mile section (Basin to Halburton - ring for details). Lakeside: Open all year, Weekends full members only, Maximum five day permits per day, *Methods:* Canal Methods: Any. Restrictions: Fish from permanent pegs, No night fishing, No cars on bank, No digging of banks or excessive clearance of vegatation. Lakeside Methods: Any. Restrictions: No night fishing, No boilies, Trout pellets or nuts, One rod only, Fishing from permanent pegs, No dogs, Nets to be dipped. Ring Exe Valley Angling for full details

West Pitt Farm Fishery
Contact: Mr Rodney Crocker, Uplowman, Nr. Tiverton, EX16 7DU, 01884 820296, rodc.hols-fishing@claramail.com, *Water:* 3 lakes up to 1.25 acres, *Species:* Common & Mirror Carp, Bream, Tench, Roach, Rudd, Crucians, Golden Tench, Chub, Golden Orfe, *Permits:* Self service day tickets £4.50 per day (correct money please), *Charges:* £4.50/day,. £3.50 evenings, *Season:* All year, no closed season, *Methods:* No Boilies, Barbless Hooks. Nets to be dipped. Groundbait in moderation

Torrington

Bakers Farm
Contact: Mr & Mrs Ridd, Bakers Farm, Moortown, Torrington, EX38 7ES, 01805 623260, *Water:* 1 acre lake, *Species:* Mirror & Common Carp, Tench, Roach & Rudd, *Charges:* £4/rod/day, *Methods:* Barbless Hooks, No large Carp in keepnets

Darracott
Contact: South West Lakes Trust, 01837 871565, info@swlakestrust.org.uk, *Water:* Ranger Tel 01288 321262, *Species:* Roach up to 1lb. Mixed bags to 20lb plus of Roach, Rudd, Bream and Tench. Perch to 2.25lb. Carp to 15lb, *Permits:* See South West Lakes Trust coarse advert, *Charges:* Full day £4.50, Concession £3.50, 24 Hour £8.50, Season Day £80, Season Concession £60, Season Child (under 16) £35, Season Day & Night £120, Additional Fisheries £20 each, *Season:* Open all year 24 hours a day, *Methods:* No child under 14 years may fish unless accompanied by an adult over 18 years. No child under 16 may fish overnight unless accompanied by an adult over 18 years, and then only with permission of parent or legal guardian (letter to this effect must be produced)

Great Torrington Anglers Association (Coarse)
Contact: Paul Martin, 67 Calf Street, Torrington, EX38 7BH, 01805 623658 Fax:01805 623658, paul@olmargames.fsbusiness.co.uk, *Water:* Coarse fishing on local reservoirs, open to anglers from Torrington and surrounding areas, *Permits:* No day tickets sold by club, *Charges:* Annual membership Adult £5.00, Junior £3.00

Stevenstone Lakes
Contact: Alan & Rebecca Parnell, Deer Park, Stevenstone, Torrington, EX38 7HY, 01805 622102, parnellaj@yahoo.co.uk, *Water:* Three lakes, total of six acres in a parkland setting, *Species:* Mirror Carp 23lb, Common 13lb, Tench 6lb, Rudd 1lb, Eels 3lb, *Charges:* Contact Alan & Rebecca Parnell, *Season:* Open all year, 7am to sunset, *Methods:* Barbless hooks only, no boilies, no nut type baits, no fish over 2lb in keepnets, no dogs, no litter. Unhooking mats essential

Winkleigh

Okehampton Coarse Fishing Club
Contact: M.J. Cowley, The Barton, Belstone, Okehampton, EX20 1RA, 01837 840371, *Water:* Enclosed still water. Brixton Barton Farm, *Species:* Common Carp to 8lb, Roach, Rudd, *Permits:* Fishing only with a member, *Charges:* £3.50, *Season:* 12 months, sunrise to sunset, *Methods:* Barbless hooks. No fish over 2lb in keepnets

Stafford Moor Fishery
Contact: Andy or Debbie Seery, Dolton, Winkleigh, EX19 8PP, Tel/Fax: 01805 804360, *Water:* 6 acre specimen lake, 100 pegs match fishery (bookings available); 2 acre pleasure lake, *Species:* Carp 30lb, Tench, Bream, Roach, Rudd, Eels, *Permits:* At lodge at Stafford Moor, *Charges:* £5 pleasure/day, £3.50 conc./OAP/Junior; £6 specimen/day, £4 conc./OAP/Junior, *Season:* All year, *Methods:* The method is banned, max. 6 pints of bait (incl. 2 pints of Trout pellets), max. 2 kg groundbait, barbless hooks from size 16 upwards (max. size 6), night fishing by arrangement

Yelverton

Coombe Fisheries
Contact: Mr Stephen Horn, Yelverton, Nr Plymouth, 01822 616624, , stephenchorn@cs.com, *Water:* Two 1 acre lakes, *Species:* Coarse fish: Rudd, Roach, Tench, Bream + various Carp (24lb), *Permits:* Local Post Office and also mobile phone 07788 715470. *Charges:* £4/day, £2.50/evening, *Season:* No close season, Dawn to dusk, *Methods:* Barbless hooks, No peanuts

DEVON
Stillwater
Trout

Ashburton

Venford
Contact: South West Lakes Trust, 01837 871565, info@swlakestrust.org.uk, *Species:* Brown Trout, *Charges:* Free to holders of a valid Environment Agency Licence, *Season:* 15 March - 12 October, *Methods:* Angling by spinning, bubble float & bait

Axminster

Lower Bruckland Fishery
Contact: David Satterley, Lower Bruckland Farm, Musbury, Axminster, EX13 8ST, (01297)552861, Fax: 551197, *Water:* 2x 2 acre lakes, *Species:* Tringle Lake: Rainbows to 30lb & Wild Browns, Serpentine Lake: Rainbows, *Permits:* Available at Angler's Hut by car park, *Charges:* Tringle: £16/day, £12/half day, £8/evening - Serpentine: 4-fish £15, 2-fish £12.50, *Season:* All year (Serpentine opens 1 April 2001), *Methods:* Tringle: Catch & Release, max hook 10, Barbless - Serpentine: Catch & Keep, any method except Spinners

Barnstaple

Blakewell Fisheries
Contact: Mr Richard & John Nickell, Blakewell Fisheries, Muddiford, Barnstaple, EX31 4ET, 01271 344533, blakefish@sosi.net, *Water:* 5 Acre Lake, *Species:* Rainbow, Brown & Brook Trout, *Charges:* 5 Fish £22, 4 Fish £19, 3 Fish £17, 2 Fish £15, *Season:* All Year, *Methods:* Fly Only

Beaworthy

South Hay Fishery
Contact: Gill and Reg Stone, South Barn Farm, South Hay, Shebbear, Beaworthy, 01409 281857, R.D.Stone@btinternet.com, *Water:* 2 acre Trout lake, 2 Miles of River Torridge, *Species:* Rainbow Trout (lake), Brown Trout, Sea Trout, Salmon (river), *Charges:* Lake £5 per day plus £1.50 per lb, River £10 per day, *Season:* Lake - all year, River - Mid March to End September, *Methods:* Fly only.

Bideford

Fosfelle Country House Hotel (Game)
Contact: Hartland, Bideford, 01237 441273, *Water:* Approx half acre, *Species:* Rainbow & Golden Trout, *Charges:* £7.50 half day - 2 Trout, *Season:* Open all year, *Methods:* Displayed on board

Torridge Fly Fishing Club
Contact: Mr W.H. Akister (secretary), Ebroch, North Down Rd, Bideford, EX39 3LT, 01237 475906, *Water:* 2 x 4 acre reservoirs situated 2 miles east of Bideford, *Species:* Stocked Rainbow Trout from 1.5 to 6lb. Natural Browns to 5lb, *Permits:* 2 day tickets allowed each day, *Charges:* Day tickets: £8 per day (3 fish limit) to be obtained at Summerlands Fishing Tackle, Westward Ho!, Tel. 01239 471291; Season tickets: £125 (waiting list: membership limited to 25), *Season:* 14th April - 16th December for Rainbow Trout, 14th April - 30th September for Brown Trout, *Methods:* Floating Fly Lines only

Chagford

Fernworthy
Contact: South West Lakes Trust, 01837 871565, info@swlakestrust.org.uk, *Species:* Brown Trout, *Permits:* Self Service Kiosk, *Charges:* Full day £9, Season £120, Reduced day £7, Season £90, Child/Wheelchair £2, Season £30, *Season:* Opens 1 April 2001 - 12 October, *Methods:* Catch & Release operates. Barbless hooks only

DEVON - STILLWATER TROUT

Christow

Tottiford

Contact: South West Lakes Trust, 01837 871565, info@swlakestrust.org.uk, *Water:* Ranger Tel 01647 277587, *Species:* Brown Trout Boat Fishery, fish to 6lb, *Permits:* Kennick Self Service, *Charges:* £16 for boat & fishing, *Season:* Opens 15 March 2001 - 12 October, *Methods:* Boat only Fishery. Fly fishing only. Catch & release allowed with barbless hooks

Chudleigh

Kennick

Contact: South West Lakes Trust, 01837 871565, info@swlakestrust.org.uk, *Water:* Ranger Tel 01647 277587, *Species:* Premier Rainbow Fishery Bank & Boat, *Permits:* Self Service Kiosk - Boats may be booked in advance: 01647-277587, *Charges:* Full day £15.75, Season £385. Reduced day £12.50, Season £290, Child/Wheelchair £3, Season £90. Evening Monday - Friday £12.50. Season Permits can be used on any Premier Fishery only. Boats £9.50 per day inc. 2 fish extra to bag limits. 'Wheelie Boat' available for disabled anglers (must be booked at least 48 hrs in advance), *Season:* Opens 24 March 2001 - 31st October, *Methods:* No child under 14 years may fish unless accompanied by an adult over 18 years

Kennick Fly Fishers Association

Contact: Mike Boston, 5 Shirburn Rd, Torquay, TQ1 3JL, 01803-325722, *Water:* 45 acres, *Species:* Rainbow + wild Brown Trout, *Permits:* Club members able to obtain SWLT discounted tickets, *Charges:* Membership fee for club is £8 annual subscription, *Methods:* i.a.w. SWLT byelaws

Cullompton

Goodiford Mill Fishery

Contact: David Wheeler, Goodiford Mill, Kentisbeare, Cullompton, EX15 2AS, 01884 266233, *Water:* 2 Lakes in 4.5 acres, *Species:* Rainbow & Brown Trout, *Charges:* £18 - 4 fish, £15 - 3 fish, Evening £13 - 2 fish, £7 to fish & £1.60/lb, *Season:* All year, *Methods:* Max 10 longshank.

Hatherleigh

Half Moon Fishery (Trout Lake)

Contact: Half Moon Inn, Sheepwash, Nr Hatherleigh, EX21 5NE, (01409) 231376, *Fax:* 231673, lee@halfmoon.demon.co.uk, *Water:* See also entry under Torridge. 3x 2 acre Trout lakes, *Species:* Rainbow Trout up to 3lb, *Permits:* Day tickets available to residents and non-residents, *Charges:* £10/2-fish, £15.50/4-fish

Holsworthy

Mill Leat Trout Fishery

Contact: Mr Birkett, Thornbury, Holsworthy, EX22 7AY, 01409 261426, cottages@mill-leat.fsnet.co.uk, *Water:* Two lakes totalling 3 acres, *Species:* Rainbow Trout, *Charges:* £5 plus £1.50 per lb. No Limit, *Season:* 1st April - 31st October, *Methods:* Fly only

Honiton

Hollies Trout Farm

Contact: Bobby Roles, Sheldon, Honiton, EX14 4QS, 01404 841428, lacy121@clara.net, *Water:* Spring fed lake, *Species:* Rainbow & Brown Trout, *Charges:* Full day £19/4-fish or £15/3- 4 hours (£3 after 5pm) and fish at £1.75/lb. £4.50 - 4 hours (£3 after 5pm) and fish at £1.75/lb, Concessions for OAP's and under 12's, *Season:* Open all year dawn to dusk, *Methods:* Fly only, dry or wet

Otter Falls

Contact: David Courtney, Old Spurtham Farm, Upottery, EX14 9QD, 01404 861634, *Water:* Two 2 acre lakes, *Species:* Rainbow Trout, *Permits:* As above, *Charges:* £25 Full day, £15 Half day. Catch and release, *Season:* No closed season - essential to book - bookings only, *Methods:* Barbless hooks.

Stillwaters

Contact: Michael Ford, Lower Moorhayne Farm, Yarcombe, Nr Honiton, EX14 9BE, 01404 861284, info@land-own.demon.co.uk, *Water:* 1 acre lake. 1 Sea Trout rod on River Axe at the Sea Pool, *Species:* Trout & Sea Trout, *Charges:* From £10, *Season:* March 1st - November 1st, *Methods:* Fly only

Ivybridge

Mill Leat Trout Farm

Contact: Chris Trant, Ermington, Nr Ivybridge, PL21 9NT, 01548 830172, chris@millgallery.com, *Water:* 0.75 Acre lake, *Species:* Rainbow Trout average 2 to 4.5lb, *Permits:* EA Licence required, *Charges:* 2 fish £9, 4 fish £16 or £3 charge then £1.50/lbs, *Season:* Open all year - booking advisable, *Methods:* No lures

Kingsbridge

Valley Springs (Trout)

Contact: J. Bishop, Sherford, Nr Kingsbridge, TQ7 2BG, 01548 531574, *Water:* 2 Lakes totalling approx 3 acres, *Species:* Rainbow & Brown Trout, *Charges:* £7/visit + £2/lb, *Season:* Open all year, *Methods:* Barbless hooks, Traditional fly fishing methods only

Newton Abbot

Watercress Fishery

Contact: Mr Paul Cook, Kerswell Springs, Chudleigh, Newton Abbot, TQ13 0DW, 01626 852168, watercress.fishery@btinternet.com, *Water:* 3 spring fed lakes totalling approx 5 acres. Alder lake specimen lake +3lb Tiger, Brown, Brook & Rainbow, *Species:* Rainbow, Brown, Tiger and Brook Trout, *Permits:* On site. No EA rod licence required, *Charges:* Day £20 - 5 fish, £17 - 4 fish, half day £14 - 3 fish, £11 - 2 fish; Alder lake (specimen lake +3lb) 4-fish/£30, 2-fish/£17, *Season:* Open all year, 8am to 1 hour after sunset, *Methods:* Alder lake - specimen lake

Okehampton

Meldon

Contact: South West Lakes Trust, 01837 871565, info@swlakestrust.org.uk, *Species:* Brown Trout, *Charges:* Free to holders of a valid Environment Agency Licence, *Season:* 15 March - 12 October, *Methods:* Angling by spinning, fly or bait

Roadford

Contact: South West Lakes Trust, 01837 871565, info@swlakestrust.org.uk, *Water:* Ranger Tel 01409 211507, *Species:* Brown Trout Fishery - Boat & Bank (boats may be booked in advance: 01409 211507), *Permits:* Angling & Watersports Centre at Lower Goodacre, *Charges:* Full day £12, Season £280,

Reduced day £10, Season £225, Child/ Wheelchair £3, Season £60, Evening Mon-Fri £9.50. Boats £9.50 per day, *Season:* Opens 24 March 2001 - 12th October, *Methods:* Fly fishing only. Catch and release operates - Barbless hooks only. No child under 14 years may fish unless accompanied by an adult over 18 years

Roadford Flyfishing Club
Contact: Mr M.F. Whyatt (Treasurer), Appletree Cottage, Stapledon Farm, Holsworthy, EX22 6NS, 01409 254606, dibble@myfishandfly.net, *Water:* Roadford Reservoir, *Species:* Wild Brown Trout only (1999-2000 season record 8lb 4oz), *Permits:* Discounted day tickets available from club treasurer (Sec. R.J.Dibble, 01822-834188), *Charges:* £6 Adult membership, £2 junior, £5 per day for members use of electric outboard motor boat, *Season:* Open from March 21st to second week of October, *Methods:* Bag limit 4 fish over 10 inches, Catch and release practiced, Barbless/ crushed barb hooks only, Boats available

Plymouth
Drakelands
Contact: Mr Elford, Higher Drakelands, Hemerdon, Plympton, Plymouth, 01752 344691, *Water:* 1.75 acre lake, *Species:* Brown Trout, Rainbow Trout, *Charges:* Ticket to fish £3 plus fish @ £1.85/lb, 1/ 2 day ticket £11 - 4 hrs (2 fish), £14.50 - 6 hrs (3 fish), £18 - 8 hrs (4 fish), £21 - 8 hrs (5 fish), *Season:* Open all year, Tuesday - Sunday, *Methods:* Barbless hooks only.

Seaton
Wiscombe Park Fishery (Trout Lakes)
Contact: Mike Raynor, Wiscombe Park Fishery, Colyton, EX24 6JE, 01404 871474, michael@wiscombe.globalnet.co.uk, *Water:* Two half Acre lakes, *Species:* Rainbow Trout, Brown Trout, *Permits:* Self-service (No booking), *Charges:* £17/ day (8 fish limit), £12/4hrs (3 fish), £8.50/2 hrc (2 fish), Children u.15 free (accompanied by permit holding adult), *Season:* All year, *Methods:* Fly fishing (singles)

South Brent
Avon Dam
Contact: South West Lakes Trust, 01837 871565, info@swlakestrust.org.uk, *Species:* Brown Trout, *Charges:* Free to holders of a valid Environment Agency Licence, *Season:* 15 March - 12 October, *Methods:* Angling by spinning, fly or bait

Hatchlands Trout Lakes
Contact: Malcolm Davies, Greyshoot Lane, Rattery, South Brent, TQ10 9LL, 01364 73500, *Water:* 6 acres, 2 lakes, *Species:* Rainbow, Brown and Brook Trout, *Permits:* No EA Permit required, *Charges:* Prices from £8 for 2 fish. Other prices on application. Sporting ticket from £15, *Season:* Open all year, *Methods:* Barbless hooks on catch and release

Somerswood Lake
Contact: S.A. Goodman, Brent Mill Farm, South Brent, TQ10 9JD, 01364 72154, *Water:* 2 acres in Avon valley, *Species:* Rainbow Trout, *Permits:* At farmhouse, *Charges:* Full day £16 for 4 fish, 1/2 day £10 for 2 fish, *Season:* Open all year, *Methods:* Fly

South Molton
Wistlandpound
Contact: South West Lakes Trust, 01837 871565, info@swlakestrust.org.uk, *Water:* Ranger Tel 01288 321262, *Species:* Intermediate Rainbow Trout Fishery. Trout to 6lb, *Permits:* Post Office in Challacombe (01598) 763229, The Kingfisher, Barnstaple, (01271) 344919. Camera & Picture, Combe Martin (01271) 883275, Variety Sports, Ilfracombe (01271) 862039, *Charges:* Full day £10.50, Season £190, Reduced day £9.50, Season £170, Child/ Wheelchair £2, Season £40, *Season:* Opens 15 March - 12th October, *Methods:* Fly fishing only. Catch and release - barbless hooks

Tavistock
Milemead Fisheries
Contact: Mr Harry Dickens, Mill Hill, Tavistock, PL19 8NP, 01822 610888, *Water:* 2 acre spring fed lake, max 10 anglers at any one time, *Species:* Rainbow and Brown Trout from 1.5lb to 10lb, *Permits:* Available from lakeside tackle + bait shop, *Charges:* Please phone for details, *Season:* Open all year 8.30 am to dusk, *Methods:* Fly fishing only, no catch and release, please read the rule boards

Tavistock Trout Farm & Fishery
Contact: Abigail Underhill, Parkwood Road, Tavistock, PL19 9JW, 01822 615441, *Water:* 5 Lakes totalling approx 4 acres, *Species:* Rainbow Trout, Brown Trout, *Charges:* Full day 4 fish permit - Osprey Lake £34, Full day 4 fish Kingfisher + Heron £16.50, *Season:* Open all year 8am - dusk, *Methods:* Max hook size 10

Tiverton
Bellbrook Valley Trout Fishery
Contact: Mike Pusey, Bellbrook Farm, Oakford, Tiverton, EX16 9EX, 01398 351292, mike_pusey@notes.interliant.com, *Water:* 6 Lakes totalling 5.5 acres plus members lake 1.25 acres, *Species:* Rainbow Trout (25lb 12oz), Goldies (14lb 2oz), Exmoor Blue (8lb 6oz) and Wild Brown Trout (7lb 8oz), *Charges:* Normal lakes from £6 + pay by weight (evening) to specimen lakes £39/day (4 fish), Super specimen tickets from £69. Many other tickets available plus Bellbrook Valley Flyfishers membership with a host of benefits, *Season:* Open all year 8.00am / dusk (No later than 9.00pm), *Methods:* Fly only, some catch & release available

Torrington
Great Torrington Anglers Association (Trout)
Contact: Paul Martin, 67 Calf Street, Torrington, EX38 7BH, 01805 623658 Fax:01805 623658, paul@olmargames.fsbusiness.co.uk, *Water:* Fly fishing on local reservoirs and canal fishing, *Permits:* No day tickets sold by club, *Charges:* Annual membership Adult £5-00, Junior £3-00

Totnes
Newhouse Fishery
Contact: Adrian Cook, Newhouse Farm, Moreleigh, Totnes, 01548 821426, *Water:* 4 Acre lake, *Species:* Rainbow Trout, Brown Trout, *Permits:* At above. No EA rod licence required, *Charges:* 5 Fish £20, 4 Fish £17, 3 Fish £14, 2 Fish £11, *Season:* Open all year, *Methods:* Fly only, Barbed hooks

Winkleigh

Stafford Moor Fishery

Contact: Andy or Debbie Seery, Dolton, Winkleigh, EX19 8PP, Tel/Fax: 01805 804360, *Water:* 4 lakes: 2x 1.5 acres, 1x 8 acres, 1x 2 acres, *Species:* Rainbow (Blues & Golds) + Brown Trout, *Permits:* At lodge at Stafford Moor, *Charges:* One charge of £6 to fish (incl. 1st fish), then £5 per fish, *Season:* Open all year, *Methods:* Fly only

Yelverton

Burrator

Contact: South West Lakes Trust, 01837 871565, info@swlakestrust.org.uk, *Species:* Low Cost Rainbow & Brown Trout, *Permits:* Esso Garage, Yelverton, *Charges:* Full day £9, Season £120, Reduced day £7, Season £90, Child/ Wheelchair £2, Season £30, *Season:* Opens 15 March 2001 - 12th October, *Methods:* Catch & Release operates. Barbless hooks only

DORSET
River Fishing

THE 'HAMPSHIRE' AVON

For detailed description of the Hampshire Avon and tributaries, see under Hampshire River fishing.

RIVER AVON PEWSEY - CHRISTCHURCH

Fisheries located between Pewsey and Salisbury are predominantly managed for Brown Trout fly fishing. A mixture of Coarse, Salmon and Trout fishing is available on the main river between Salisbury and Christchurch.

Christchurch Angling Club (Game)

Contact: S. Richards, 15 Roeshot Crescent, Highcliffe, Dorset, BH23 4QH, 01425 279710, steve@christchurchanglingclub.fsnet.co.uk, *Water:* Largest club on the River Avon, mainly mid/lower Avon, Burgate-Christchurch, also Fishing on River Stour between Gains Cross and Christchurch. Stillwater Game fishing at Cranebrook and other stillwaters. Sea

Trout at Christchurch Harbour. Please telephone the secretary for full details, *Species:* Salmon, Sea Trout, Rainbow Trout & Brown Trout, *Permits:* From the Secretary, or direct from local Tackle shops, *Charges:* Adult £95, Junior £38, Concession £60, (joining fee £15 adult, £6 junior), *Season:* Rainbow Trout all year round. Brown Trout: 1st April to 15th October; Salmon 1st Feb. to 31st Aug, Sea Trout 1st July 31st Oct, *Methods:* See rules for individual waters

Royalty Fishery

Contact: Davis Tackle, 75 Bargates, Christchurch, 01202 485169, davis@bonefishadventure.com, *Water:* Approx.1 ml of double bank fishing. Lowest beat on river. Controlled by Christchurch Angling Club as of 1 April 2001. *Species:* Roach 3lb, Chub 8lb, Dace 12oz, Barbel 13lb 12oz, Pike 38lb, Bream 11lb, Perch 4lb, Carp 31lb, Tench 7lb, Salmon 30lb, Sea Trout 14lb, *Charges:* please phone 01202 485169, *Methods:* No spinning, no night fishing.

Winkton Fishery

Contact: Davis Tackle, 75 Bargates, Christchurch, 01202 485169, *Water:* Approx 1 mile of fishing. Lower river near Christchurch, *Species:* Roach, Chub, Dace, Barbel, Pike, Bream, Perch, Carp, Salmon, Sea Trout, Brown Trout, *Charges:* Please call 01202 485169, *Methods:* No spinning, no night fishing (except for Sea Trout by arrangement)

FROME

The Frome rises through chalk on the North Dorset Downs near Evershot, and flows south through Dorchester, and finally Wareham, where it confluences with the River Piddle in Poole harbour. The River Frome is well known for its excellent Salmon, Brown Trout and Grayling fishing. There are also good numbers of coarse fish in certain areas; although access is limited sport can be very rewarding. Salmon and Trout fishing is generally controlled by syndicates and local estates.

Frome, Piddle & West Dorset Fishery Association

Contact: Mr PJ Leatherdale, Hanthorpe Cottage, Briantspuddle, Dorchester, DT2 HR, 01929-471274, *Water:* An amalgamation of riparian owners with an interest in the welfare of river fisheries in their locality. Information can be obtained concerning estate waters from the contact above

Dorchester Fishing Club

Contact: Mr J.Grindle (Hon. Sec.), 36 Cowleaze, Martinstown, DT2 9TD, 01305 889682, john@36cowleaze.freeserve.co.uk, *Water:* Approx 6.5 miles of double bank on the Frome near Dorchester, Brown Trout fly fishing, *Species:* Brown Trout, Grayling, *Permits:* John Aplin, Dorchester (01305) 266500. Web site, *Charges:* Day tickets and membership available. Please telephone for prices, *Season:* April 1st - Oct 14th, *Methods:* Dry fly and Nymph only.

River Frome (Town Section)

Contact: Purbeck Angling Centre / Deano, 01929 550770, *Water:* One mile stretch of the River Frome, *Species:* Roach, Dace, Grayling, Eels, Pike, Salmon, Trout, Sea Trout, Mullet, Bass and Flounder, *Permits:* Enquiries to Purbeck Angling Centre, *Charges:* Free fishing on public section. Enquiries to Purbeck Angling Centre, *Season:* Normal closed seasons apply

Wessex Fly Fishing & Chalk Streams Ltd. (Frome)

Water: See entry under Piddle, *Charges:* from £19 to £65

PIDDLE AND WEST DORSET STREAMS

'West Dorset' streams include the River Brit, Asker, Bride and Char. These streams are relatively short, 'steep' water courses supporting populations of mainly Brown Trout and Sea Trout. The River Piddle rises at four major springs near Alton St. Pancras, initially flowing south before turning east at Puddletown towards Poole Harbour, where it confluences with the River Frome. This is a relatively small river known primarily for its Salmon, Brown Trout and Sea Trout. Other fish species can be found in the River Piddle including, Roach, Dace, Pike and Perch. Much of the fishing is controlled by local syndicates and estate waters; further information about these groups can be obtained from the aforementioned Frome, Piddle and West Dorset Fishery Association.

Environment Agency - Piddle Fishery
Contact: Conservation Officer, Environment Agency, Rivers House, Sunrise Business Park, Blandford Forum, DT11 8ST, 01258 456080, *Water:* 3km of bank fishing on Lower Piddle, *Species:* Salmon & Sea Trout, *Permits:* 14 permits per annum, *Charges:* £199 plus vat (£34.82), subject to annual review

Wessex Fly Fishing & Chalk Streams Ltd. (Piddle)
Contact: Richard Slocock, Lawrences Farm, Tollpuddle, Dorchester, 01305 848460, *Water:* 5 Lakes & Pools totalling 4 acres for Rainbow Trout. Plus 16 Beats on Rivers Piddle & Frome for Brown Trout, *Charges:* Rivers: Minimum £19 day, Max £60, *Season:* Rivers: April 1st to October 15th, *Methods:* Fly Fishing only, Most river beats are catch & release using barbless hooks

STOUR

The River Stour in Dorset is well known by anglers across the country for quality of its fishing. Over the years many British record captures have been made here, for example the current Roach record stands at 4lb 3oz, taken from the Stour near Wimborne.

The Stour rises on the Greensand at St. Peters Pump in Stourhead Gardens and flows through Gillingham near by where it is joined by the Shreen Water and the River Lodden. The Stour stretches out for 96 km, passing through the Blackmoor Vale down to the sea at Christchurch; the total fall over this distance is approximately 230m. Other notable tributaries along its length include the River Tarrant confluencing near Spetisbury, the River Allen at Wimborne and the Moors River coming in near Christchurch. The Stour confluences with the River Avon at the 'Clay Pool' in Christchurch, before flowing into the harbour area and ultimately out into the English Channel.

Blandford & District Angling Club
Contact: Peter Brundish, 10 Windmill Road, Blandford Forum, DT11 7HG, 01258 453545, *Water:* 4 miles of Dorset Stour, *Species:* Roach to 1.5lb, Bream to 8lb 10oz, Perch to 3lb 2oz, Carp to 17lb, Chub, Pike to 25lb, *Permits:* Conyers Tackle Shop, Market Place, Blandford Tel 01258 452307. Todber Manor Fishing Tackle Shop, Tel: 01258 820384. Or from the secretary, *Charges:* Senior £27.50, O.A.P. £16.50, Junior £8.50, Day tickets £4. Please enquire for family membership, *Season:* Normal coarse season, *Methods:* Boilies banned

Dorchester & District Angling Society
Contact: W. Lucy, Secretary, 7 Celtic Crescent, Dorchester, DT1 2QJ, 01305 264873, *Water:* 4 miles on Dorset Stour, 1.5 miles Dorset Frome plus 1 lake Kingcombe. R. Brue Som + water sharing agreements and Wessex Fed. waters, *Species:* Roach, Dace, Chub, Pike, Gudgeon, Perch, Eels, Carp, Bream, Grayling, *Permits:* Anglers Tackle Store, Weymouth, Aplins Tackle Dorchester, Weymouth Angling Centre, Surplus International, Dorchester, *Charges:* £35 senior, £17.50 Senior citizen, £13 Junior (14-17), £5 Primary (10-13), Members guest tickets, no day tickets, half-year membership from December 1, *Season:* June 16th - March 14th, Stillwater open all year

Durweston Angling Association
Contact: Mr Vernon Bell (secretary), Endcote, Durweston, 01258 451317, *Water:* 2 miles Dorset Stour (including Weir & Mill Pool), *Species:* Bream, Roach, Rudd, Gudgeon, Dace, Eels, Chub, Pike, Perch, *Permits:* The White Horse Public House, Stour Paine. The Mill House, Durweston (after 9 a.m.), *Charges:* Day tickets: £3, River permit £27.50/adult, £16/youth, Charges may change in 2001, *Season:* Close season 14th March - 16th June

Gillingham & District A A
Contact: Simon Hebditch (Hon. Secretary), 5 Ham Court, Shaftsbury Rd, Gillingham, SP8 4LU, 01747 824817, ditch@ham5.fsnet.co.uk, *Water:* 7 miles Upper Stour - Gillingham to Marnhull. Turners Paddock lake at Stourhead. Mappowder Court 4 lakes at Mappowder, *Species:* River: Roach, Chub, Dace, Perch, Pike, Gudgeon, Bream. Turners Paddock: Bream, Tench. Mappowder: Carp, Crucians, Rudd, Tench, Perch, Roach, Bream, *Permits:*

The Timepiece, Newbury, Gillingham, Dorset, SP8 4HZ. Tel: 01747 823339. Mr P Stone (Treasurer). Mr J Candy, Todber Manor Fisheries Shop, Tel: 01258 820384, *Charges:* £4 day ticket for any water, Membership about £22, Juniors £11, £5 Turners Paddock, *Season:* River & Turners Paddock closed in usual close season, Mappowder Court open all year, *Methods:* Barbless hooks only at Mappowder. No livebaiting at Turners Paddock

Muscliffe & Longham
Contact: Ivor Brittain, Bournemouth, Tel/Fax: 01202 514345, bmthlodge@cwcom.net, *Water:* 1.5 miles River Stour at Muscliffe and quarter mile at Longham, *Species:* Chub, Barbel, Roach, Dace, Pike, Eels, Minnow, Gudgeon and Perch, *Permits:* Free (owned by Bournemouth Council), *Charges:* Free. E.A. licence required, *Season:* 16th June to 14th March, *Methods:* No restrictions.

Ringwood & District Angling Club (Stour)
Contact: Mr. K.J. Grozier, 11 Merlin Close, Hightown, Ringwood, BH24 3RB, 01425 471466, *Water:* 11 stretches on Stour including total control of Throop fishery and various stretches upstream Stourpaine, *Species:* Throop - Barbel to 14lb, Chub 7lb. Middle regions good general Roach, Chub, Bream, Pike, Perch, some Trout, Grayling and Carp, *Permits:* As above and local tackle shops, *Charges:* Adult £80, Junior £37, concessions for OAP's and disabled; Throop day tickets £7.50. Concessions, O.A.P's, Disabled and Juniors available from local tackle dealers, *Season:* As per coarse season, *Methods:* All on reverse of ticket.

Stalbridge Angling Society
Contact: Mr T Cairns, 35 Blackmore Rd, Stalbridge, DT10 2NU, 01963 363688, *Water:* 2.5 miles Stour, 3 Lakes (Buckland Newton), *Species:* Bream, Tench, Roach, Dace, Pike, Chub, Carp, Rudd, *Permits:* Stalbridge Angling 01963 362291, *Charges:* Senior Annual £18 no joining fee, Junior (under 17 years) & senior citizens £6 no joining fee. Husband and wife ticket £30, Reg Disabled/OAP's £6. Day Tickets £3 senior, £1 junior, *Season:* No closed season on Lakes, *Methods:* No boilies on ponds, no braided lines, no fixed method feeders or fixed leads. Full rules available with permit.

DORSET - RIVER FISHING / STILLWATER COARSE

DORSET
Stillwater
Coarse

Sturminster & Hinton A.A
Contact: R. Wylde, 38 Grosvenor Rd, Stalbridge, DT10 2PN, 01258 472788 or 01963 363291, steve@dimmer.freeserve.co.uk, *Water:* 14 miles mid River Stour, 3 small lakes (members only), *Species:* Roach, Chub, Tench, Bream, Perch, Carp, Pike, *Permits:* Harts Garden Supplies, Kevs Autos or S. Dimmer (Membership Secretary) 01963 363291(evenings), *Charges:* £4/day, £10/week, Juniors £3/ season, Adults £17.50 + £5 joining fee, *Season:* March 14th - June 16th, *Methods:* No dogs, Radios, No live baiting, No night fishing, One rod, second rod for Pike only

Throop Fisheries
Contact: Now run by Ringwood Angling Club, *Water:* See entry under Coarse Fisheries - Bournemouth. 10 miles on Dorset Stour

Wareham & District Angling Society
Contact: Mr. Burgess, BH20 4NB, 01929 550540, *Water:* River waters on North Dorset Stour and the Frome. 3 lakes Wareham area, *Species:* Coarse, *Permits:* Wessex Angling, Poole, Dorset; Dennings Tackle, Wyke Regis, *Charges:* Senior £32, Ladies / O.A.P's £16, Junior £15, Husband and Wife membership £39. (subject to confirmation). Membership runs from June 1st to May 31st, *Season:* One lake open during Coarse closed season, *Methods:* Barbless, No litter, No cans, Variations as per membership book

Wimborne & District Angling Club (Stour)
Contact: G.E.Pipet (secretary), 12 Seatown Close, Canford Heath, Poole, 01202 382123, *Water:* 10 miles River Stour, 17 lakes, 1 mile River Avon, *Species:* Trout & Coarse Fisheries, *Permits:* Certain waters are available on Guest Tickets £6 from Wessex Angling, 321 Wimborne Rd, Oakdale, Poole, *Charges:* £65 + £8 joining fee, *Methods:* Barbless hooks on Coarse stillwaters, No floating baits

Bournemouth

East Moors Lake
Contact: Mr. Nicolas Hoare, East Moors Farm, East Moors Lane, St. Leonards, Ferndale, Nr Bournemouth, 01202 872302, *Water:* 1.5 acre lake, *Species:* Carp: common, Mirror, ghost, leather, purple blushing; Tench, Gold Tench, Roach, Perch, Rudd, Chub & Pike, *Charges:* Members only, Country/ Holiday membership available - see website or phone, *Methods:* Barbless hooks only, no boilies, no keepnets, no dogs. Children under 14 must be accompanied by adult

Throop Fisheries (Coarse Lake)
Contact: Now run by Ringwood Angling Club. *Water:* Northern edge of Bournemouth. 10 Miles of river bank on Dorset Stour + Stillwater Mill Pool, *Species:* Barbel, Chub, Carp, Roach, Tench, Perch, Dace, Pike, *Permits:* Yeovil Angling Centre - Tel. 01935 476777, Ringwood Tackle - Tel. 01425 475155, Bournemouth Fishing Lodge - Tel. 01202 514345, *Charges:* Prices on application + list, *Season:* 16th June - 14 March (Open every day between these dates), *Methods:* No night fishing.

Bridport

Mangerton Valley Coarse Fishing Lake
Contact: Clive & Jane Greening, New House Farm, Mangerton Lane, Bradpole, Bridport, DT6 3SF, 01308 458482, jane@mangertonlake.freeserve.co.uk, *Water:* 1.6 acre lake, *Species:* Carp to 20lb (Common and Mirror), Roach, Tench, Bream, *Permits:* From Post Office, *Charges:* £4.50 day, £3 half day, £2 evening, *Season:* Possibly closed March-April-May (please ring first), *Methods:* Barbless hooks. No boilies or beans. No nuts. No dogs. Night fishing by arrangement. All chidren under 12 to be accompanied by an adult

Christchurch

Avon Tyrrell Lakes
Contact: Richard Bonney, Avon Tyrrell House, Bransgore, Christchurch, BH23 8EE, 01425 672347, info@avontyrrell.org.uk, *Water:* Two lakes totalling approx 2.5 acres, *Species:* Carp, Tench, Roach, Bream, Perch and Rudd, *Permits:* On site from reception, *Charges:* £5 Day Tickets Adults. £2.50 Juniors(Under 16).Season Tickets also available, please note Night Fishing only available on a season ticket, *Season:* Open mid June to Mid March 8am to 8pm, *Methods:* Barbless Hooks, No keepnets, No nut baits. See rules on site

Christchurch Angling Club (Coarse Ponds)
Contact: S. Richards, 15 Roeshot Crescent, Highcliffe, Dorset, BH23 4QH, 01425 279710, steve@christchurchanglingclub.fsnet.co.uk, *Water:* Various coarse ponds. See entry under Hampshire Avon, *Methods:* See rules for individual waters

Hordle Lakes
Contact: M.F. Smith, Hordle Lakes, Golden Hill, Ashley Lane, Hordle, Nr New Milton, 01590 672300, *Water:* Seven spring fed lakes set in 11 acres, *Species:* Double figure Carp. Tench, Roach, Rudd, Bream and Perch, *Charges:* Adults £6 per day. Kiddies pool £2, *Season:* Open all year 8am to dusk, *Methods:* All fish to be returned immediately. No groundbaiting, loose feeding only. Barbless hooks only, no larger than size 6. No Boilies, beans, nuts, Trout bait or floating crust/biscuit. Full rules at the fishery.

Mudeford Wood Angling Club
Contact: Davis Tackle, 75 Bargates, Christchurch, 01202 485169, *Water:* Half acre lake, *Species:* Carp, Tench, Roach, *Permits:* Davis Tackle, Christchurch. Limit of 4 day tickets per day, *Charges:* £5 per rod per day, *Season:* Closed 31st March 2000 - 16th June 2000, fishing from 7am till one hr after sunset, *Methods:* Barbless hooks only, No boilies

Orchard Lakes

Contact: Mr R Southcombe, New Lane, Bashley, New Milton, BH25 5TD, 01425 612404, *Water:* 3 small lakes, largest 2 acres, *Species:* Carp, Tench, Bream, Roach, Rudd, Perch, *Permits:* Day tickets on the bank, *Charges:* From £5/day main & Tench lake; £4 on Match Pool, *Season:* Open all year 7am to dusk, *Methods:* Barbless hooks only. No keepnets

Sopley Farm PYO

Contact: Sopley Farm PYO, Sopley, Christchurch, 01425 672451, *Water:* 8 acre lake. 1000 yard perimeter, *Species:* Carp, Bream, Roach, Rudd, *Permits:* At each PYO Farm Shop, *Charges:* £40 Season. £5 Day. £3 Half Day. £3 day OAP and u14, *Season:* June to October when PYO's are open. 9.30am to 6.30pm, *Methods:* Barbless Hooks. No keepnets.

Whirlwind Lake

Contact: Mr & Mrs Pillinger, Whirlwind Rise, Dudmore Lane, Christchurch, BH23 6BQ, 01202 475255, *Water:* Secluded lake, *Species:* Common, Crucian and Mirror Carp, Roach, Rudd, Tench, Chub etc, *Permits:* On site and local fishing tackle shops. Davis Tackle, 75 The Bargates, Christchurch 01202 485169. Pro Tackle, 258 Barrack Road, Christchurch 01202 484518. Advanced booking advisable, limited number available, *Charges:* Adults £6.50 day ticket. £5 half day (Limited places). Children (must be accompanied) £4 day, £2.50 half day, *Season:* Open all year, *Methods:* Barbless hooks only. No keepnets, No boilies.

Cranborne

Gold Oak Fishery

Contact: Mr J Butler, Gold Oak Farm, Hare Lane, Cranborne, 01725 517275, *Water:* 7 small lakes, *Species:* Carp to 20lb, Green + Golden Tench to 5-6lb, Perch 2.5lb, Roach 2lb, Chub 3lb, Bream 3lb, *Charges:* Summer day - £7 Adult, £5 Junior. 1/2 day - £5 Adult, £3 Junior. Eve £3 Adult, £1 Junior. Winter day - £5 Adult, £3 Junior. 1/2 day - £3 Adult, £2 junior, *Season:* All year, *Methods:* No large fish in keepnets, Barbless hooks, Dogs on lead.

Martins Farm Fishery

Contact: Mr Ball, Martins Farm, Woodlands, Nr Verwood, 01202 822335, *Water:* 2.5 acre spring fed lake, *Species:* Carp, Tench, Perch, Roach, Rudd, *Permits:* Tel: 01202 822335, *Charges:* £6 Adult day ticket, £3 Juniors, *Season:* Closed 16th March - 16th June, *Methods:* No keepnets, barbless hooks, No hemp/boilies.

Wimborne & District Angling Club (Coarse Lakes)

Contact: G E Pipet (secretary), 12 Seatown Close, Canford Heath, Poole, BH17 8BJ, 01202 382123, *Water:* 1 mile River Avon. 12 coarse lakes, 5 Trout lakes. See also entry under Stour, *Species:* Mixed Coarse, *Permits:* Certain waters are available on guest tickets. £6 from Wessex Angling, 321 Wimborne Rd, Oakdale, Poole, *Charges:* £65 plus £8 joining fee, *Methods:* Barbless hooks on coarse stillwaters. No floating baits

Dorchester

Dorchester & Dist. Angling Society (Coarse Lake)

Contact: W. Lucy, Secretary, 01305 264873, *Water:* See entry under Stour; One coarse lake at Kingcombe

Hermitage Lakes (Coarse)

Contact: Nigel Richardson, Common Farm, Hermitage, Cerne Abbas, Dorchester, 01963 210556, *Water:* Half acre lake, *Species:* Carp, *Charges:* Day ticket £4, *Season:* Closed 14th March - 16th June, *Methods:* Barbless hooks, No keepnets.

Luckfield Lake Fishery

Contact: John Aplin, 1 Athelstan Road, Dorchester, DT1 1NR, 01305 266500, *Water:* 1.5 acre clay pit in beautiful surroundings, *Species:* Carp - 23lb, Tench - 9lb+, Roach - 3lb+, *Permits:* As above, *Charges:* Day £5, Night £6, 1/2 season £30, Full season £60, *Season:* 16th June - 14th March, *Methods:* No keepnets, Barbless hooks.

Pallington Lakes

Contact: Mr. Simon or Mrs. Tini Pomeroy, Pallington, Dorchester, DT2 8QU, 01305 848141 / 07887 840507, pallatrax@aol.com, *Water:* 3 lakes and a stretch of the River Frome, *Species:* Lakes: Carp to 30lb 12oz, Tench to 12lb 3oz, Perch to 4lb 13oz, Grayling to 3lb

4oz, Roach, Bream, Chub, Rudd, *Permits:* As above, also mobile: 07887 - 840507, *Charges:* Lakes: Day £7, Evening £4, 24 hours £13. Juniors half price. River by arrangement, *Season:* All year round, *Methods:* Barbless hooks, No keepnets. No groundbait. No nut baits. All anglers must be in possesion of a fish antisceptic. All Carp anglers must have min. 36" landing net and unhooking mat

Gillingham

Culvers Farm Fishery

Contact: V.J. Pitman, Culvers Farm, Gillingham, SP8 5DS, 01747 822466, *Water:* One 1.5 acre lake. One 3 acre lake, *Species:* Carp, Bream, Roach and Tench, *Charges:* Day £5. Half Day £3. OAP's and under 16 £3 all day, *Season:* Open all year. No night fishing, *Methods:* Barbless hooks only. No Boilies. No keepnets allowed on Middle Mead. Lower Mead - keepnets permitted.

Gillingham & District A A (Coarse Lakes)

Water: See entry under Stour. 5 lakes

Lyme Regis

Wood Farm Caravan Park

Contact: Ian Pointing, Axminster Road, Charmouth, DT6 6BT, 01297 560697, holidays@woodfarm.co.uk, *Water:* 2 ponds totalling approx 1 acre, *Species:* Carp, Rudd, Roach, Tench & Perch, *Permits:* Rod Licences sold, *Charges:* £3.30 day ticket. £13.50 week. £29 season, *Season:* All year, *Methods:* No boilies, keepnets. Barbless hooks only

Stalbridge

Stalbridge Angling Association

Contact: Mr T Cairns, 35 Blackmore Rd, Stalbridge, DT10 2NU, 01963 363688, *Water:* See entry under Stour. 3 ponds

Sturminster Newton

Sturminster & Hinton A.A (Coarse Lakes)

Water: See entry under Stour. 3 small lakes (members only)

DORSET - STILLWATER COARSE / STILLWATER TROUT

Todber Manor Fisheries
Contact: John Candy, Manor Farm, Todber, Sturminster Newton, DT10 1JB, 01258 820384, *Water:* Two acre canal style lake; one acre Specimen Lake; 2x 1 acre small Carp lakes & other species i.e. Roach, Tench, Rudd, *Species:* Roach, Skimmers, Tench, Gudgeon, Crucians, Perch and Barbel. Specimen Lake Carp 20lb plus, Pike 20lb plus, *Permits:* As above, *Charges:* £4 per day. Specimen Lake £20 for 24 hours, *Season:* Open all year, *Methods:* Barbless hooks only. No keepnets on specimen lake

Wareham
Wareham & District Angling Society (Coarse Lakes)
Water: See entry under Stour - 3 lakes

Weymouth
Osmington Mills Holidays
Contact: Reception, Osmington Mills, Weymouth, DT3 6HB, 01305 832311, *Water:* 1 Acre Lake, *Species:* Carp, Tench, Bream, Roach, *Permits:* Caravan Park reception, On bank, *Charges:* £5 per day Adults, £2.50 under 16, £2.50 Evening ticket after 5 p.m, *Season:* May 23rd - March 15th, *Methods:* Barbless hooks, No keepnets, No particle bait.

Radipole Lake
Contact: Mr D.Tattersall, Council Offices, North Quay, Weymouth, DT4 8TA, 01305 206234, davidtattersall@wpbc.weymouth.gov.uk, *Water:* 70 acres plus, *Species:* Carp to 20lb, Eels, Roach to 2lb, Dace, Pike, Mullet, *Permits:* Anglers Tackle Store, 64 Park Street, Weymouth, 01305 782624. Weymouth Angling Centre, 24 Trinity Road, Weymouth 01305 777771, *Charges:* Day Junior £1.80, Adult £3.80, 60+ £2.70; Monthly & annual available, *Season:* 16th June - 14th March, *Methods:* 2 Rod max, Barbless hooks only, No bivvies

Warmwell Holiday Park
Contact: John Aplin - Fishery Manager, Warmwell, Nr Weymouth, DT2 8JE, 01305 257490 or 0589 680464, *Water:* 3 lakes. 2 acre specimen lake - 20 swims pre-booking only. 2 mixed fishing lakes, *Species:* Carp to 40lb. Perch to 4lb, Rudd, Crucians, Eels, *Permits:* Very limited winter day tickets available from fishery manager on number above, *Charges:* Day tickets £20 for 12 hours, dawn to dusk, *Season:* Winter season dawn to dusk, *Methods:* Barbless hooks. No nuts, beans or pulses. 2 rods max. No keepnets. No remote control boats. Unhooking mats must be used. Minimum 10lb line.

Wimborne
Crooked Willows Farm
Contact: Mr & Mrs VJ Percy, Mannington, Wimborne, BH21 7LB, 01202 825628, *Water:* 1.5 acres, *Species:* Carp to 20lb, Tench to 6lb, Chub 4lb, Roach, Rudd + Crucians, *Permits:* Available on bank, *Charges:* £4/day, Juniors £2, *Season:* Dawn to Dusk all year round, *Methods:* Barbless hooks only, no groundbait, NO keepnets

Environment Agency - Little Canford Ponds
Contact: Conservation Officer, Environment Agency, Rivers House, Sunrise Business Park, Blandford Forum, DT11 8ST, 01258 456080, *Water:* Approx. 2 acres, *Species:* Carp, Bream, Roach, Perch Tench, Rudd, Pike, *Charges:* Adult £42, Conc. £21, Junior £21, under 12 years free (subject to annual review)

Whitemoor Lake
Contact: 400 Colehill Lane, Colehill, Wimborne, BH21 7AW, 01202 884478, *Water:* 2 Acre lake + half acre canal, *Species:* Carp 25lb, Tench 7lb, Perch 4-9lbs, Roach 2lb, Rudd 1-8lbs, *Permits:* Minster Sports (Wimborne), Bournemouth Fishing Lodge (Bournemouth), *Charges:* Adults £5-00, Juniors £3-00, O.A.P's £4-00, *Season:* No close season, *Methods:* No barbed hooks, No keepnets

DORSET Stillwater Trout

Beaminster
Knights in the Bottom Lakes
Contact: Jill Haynes, Knights in the Bottom, Hooke, Beaminster, DT8 3PG, 01308 862157, *Water:* 3 Lakes, 3.5 acres of water, *Species:* Trout, *Charges:* On application, *Season:* April - October, *Methods:* Fly Only.

Bridport
Mangerton Mill
Contact: Mr Harris, Mangerton Mill, Mangerton, Bridport, DT6 3SG, 01308 485224, *Water:* 1 Acre lake, *Species:* Rainbow Trout, *Permits:* Post Office, *Season:* 1st April - 31st December, *Methods:* Max hook size 10

Cranborne
Wimborne & District Angling Club (Lakes)
Contact: Mr J Burden, 35 Hardy Crescent, Wimborne, BH21 2AR, 01202 889324, *Water:* 5 Trout lakes plus Brown Trout on the River Avon. See also entry under Stour

Dorchester
Flowers Farm Fly Fishers
Contact: Alan.J.Bastone, Flowers Farm, Hilfield, Dorchester, DT2 7BA, 01300 341351, *Water:* 5 lakes total 3.75 acres, *Species:* Rainbow & Brown Trout. Best fish 14lb 2oz Rainbow in 1999 and 4lb 8oz Brown in 1998, *Permits:* Some 25 and 50 fish tickets available. Prices on request (Tel/Fax: 01300-341351), *Charges:* £18 per day, £14 half day, £10.50 evening, *Season:* Open all year 5.30am to dusk, *Methods:* Single fly, Max size 10, Bank fishing only

Hermitage Lakes (Trout)
Contact: Nigel Richardson, Common Farm, Hermitage, Cerne Abbas, Dorchester, 01963 210556, *Water:* 3 half acre lakes, *Species:* Rainbow & Brown Trout, *Charges:* Day (4 fish) £15, Half day (3 fish) £12, Evening (2 fish) £9, *Season:* Open all season, *Methods:* Max size 10 longshank.

Wessex Fly Fish. Trout Lakes & Chalk Streams Ltd

Contact: Tollpuddle, *Water:* See entries under Piddle and Frome. 5 clearwater lakes and pools totalling 4 acres, *Charges:* Lakes: Day £26, £22/6hrs, £18/4hrs, £15/evening, conc. £16, *Season:* Lakes: March 1st - January 15th

Lyme Regis
Amherst Lodge

Contact: Darren Herbert, Amherst Lodge, Uplyme, Lyme Regis, DT7 3XH, 01297 442773, *Water:* 6 spring fed Trout lakes, *Species:* Rainbow to 14.5lb and Brown Trout, *Permits:* Go to rod room on arrival, *Charges:* From £13 for catch & keep, from £8 for catch & release, *Season:* Open all year, Dawn to dusk, Must book if arriving before 8.00am, *Methods:* All conventional methods acceptable, No spinning, Bait etc.

Wimborne
Whitesheet Trout

Contact: P. Cook, Whitesheet Farm, Holt, Wimborne, BH21 7DB, 01202 883687, *Water:* 3 lakes totalling 7 acres, *Species:* Rainbow + Brown Trout, *Permits:* On site, *Charges:* 25-fish ticket: £175; membership ticket: £50/season; day ticket with membership: 5-fish/£20, 3-fish/£15, 2-fish/£12; day ticket: 5-fish/£25, 3-fish/£20, 2-fish/£15, *Season:* Open all year dawn to dusk, *Methods:* Fly only

GLOUCS Stillwater Coarse

Cirencester
Swindon Isis Angling Club Lake No1

Contact: Peter Gilbert, 31 Havelock St, Swindon, SN1 1SD, 01793 535396, *Water:* 6 acre mature gravel pit at Cotswold Water Park (Water Park Lane 19), South Cerney, Cirencester, *Species:* Tench (9lb) lake with Carp to 30lb, Rudd to 2lb12oz, odd big Bream, usual Roach and Perch + good Pike, *Permits:* Tackle shops in Swindon, Cirencester, Chippenham and Calne, *Charges:* Club *Permits:* Senior £29.50. OAP and disabled £12. Juniors £8. The club permit contains two free day tickets and more day tickets can be obtained for £5 each; year starts 1 April, *Season:* Open all year round. Club cards start 1st April, *Methods:* No bans

Fairford
Milestone Fisheries (Coarse)

Contact: Sue or Bob Fletcher or Andy King, London Road, Fairford, GL7 4DS, 01285 713908, *Water:* 3.5 acre mixed coarse lake. 56 acre Pike lake, *Species:* Well stocked with Carp 26lb, Tench 9.5lb, Bream 11lb, Roach 3.5lb, Rudd, Perch 4.5lb. Separate 56 acre Pike lake 33lb, *Permits:* Day tickets available from fishery office - above address (also fax: 01285-711113), *Charges:* £5.00 per day (2 rods) Junior £3.00 per day, £8 day & night. Pike lake - Day ticket £8, Night ticket £8, day & night ticket £13, *Season:* No closed season, open every day except Dec 25th. Night fishing by arrangement. Pike lake Open from 1st October to end of April, *Methods:* No keepnets, no dogs, barbless hooks only. Pike lake - Barbless & semi - barbless hooks, Minimum of 12lb b.s. line. Traces min 18lbs, 36 soft mesh landing net, unhooking mat, strong wire cutters.

Gloucester
Huntley Carp Pools

Contact: John Tipper - Frank Morris, 14 Thoresby Ave, Tuffley, Gloucester, GL4 0TE, 01452 505313 Fax:01452 618708, *Water:* 2 x 4 acre lakes. 1 with Carp to 25lb. 1 with general fish, Carp, Tench, Perch, Bream, Roach, Rudd, Crucian, *Species:* Carp: to 25lb. Coarse: Carp to 20lb, Bream 4lb, Perch 3lb, Tench 5lb, Roach/Rudd 2.75lb, *Permits:* Only from above, *Charges:* To be advised, *Season:* 16th June - 30th April, *Methods:* No keepnets, barbless hooks.

GLOUCS Stillwater Trout

Fairford
Milestone Fisheries (Trout Lakes)

Contact: Sue or Bob Fletcher or Andy King, Milestone Fisheries, London Road, Fairford, GL7 4DS, 01285 713908, fax 1285 711111, *Water:* 10 acre lake and 2 acre lake, *Species:* 10 acre lake: Brown Trout, Rainbow Trout 2lb - 20lb. 2 acre lake: Rainbow Trout 1lb - 1.25lb (bank fishing only). Also Blue/Golden Trout and doubles only pool 10lb - 23lb, *Permits:* Day tickets & Season tickets plus a limited number catch and release (take first fish - not available when water temperature is high). *Charges:* 10 acre lake: Day & season tickets. Bank (Boats & Float tube for hire) Day ticket 5 fish £30, 1/2 day 3 fish £20.2 Acre lake: bank fishing only. Catch and take only £12 for 5 fish (top pool), *Season:* No closed season (Return all browns), *Methods:* Catch & take or Catch & release on ten acre lake only. (Barbless hooks on Catch & release), Fly fishing only

HAMPSHIRE - RIVER FISHING / STILLWATER COARSE

HAMPSHIRE
River Fishing

THE 'HAMPSHIRE' AVON

The River Avon is one of England's most famous rivers, and is revered by all anglers for the quality of fish that live in it. This river creates a certain mystique that captivates the attentions of fishers from all walks of life.

The River Avon rises in the Vale of Pewsey and, with its tributaries the Bourne and Wylye, drains the chalk of Salisbury Plain. The River Nadder, which is joined by the Wylye near Salisbury, drains the escarpment of the South Wiltshire Downs and the Kimmeridge clays of the Wardour Vale. The River Ebble and Ashford Water also drain the South Wiltshire Downs and join the Avon downstream of Salisbury and Fordingbridge respectively.

Below Fordingbridge, a number of streams drain the New Forest area. The Avon finally drains into Christchurch harbour, where it is joined by the Rivers Stour and Mude before discharging into the English Channel.

AVON HAMPSHIRE
Britford (Coarse)
Contact: London Angler's Association, Izaak Walton House, 2A Hervey Park Road, London, E17 6LJ, 02085 207477, *Water:* Several stretches of the Hampshire Avon, *Species:* Roach 3lb, Barbel 10 lb, Chub 7 lb, plus specimen Dace, Grayling, Perch & Pike, *Permits:* Members only, Address as above, *Charges:* Senior: £35 - Junior, OAP, reg. disabled: £18.50 - Husband & wife: £52 - Club affiliated membership available on request, *Season:* Current EA byelaws apply, *Methods:* See members handbook
Britford (Game)
Contact: London Angler's Association, Izaak Walton House, 2A Hervey Park Road, London, E17 6LJ, 02085 207477, *Water:* Several stretches of the Hampshire Avon, *Species:* Trout & Salmon, *Permits:* Members only, Address as above, *Charges:* Senior: £35 - Junior, OAP, reg. disabled: £18.50 - Husband & wife: £52 - Club affiliated membership available on request, *Season:* Current EA byelaws apply, *Methods:* See members handbook

Christchurch Angling Club (Coarse River)
Contact: S. Richards, 15 Roeshot Crescent, Highcliffe, Dorset, BH23 4QH, 01425 279710, steve@christchurchanglingclub.fsnet.co.uk, *Water:* Largest club on the River Avon, mainly mid/lower Avon, Burgate - Christchurch, including the Royalty Fishery as of 1.4.01, also Fishing on River Stour between Gains Cross and Christchurch plus various coarse ponds including Blashford and Ivy Lakes. Please telephone the secretary for full details, *Species:* Roach (3lb), Chub (7lb), Dace (1lb), Barbel (14lb), Pike (30lb), Bream (11lb), Perch (4lb), Carp (40lb), Eels (5lb), Cucian Carp (4lb), Grayling (3lb), Tench (9lb), *Permits:* Day tickets available for Rivers & Stillwaters from the Secretary or direct from local Tackle Shops, *Charges:* Adult £95, Junior £38, Concession £60, (joining fee £15 adult, £6 junior), *Season:* Coarse: 16th June to 15th March. Salmon: 1st Feb to 31st August. Rainbow Trout all year round. Brown Trout: 1st April to 15th October, *Methods:* See rules for individual waters
Ringwood & District Angling Club (Hampshire Avon)
Contact: Mr K J Grozier, 11 Merlin Close, Hightown, Ringwood, BH24 3RB, 01425 471466, *Water:* Between - Severals fishery at Ringwood upstream to Burgate including Ibsley, *Species:* Barbel to 14lb, Chub to 7lb, Roach 3lb+, Pike 30lb+, Bream 10lb+, Perch, Carp, Dace, Salmon, Sea Trout, Brown Trout, *Permits:* As above and local tackle shops, *Charges:* Adult £80, Junior £37, Concessions, O.A.P.'s, Disabled £55 (Joining fee-£15 adult, £5 junior). Severals day tickets £7.50. Concessions for O.A.P.'s, Disabled, Juniors. Prices subject to seasonal review, *Season:* Slight variaions to coarse season due to Salmon fishing, Current E.A. byelaws apply

HAMPSHIRE
Stillwater
Coarse

Fordingbridge
Cranborne Fruit Farm
Contact: Cranborne Fruit Farm, Alderholt, Fordingbridge, 01425 672451, *Water:* 3 acre lake, *Species:* Carp, Bream, Roach, Rudd, *Permits:* At each PYO Farm Shop, *Charges:* £40 Season. £6 Day. £4 Half Day. £3 day OAP and u14, *Season:* June to October when PYO's are open. 9.30am to 6.30pm, *Methods:* Barbless Hooks, No keepnets
New Forest Water Park
Contact: Mark Jury, Hucklesbrook Lakes, Ringwood Road, Fordingbridge, SP6 2EY, 01425 656868, info@newforestwaterpark.co.uk, *Water:* 19 acre lake, 11 acre lake, *Species:* Pike to 35lb + Carp to 40lb in 11 acre lake. Carp to 32lb, Tench to 10lb, Roach to 3lb, Rudd to 2lb in 19 acre lake, *Permits:* From Clubhouse (After 9 a.m.) or on bank, *Charges:* £5 for 2 rods day ticket, £15 for 24hrs, *Season:* All year round, *Methods:* Barbless hooks, No nut baits, No keepnets, No live bait

Ringwood
Blashford & Ivy Lakes
Water: Series of former Gravel Pits. Fishing available to members of Christchurch Angling Club. See entry under Hampshire Avon
Hurst Pond
Contact: Ringwood Tackle, Tel: 01425 475155, bmthlodge@cwcom.net, *Water:* 1.5 acre pond at Hedlands Business Park, Blashford, Ringwood, *Species:* Carp 18lb, Tench 6.5lb, Roach 2.5lb, Rudd 2lb, Perch 3lb 12oz, Crucians 2.5lb, Eels 5lb, *Charges:* £5 per day, £3.50 Concessions. Limited night fishing, £10 - 24hr ticket, *Season:* Open all year

Ringwood & District Angling Club (Coarse Lakes)
Contact: Mr K J Grozier, 11 Merlin Close, Hightown, Ringwood, BH24 3RB, 01425 471466, *Water:* 4 lakes at Hightown + Northfield on outskirts of Ringwood, *Species:* Hightown - Mixed fishery with Carp to 36lb, Tench, Bream, Roach, Rudd, Pike, Eels. Northfield - Big Carp to 30lb, Tench to 12lb, Bream, Roach, Rudd, Pike, *Permits:* From above and local tackle shop, *Charges:* Adult £80, Junior £37, concessions for OAP's and disabled; day tickets £7.50 plus night options available at Ringwood Tackle, West St, Ringwood, 01425-475155. Prices may change for 2000, please enquire, *Season:* All year fishing available, *Methods:* All on reverse of ticket

HAMPSHIRE Stillwater Trout

Fordingbridge
Damerham Fisheries
Contact: Mike Davies, The Lake House, Damerham, Fordingbridge, SP6 3HW, 01725 518446, *Water:* 6 lakes. 1.5 mile Allan River, *Species:* Rainbow Trout (Sandy, Lavender, White + Electric Blue Rainbow Trout), *Permits:* Season Rods, *Charges:* Full Rod £1,500 (32 days), ½ Rod £750 (15 days), ¼ Rod £600 (10 days). Please phone to confirm prices, *Season:* March - October, *Methods:* Fly only
Rockbourne Trout Fishery
Contact: Rockbourne Trout Fishery, Rockbourne Road, Sandleheath, Fordingbridge, SP6 1QG, 01725 518603, rockbourne@talk21.com, *Water:* 6 Spring fed lakes & 3 chalkstream beats on the Sweatford water, *Species:* Rainbow / Brown Trout, Triploids, *Permits:* From the fishery, *Charges:* Day ticket 5 fish limit £38, Half day 4 fish limit £32, 3 fish half day £25, Evening ticket 2 fish limit £16. Junior/ Novice lake: 1 fish (catch and release) half day £7.50. From March 1st 2001: 5-fish/£40, 4-fish/£34, 3-fish/£27, 2-

fish/£18. Junior/Novice lake: £8/half day, adults £10, *Season:* All year, *Methods:* Fly only, max hook size 10lb, no droppers, tandem/double/treble hooks, no dogs

Stockbridge
John O ' Gaunts
Contact: Mrs E Purse, 51 Mead Road, Chandlers Ford, SO53 2FB, 01794 388130 or 02380 252268, *Water:* 2 Lakes approx 7 acres in Test Valley, *Species:* Rainbow Trout (various sizes), *Permits:* Available from Fishery Tel: 02380 252268 or 01794 388130, *Charges:* £32/day-4-fish, £18/half day-2-fish, *Season:* February 1st - November 30th inclusive, *Methods:* Fly and Nymph only

SOMERSET River Fishing

AXE
The River Axe emerges from the Mendip Hills at Wookey Hole and from here to below Wookey the river is Trout water. The river deepens as it crosses low lying land at the foot of the Mendips to the sluices at Bleadon and Brean Cross, the tidal limit. Fish species in the lower reaches include Bream, Roach, Tench, Dace and Pike.

Taunton Fly Fishing Club
Contact: M.G. Woollen, Graylings, Frog Lane, Chard, TA20 3NX, 01460 65977, *Water:* Large sections Rivers Tone and Axe plus Otterhead Lakes, *Species:* Sea Trout, Brown Trout, Grayling, *Permits:* For Otterhead Lakes: Topp Tackle, Station Rd. Taunton; Enterprise Angling, East Reach, Taunton, *Charges:* Full Club Membership: £110 - Otterhead Day tickets: £5, *Season:* 1st April - 15th October, *Methods:* Fly only.

Weston-super-Mare A.A
Contact: Weston Angling Centre, 25a Locking Road, Weston-super-Mare, BS23 3BY, 01934 631140, *Water:* River Axe, River Brue, South Drain, North Drain. Summer Lane Pond, Locking Pond, *Species:* Bream, Tench, Roach, Carp, Gudgeon, Perch, Rudd, some Dace, Chub, *Permits:* Weston Angling Centre, *Charges:* Season £20, Week £10, Day £4, *Season:* Old River Axe, Summer Lane and Locking Ponds - year round, *Methods:* No boilies, No nuts.

BARLE
Dulverton Junior Fishing
Contact: P. Veale, Lance Nicholson Fishing, Tackle and Guns, 9 High Street, Dulverton, TA22 9HB, 01398 323409, lancenich@lancenich.f9.co.uk, *Water:* 540 metres of single bank on the River Barle, *Species:* Brown Trout, *Permits:* From above, *Charges:* Free to persons under 16. EA licence required, *Season:* As current Byelaws, *Methods:* As current Byelaws
Fly Fishing in Somerset (Barle)
Contact: R.M. Gurden, 01643-831318 or 07974-539263, complete.angling@virgin.net, *Season:* March 15th - September 30th, *Species:* Wild Brown Trout + Salmon, *Water:* 11km Barle, *Permits:* Day tickets, Salmon only when members beats become available.

BRAY
Nick Hart Fly Fishing (Bray)
Contact: Nick Hart, Exford View, 1 Chapel Street, Exford, Minehead, TA24 7PY, 01643 831101 or 0797 1198559, nick@hartflyfishing.demon.co.uk, *Water:* 1 mile on Bray (Please see entry under Devon River Fishing - Torridge), *Species:* Brown Trout to 1lb, Sea Trout to 5lb, *Permits:* From Nick Hart Fly Fishing, *Charges:* £10/day Trout, £15/ day Sea Trout (night fishing allowed), *Season:* 15 March - 31 September, *Methods:* Fly only, Catch & Release of Trout preferred

SOMERSET - RIVER FISHING

BRIDGWATER AND TAUNTON CANAL

Cut in 1827 the canal provided a good commercial waterway between the two towns. The canal has been recently restored for navigation but there is only infrequent boat traffic. The canal offers excellent coarse fishing from the towpath for Roach, Bream, Tench, Rudd, Perch & Pike.

HUNTSPILL RIVER / SOUTH DRAIN / CRIPPS RIVER / NORTH DRAIN

The Huntspill River is a man made drainage channel, excavated in the 1940s and connected to the River Brue and South Drain via the Cripps River. The North Drain was dug c1770 to drain low lying moors to the north of the River Brue. The Huntspill is a notable coarse fishery and is often the venue for national and local match fishing competitions. Catches consist primarily of Bream and Roach. The North and South Drain and Cripps River contain similar species and also offer good sport for the coarse angler.

Bridgwater Angling Association
Contact: Mr M Pople, 14 Edward Street, Bridgwater, TA6 5EU, 01278 422397, *Water:* 6 miles on the Bridgwater & Taunton Canal, Fishing on the Rivers Cripps, North & South Drain, King's Sedgemoor Drain, Langacre Rhine & The Huntspill. Stillwater fishing at Combwich, Walrow, Dunwear & Screech Owl, *Species:* All types of Coarse Fish, *Permits:* Available from Tackle outlets throughout Somerset area including Somerset Angling, 74 Bath Rd, Bridgwater, Tel: 01278 431777 & Thyers Tackle, 1a Church Street, Highbridge, Tel: 01278 786934. Further information on Bridgwater A.A. available from Watts News, Edward Street, Bridgwater. Open: Mon-Sat 5am-7pm, Sunday 5am-4pm. Tel: 01278 422137, *Charges:* Adult season £23, Junior (12-17yrs) £6, Senior Citizens £6, Disabled £6, Junior (7-11yrs) £3. Prices may increase in 2001. Day tickets £3.50, enquire at outlets, *Season:* E.A. byelaws apply, *Methods:* Full rules and map with permits

Taunton Angling Association
Contact: Mr. D. Bridgwater, 3 Laurel Villas, Bishops Hull, Taunton, 01823 271835, kgregson@compuserve.com, *Water:* 7 miles on Bridgewater & Taunton Canal, 6 miles on River Tone, West Sedgemoor Drain, Walton & King Stanley Ponds, Wellington Basins, *Species:* Roach 2lb, Bream 7lb, Eels 2lb, Rudd 1.5lb, Perch 2lb, Pike 20lb, Tench 6lb, *Permits:* Topp Tackle, 63 Station Road, Taunton, (01823) 282518. Enterprise Angling (01823) 282623, *Charges:* Season £21; Day tickets £4 Senior, £2 Junior, *Season:* Closed 14th March - 16th June, Ponds open all year, *Methods:* Barbless hooks on stillwaters

BRISTOL AVON

The River Avon flows from its sources near Sherston and Tetbury to its confluence with the Severn at Avonmouth some 117 kilometres and is fed by many tributaries on its way. The headwaters of the River Avon, the Tetbury and Sherston branches join at Malmesbury. Both are important Trout streams where fishing is strictly preserved and there is little opportunity for the visiting angler to fish these waters.

Bristol, Bath & Wiltshire Amalgamated Anglers
Contact: Jeff Parker, 16 Lansdown View, Kingswood, Bristol, BS15 4AW, 0117 9672977, *Water:* Approx 80 miles Coarse Fishing on Bristol Avon & Somerset Rivers & Streams. Stillwaters at Lyneham, Calne, Malmesbury, Bath and Pawlett near Bridgwater. Trout only water on Cam Brook. Too much to list here, please contact the secretary for full details, *Species:* All coarse species, *Permits:* Full Membership available from the Secretary. Veterans over 70 years may apply in writing for free full membership sending SAE to Secretary. Full members only may fish at Tockenham Resevoir, Burton Hill lake at Malmesbury & Shackells Lake. Day Tickets for all waters except Burton Hill & Tockenham are available at Tackle Shops. Limited night fishing, *Charges:* Adults £30 (discount for early purchase), concessions £10; night fishing full members £50 per season, *Methods:* No metal cans/glass bottles in possesion; no fresh water fish as live bait, max. 2 rods per angler / full rules on application

Malmesbury to Chippenham
Coarse fisheries predominate in this section, although Trout are stocked by fishing associations in some areas. Arguably one of the best fisheries in the country, this section contains a wide range of specimen fish. Local records include: Roach 3lb 2oz, Perch 3lb 3oz, Tench 8lb 5 1/2oz, Bream 8lb 8oz, Dace 1lb 2oz, Chub 7lb 10oz, Carp 20lb 8 1/4oz and Pike 33lb 3oz. Also many Barbel to 12lb have been reported.
Chippenham to Bath
Upstream from Staverton to Chippenham the Avon continues to be an important coarse fishery, both for the pleasure angler and match fisherman. The river flows through a broad flood plain and provides a pastoral setting. In the faster flowing sections Chub, Roach, Dace and Barbel can be caught in good numbers. This year saw the local Barbel record bettered with a fish of 15lb 9 1/2oz, also a Bream of nearly 10lb was reported.
Bath to Hanham
Between Hanham and Bath much of this length retains a rural character and is an important coarse fishery used by pleasure and match anglers. The National Angling Championships have been held here. Roach, Bream and Chub are the main catches and, in some favoured swims, Dace. Very good catches of Bream are to be had with specimen fish. 'Free' fishing is available through Bath from the towpath side between Newbridge and Pulteney Weir. Carp of 20lb have been reported caught downstream of Pulteney and Keynsham Weirs.
Hanham to Avonmouth
Between Netham Dam and Hanham Weir the river is affected by spring tides. The water has a very low saline content and this length of river provides reasonable coarse fishing. Below Netham Dam the river contains mostly estuarine species but some Sea Trout and Salmon have been seen.

Avon Valley Country Park (River Avon)
Contact: Bath Rd, Keynsham, Bristol, BS31 1TP, 0117 9864929 Fax:0117 9864041, *Water:* 1.5 miles on River Avon, *Species:* Tench & Coarse fish, *Permits:* From above, *Charges:* £3.95 Adult entrance to park (includes ticket to fish), £2.95 Child, £3.45 Senior Citizen, *Season:* Park open: Easter - 1st November 10am - 6pm. Current E.A. Byelaws apply on the river

Bristol City Docks Angling Club

Contact: Bob Taylor, 27 Flaxpits Lane, Winterbourne, Bristol, BS36 1LA, 01454 773990, rtbr20912@cableinet.co.uk, *Water:* 3 miles on Bristol Avon from Chequers Weir to Netham. Feeder canal (Netham - docks), Bristol Docks system, *Species:* Skimmers, Bream, Roach, Dace, Chub, Pike, Eels, Carp, Tench and Perch, *Permits:* All Bristol tackle shops and Harbour Masters office, or from secretary above on 01454 773990 or 07909 806451, *Charges:* Season: Senior + 2 Juniors under 12 £14, Seniors £12, Concessions, Disabled, Juniors, O.A.P's £6, Day tickets in advance: Seniors £2.50 + Concessions £1, Day tickets on the bank issued by Bailiff: Seniors £5, Juniors/Conc £2, *Season:* 1st April - March 31st inclusive, River - normal close season applies; Docks and Feeder Canal open all year, *Methods:* Docks: Pole and Feeder. Pole & Waggler on Feeder Canal. All normal river tactics on the Avon. Daily update information from Tony on 0117 9517250

PSV Angling Club

Contact: Mike Shillaber, 44 Fonthill Road, Southmead, Bristol, BS10 5SP, 0117 9078492, sck2@hotmail.com, *Water:* PSV Angling Club do not have any specific waters, they control the use of fishing permits for Bristol Docks. Regular matches around Bristol area

BRISTOL FROME

The Bristol Frome rises at Dodington and offers a fair standard of coarse fishing on the lower sections. The upper section contains limited stocks of Brown Trout, Roach and Perch. This tributary of the River Avon is culverted beneath Bristol and discharges into the Floating Harbour.

Frome Angling Association (River)

Contact: Roger Lee, 51 Welshmill Lane, Frome, BA11 3AP, 01373 461433, *Water:* 12 miles River Frome - 10 acre lake, *Species:* River: Roach, Chub, Bream. Lake: Tench, Carp, Roach, Pike, *Permits:* Haines Angling, Christchurch Street West, Frome, *Charges:* £10 Senior, £5 Junior U/16, O.A.P's £1.50, Day tickets £2, *Season:* 16 June to March 14, unless changes in legislation occur, *Methods:* No restrictions

Frome Vale Angling Club

Contact: S. Coles (secretary), 2. Burrough Way, Winterbourne, Bristol, BS36 1LE, 01454-778095, *Water:* 1 mile River Frome; half acre lake (Winterbourne); 1 acre lake at Brimsham Park, Yate Bristol, *Species:* Carp, Roach, Bream, Tench, Pike, Perch, Chub - Brimsham Park lake: Carp, Roach, Rudd, Bream, Perch, *Permits:* As above or from Mr. I. Moss, 69 Long Rd, Mangutsfield, Bristol, *Charges:* Per Season: Seniors £15 - Juniors £7 - OAP's/Disabled £5. Day tickets not available, *Season:* From June 16th - March 14th. Closed season March 15th - June 15th, *Methods:* Barbless hooks on all waters. Lakes: barbless hooks, no floating baits, no keepnets, hooks no larger than size 10, no cereal ground baits

RIVER BOYD

The River Boyd rises just south of Dodington and joins the Bristol Avon at Bitton. In the middle and lower reaches coarse fish predominate. The upper reaches above Doynton contain Brown Trout.

BY BROOK

The Broadmead and Burton brooks together form the By Brook which flows through Castle Combe and is joined by several smaller streams before entering the River Avon at Bathford. Brown Trout predominate above the village of Box, mostly small in size but plentiful in number. At Box and below the fishery is mixed and Dace to 14oz and Roach of 2lb are not uncommon.

RIVER MARDEN

The River Marden is fed by springs rising from the downs above Cherhill and joins the River Avon upstream of Chippenham. Brown Trout occur naturally in the upper reaches. Downstream of Calne coarse fish predominate and weights of more than 30lb are regularly caught in matches. The Marden Barbel record currently stands at over 10lb.

SOMERSET FROME

The Somerset Frome is the main tributary of the Bristol Avon. It drains a large catchment area which is fed from the chalk around Warminster and limestone from the eastern end of the Mendips. There are numerous weirs and mills mostly disused. The tributaries above Frome provide ideal conditions for Brown Trout with fishing on the River Mells. The middle and lower reaches provide excellent coarse fishing.

Avon & Tributaries Angling Association

Contact: Mr Miller (Secretary), 5 William St, Bath, BA2 4DE, *Water:* Somerset Frome, Cam, Wellow, Midford Brooks, *Species:* Coarse, *Charges:* No day tickets, guest ticket from individual members, *Season:* In rules, *Methods:* In rules

MIDFORD BROOK

The Midford Brook runs through well wooded valleys with mostly mixed fishing on the lower reaches and Trout fishing in upper reaches. The largest Brown Trout recorded weighed 5lb 6oz.

KENNET AND AVON CANAL

There are some 58 kilometres of canal within the Bristol Avon catchment area which averages one metre in depth and thirteen metres in width. The Kennet & Avon Canal joins the River Avon at Bath with the River Kennet between Reading and Newbury. The canal was opened in 1810 to link the Severn Estuary with the Thames. The canal, now much restored, provides excellent fishing with Carp to 25lb, Tench to 5lb also Roach, Bream, Perch, Rudd, Pike and Gudgeon.

Bathampton Angling Association

Contact: Dave Crookes, 25 Otago Terrace, Larkhall, Bath, BA1 6SX, 01225 427164, *Water:* 2 Acre lake at Newton Park, 3 Lakes - Total 10 acres at Hunstrete, Lydes Farm Lake. 6 Miles Kennet & Avon canal Bath to Limpley Stoke, 3 Miles River Avon Kelston to Bath, 2 Miles River Avon at Claverton, 5 Miles Trout fishing on Box Brook (Fly Only). 1 mile of River Chew, Compton Dando, Keynsham, *Species:* Carp, Tench, Bream, Roach, Dace, Barbel, Perch, Chub.Trout, *Permits:* Tackle Shops in Bristol & Bath area, *Charges:* Adults £20, Lady & Gent combined £28, Juniors (Under 17) £5.50, O.A.Ps

£4.50, Registered disabled £5.50, *Season:* All year on lakes. River season details and maps of lakes on request, *Methods:* Barbless hooks, No keepnets as indicated in membership card at Newton Park Lakes and Huntstrete Lakes

BRUE

The River Brue is a Trout fishery from its source above Bruton to Lovington. From here to Glastonbury a number of weirs provide areas of deep water and coarse fish predominate, notably Chub and Roach, together with Bream, Dace and Pike. Similar species may be found between Glastonbury and Highbridge where the river is channelled across the Somerset Levels and connected with a number of drainage channels such as the Huntspill River and North Drain.

Glaston Manor Association
Contact: J. Ogden, 10 Dovecote Close, Farm Lane, Street, *Water:* Brue - approx. 15 miles both banks; 2/3 miles on Sheppey plus S. Drain from Catcott Bridge back to source, *Species:* Roach, Chub, Bream, Dace, Perch, Gudgeon & Pike, *Permits:* Thatchers Tackle, Wells. Street Angling, High St, Street, Somerset Tel: 01458 447830, *Charges:* Day ticket £4, Junior membership £5, Senior membership £16, OAP and disabled £8, *Season:* Current EA byelaws apply, *Methods:* No live bait permitted, Full rules on day ticket

Merry Farm
Contact: Peter Dearing, Merry Lane, Basonbridge, nr. Highbridge, TA9 3PS, 01278-783655, *Water:* 600 yds, *Species:* Pike +20lb, Carp +20lb, Perch +2.5lb, large bags of Roach & Bream, *Permits:* Collected at swim, *Charges:* £1/rod, *Season:* June-March, usual close season applies, *Methods:* No restrictions

CAM AND WELLOW BROOKS

The Cam and Wellow Brooks, rising on the north side of the Mendip Hills, flow through what was a mining area and now provide good quality Trout fishing controlled by local fishing associations.

Cameley Lakes (River Cam)
Water: See entry under stillwater Trout, Bristol. Fishing on River Cam

CHEW

The River Chew rises near Chewton Mendip and flows through the Bristol Waterworks Reservoirs at Litton and Chew Valley Lake. The river continues through Chew Magna, Stanton Drew, Publow, Woolard and Compton Dando to its confluence with the River Avon at Keynsham. A mixed fishery for most its length and is particularly good for Roach, Dace and Grayling below Pensford.

Keynsham Angling Association
Contact: Mr K. N. Jerrom, 21 St Georges Road, Keynsham, Bristol, BS31 2HU, 01179 865193, *Water:* Stretches on the Rivers Avon and Chew, *Species:* Mixed, *Charges:* Members only fishing. Membership details from secretary or Keynsham Pet & Garden Centre, tel: 01179 862366. Adult membership £12. Juniors, OAPs, disabled £4, *Season:* Current EA byelaws apply, *Methods:* Details in members handbook. On Rivers Chew and Avon there are no restrictions other than current E.A. byelaws.

Knowle Angling Association
Contact: Keith Caddick, 41 Eastwood Crescent, Brislington, Bristol, BS4 4SR, 01179 857974, derek.ezekial@adsweu.com, *Water:* 5 miles of upper and lower River Chew. Also 3 Trout lakes, *Species:* Rainbow and Brown Trout up to 8lb. Planned stocking of 4,600 for 2001 season, *Charges:* £65 annual membership, *Season:* 2 lakes all year round. 1 reservoir April to end December, *Methods:* Fly only on lakes and upper Chew

EXE & TRIBUTARIES

See detailed description under Devon River Fishing.

Broford Fishing
Contact: P. Veale, Lance Nicholson Fishing, Tackle & Guns, 9 High Street, Dulverton, TA22 9HB, 01398 323409, lancenich@lancenich.f9.co.uk, *Water:* Approx 5 miles bank fishing on Little Exe, *Species:* Wild Brown Trout with occasional Salmon, *Permits:* As above, *Charges:* £10 per day, *Season:* 15th March - 30th September, *Methods:* Fly Only

Carnarvon Arms Hotel
Contact: Dulverton, TA22 9AE, 01398 323302, carnarvon.arms@virgin.net, *Water:* Fishing on Rivers Exe & Barle, *Species:* Salmon & Wild Brown Trout, *Charges:* Please Telephone for details

Fly Fishing in Somerset (Exe)
Contact: R.M. Gurden, 01643-831318 or 07974-539263, complete.angling@virgin.net, *Season:* March 15th - September 30th, *Species:* Wild Brown Trout, Salmon early and late season, *Water:* Little Exe, 3/4 mile double bank, Catherines Brook 3/4 mile double bank, *Permits:* Day + season tickets available

Nick Hart Fly Fishing (Exe)
Contact: Nick Hart, Exford View, 1 Chapel Street, Exford, Minehead, TA24 7PY, 01643 831101 or 0797 1198559, nick@hartflyfishing.demon.co.uk, *Water:* 1.5 miles of Upper Exe, 3 miles of Middle Exe, *Species:* Up.Exe: Trout to 1lb, Mid.Exe: Salmon to double figures, *Permits:* From Nick Hart Fly Fishing, *Charges:* Trout: £15/day, Salmon: £35/day, *Season:* 15 March - 31 September, *Methods:* Up.Exe: Fly only, Barbless hooks, Catch & Release - Mid.Exe: Spin or.Fly Fish year round

ISLE

The River Isle rises near Wadeford and soon after its source is joined by a tributary from Chard Lake. Trout are found as far as Ilminster but below the town coarse fish predominate. The profile of the river is fairly natural though a number of shallow weirs provide increased depth in places. Species caught in the lower stretches include Chub, Dace and Roach.

Chard & District Angling Club
Contact: Mr Braunton, Planet Video & Angling, 19a High Street, Chard, TA20 1QF, 01460 64000, *Water:* Approx 3 miles on the River Isle. Also Chard Reservoir and Perry Street Pond, see entry under coarse fishery, *Species:* Dace, Roach, Chub, Perch, Bream, Gudgeon, *Permits:* Planet Video & Angling, 19a High Street, Chard, Somerset TA20 1QF. Tel: 01460 64000, *Charges:* Membership £12 per year, concessions juniors, OAP's and ladies; includes coarse stillwater Perry Street Pond. No day tickets Perry Street or river, *Season:* Closed season 14th March to 16th June

Ilminster & District A.A

Contact: P. Lonton, Marshalsea, Cottage Corner, Ilton, Ilminster, 01460 52519, *Water:* Approx 6 miles on the River Isle, *Species:* Roach, Chub, Perch, Bream, Dace, *Permits:* Day tickets from Ilminster Warehouse. Membership details from the secretary. Annual membership tickets from Ilminster Warehouse, Yeovil Angling Centre, The Tackle Shack, Chard Angling, Enterprise Angling, Taunton, *Charges:* £12 annual membership. Day tickets £3. Junior £2, *Season:* Current EA byelaws apply, *Methods:* Club rules apply.

Newton Abbot Fishing Association (River)

Contact: David Horder (secretary), 'Mistlemead', Woodlands, Higher Sandygate, TQ12 3QN, 01626 364173, *Water:* 1 mile stretch of the River Isle at Hambridge. See entry under Devon, Stillwater Coarse, Newton Abbot, *Season:* Rivers are controlled by the national close season for coarse fish

KENN AND BLIND YEO

The New Blind Yeo is an artificial drainage channel which also carries some of the diverted water of the River Kenn. Both waters contain good Roach with Bream, Rudd, Carp, Perch, Tench and Pike.

Clevedon & District F.A.C

Contact: Mr Newton, 64 Clevedon Rd, Tickenham, Clevedon, BS21 6RD, 01275-856107, *Water:* 6 miles - Blind Yeo / River Kenn, *Species:* Roach, Bream, Rudd, Eels, Perch, Pike, Tench, *Permits:* NSAA Permit at all local tackle shops, *Charges:* Season - Seniors: £16, Juniors/OAP/Disabled: £7; Weekly - £7; Daily - £2.50, *Season:* June 16th - March 14th inc, *Methods:* Waggler/Stick, Pole, Wedger; No live baits, no coarse fish to be used as dead bait

THE KINGS SEDGEMOOR DRAIN

The Kings Sedgemoor Drain is an artificial drainage channel dug c1790. As well as draining a large area of moor it also carries the diverted water of the River Cary and excess flood flows from the River Parrett. The KSD is a very well known coarse fishery and is used for both local and national match fishing competitions. Fish species present include Roach, Bream, Tench, Perch and Pike.

PARRETT

The River Parrett rises in West Dorset and there is some Trout fishing as far as Creedy Bridge upstream of the A303. Below this point a number of weirs and hatches result in deeper water and slower flows. The resulting coarse fishery contains a wide variety of species including Roach, Bream, Rudd, Chub, Dace, Carp, Crucian Carp and Pike. Similar species are found in the lowest freshwater section at Langport where the Rivers Isle and Yeo join the Parrett to form a wide deep river which becomes tidal below Oath Sluice.

Langport & District Angling Association

Contact: Den Barlow, Florissant, Northfield, Somerton, TA11 6SJ, 01458 272119, den@barlow65.fsnet.co.uk, *Water:* 5 miles on the River Parrett. Coombe Lake - 2.75 acres, no closed season, *Species:* All common coarse species except Barbel, *Permits:* Fosters Newsagency, Bow Street, Langport, *Charges:* Annual £11, junior £5, disabled/OAP £5.50. Weekly £5. Senior day £3, junior day £1.50, *Season:* Closed season on river only. Membership from 16th June to 15th June inc. Night fishing permitted on river only from Langport A.A. controlled banks, *Methods:* Lake: Barbless hooks, No boilies, No Carp in keepnets

Stoke Sub Hamdon & District A.A

Contact: Mr Derek Goad (Secretary), 2 Windsor Lane, Stoke-sub-Hamdon, (H.Q. Stoke Working Mens Club), *Water:* Upper Stretches River Parrett approx 10km. Also Bearley Lake, Long Load Drain (Shared Water), *Species:* Carp, Tench, Roach, Rudd, Bream, Perch, Dace, Chub, Pike, Eel, Gudgeon, Ruffe. Trout Fishing also available, *Permits:* Day and season permits from Stax Tackle, Montacute and Yeovil Angling Centre, Yeovil. Season tickets also available from secretary, *Charges:* Day ticket £4 (Bearley Lake). Season charges £10 includes cost of Bearley Lake Fishing. Juniors/OAPs £5 includes lake fishing. Juniors under 11 must be accompanied by an adult, *Season:* Trout 1st April - 31st October. Lake all year. Coarse 16th June - 14th March, *Methods:* Trout: No maggot. Lake: No boilies or nut baits, no night fishing, lake rules apply. River Coarse: No restrictions

Wessex Federation of Angling Clubs

Contact: Tom Grainger, Secretary, 14 The Ridge, Shirehampton, Bristol, BS11 0DZ, 0117 9829417, kgregson@compuserve.com, *Water:* 2 miles River Parrett, 1/2 mile River Isle, *Species:* Roach, Bream, Rudd, Chub, Carp, Tench, Perch, Gudgeon, Dace, Pike, *Permits:* Martin Brook, The Tackle Box, 1 Old Market Square, North Street, Langport, TA10 9RD, *Charges:* £2.50/day Senior, £1.00 Junior-Disabled-O.A.P's, *Season:* 16th June - 14th March, *Methods:* Live-baiting not allowed

TONE

The River Tone rises on the edge of Exmoor National Park and not far from its source it feeds into and out of Clatworthy reservoir. From here to Taunton there are some twenty miles of fast flowing Trout river, though Grayling, Dace and Roach appear near Taunton where weirs provide increased depth. Through the town and just below, Chub, Dace and Roach predominate but at Bathpool the river becomes wider, deeper and slower. Roach, Bream, Carp, Tench and Pike are the typical species in this stretch which continues to the tidal limit at New Bridge.

Taunton Angling Association (Tone)

Contact: kgregson@compuserve.com, *Water:* 6 miles on River Tone (See entry under Taunton and Bridgwater Canal), *Species:* Roach 2lb, Pike 25lb, Dace 0.5lb, Bream 10lb, Tench 3lb, Perch 3lb, Carp 25lb, *Permits:* Topp Tackle, 63 Station Road, Taunton, (01823) 282518. Enterprise Angling (01823) 282623, *Charges:* £4 day

Wellington Angling Association

Contact: M Cave, 60 Sylvan Road, Wellington, TA1 8EH, 01823 661671, *Water:* Approx 1.5 mile on River Tone, *Species:* Brown Trout, *Permits:* Membership only, *Charges:* Joining fee £10, annual membership £9, *Season:* On application, *Methods:* No spinning.

WEST SEDGEMOOR DRAIN

This artificial channel was excavated in the 1940s on the lines of existing watercourses. Coarse fish species present include Bream, Roach, Tench and Carp.

Taunton Angling Association (W. Sedgemoor Drain)
Contact: Mr. D. Bridgwater, 3 Laurel Villas, Bishops Hull, Taunton, 01823 271835, kgregson@compuserve.com, *Water:* 3 miles of West Sedgemoor Drain, easy access for disabled anglers, *Species:* Bream 5lb, Roach 1.75lb, Eels 1.5lb, Tench 7lb, Pike 16lb, Perch 2lb, Rudd 1lb, Carp 25lb, *Permits:* Topp Tackle, 63 Station Road, Taunton, (01823) 282518. Enterprise Angling (01823) 282623, *Charges:* £4 day tickets from Topp Tackle Taunton and Enterprise Angling; Club membership details from secretary

YEO
The River Yeo rises near Sherborne and between here and Yeovil the river is a coarse fishery, though tributaries such as the River Wriggle have Brown Trout. Below Yeovil a number of weirs produce areas of deep water and the resulting fishery contains good Dace together with Roach, Chub, Bream and Pike.

Ilchester & District
Contact: Mr M Barnes, 44 Marsh Lane, Yeovil, *Water:* River Yeo above and below Ilchester, *Species:* Chub, Roach, Dace, Bream, Gudgeon, Tench and Carp, *Permits:* Tackle shops in Yeovil. Yeovil Angling Centre. Stax Tackle, Montacute. Ilchester Post Office. Newsagents, Ilchester. Club Secretary, *Charges:* Season ticket £10. OAP/junior £5. Weekly ticket £3, *Season:* Open 16th June to 15th March, *Methods:* Current EA byelaws apply. Club rules on ticket and fishery map

N. Somerset Association of Anglers
Contact: Mr Newton, 64 Clevedon Rd, Tickenham, Clevedon, BS21 6RD, 01275 856107, *Water:* Blind Yeo, Kenn, Congresbury Yeo, Brue, Apex Lake, Newtown Ponds & Walrow Ponds, Tickenham Boundry Rhyne, North Drain, *Species:* Roach, Bream, Eels, Perch, Rudd, Carp, Pike, Tench, *Permits:* NSAA Permits available at all local Tackle Shops, *Charges:* Season: Seniors £16. Juniors/OAP/ Disabled £7. Weekly: £7. Day £2.50, *Season:* June 16th - March 14th inclusive. Apex Lake & Newton Ponds: June 1st - 28th February incl, *Methods:* Apex Lake + Newton Ponds: Barbless hooks, No live or dead baits, no floating baits, min. breaking strain line 2.5lb

Yeovil & Sherborne Angling Association
Contact: Alex Murray, 134 Westfield Grove, Yeovil, BA21 3DN, 01935-411238, *Water:* 4 miles rivers + discounted tickets Viaduct Fishery, *Species:* Roach, Bream, Carp, *Permits:* Membership details from above + local tackle shops, *Charges:* No day tickets. Club card £10, includes half price fishing at Viaduct

SOMERSET Stillwater Coarse

Bath
Bathampton Angling Association (Coarse Lakes)
Water: See entry under Avon. Various lakes and river fishing. 2 Acre lake at Newton Park, 3 Lakes - Total 10 acres at Hunstrete, Lydes Farm Lake, *Season:* Lydes Farm lake closed until May 2002
Frome Angling Association (Coarse Lake)
Water: 10 acre lake. See entry under Frome

Bridgwater
Avalon Fisheries
Contact: Allan Tedder (Ted), 7 Coronation Road, Bridgwater, TA6 7DS, 01278 456429, *Water:* 6 acre match Coarse + 3 acre specimen lakes, *Species:* Carp to mid 20's, Tench 7.5lb, Bream 9lb 2oz, Perch 3lb, Roach, Rudd, *Permits:* Site office and on the bank. Mobile Phone 0966 363413, *Charges:* £4 Adult, £2.50 Junior / O.A.P. / Disabled, *Season:* No closed season - Open dawn to dusk, *Methods:* Barbless on specimen lake, No floating or boilie baits on coarse lake, all nuts banned on both lakes, boilies/night fishing allowed on Carp lake only
Bridgwater Angling Association (Coarse Lakes)
Water: See entry under Taunton and Bridgwater Canal. Various stillwaters. Stillwater fishing at Combwich, Walrow, Dunwear & Screech Owl

Bridgwater Sports & Social Club
Contact: Duncan & Sandra Smith, Bath Road, Bridgwater, TA6 4PA, 01278-446215, *Water:* 3 large ponds, *Species:* Carp to 26lb, Crucian to 3lb, Bream & Roach to 1.5lb, Perch to 4lb, Tench to 5lb, *Charges:* £25/person - private members fishing, *Season:* Normal open season, *Methods:* No night fishing
Browns Pond
Contact: Phil Dodds, Off Taunton Rd (A38), Bridgwater, 01278-444145, *Water:* 2.5 acres, *Species:* Carp to 22lb, Tench to 5lb, Bream to 6lb, Perch to 2lb & Roach, *Charges:* On site. £2 per day, *Season:* Closed May, open June 1st - April 30th; dawn to dusk, *Methods:* No night fishing, barbless hooks only, no live bait, no Carp sacks
Burton Springs Fishery (Coarse Lake)
Contact: Tony Evans, Lawson Farm, Burton, Nr Stogursey - Bridgwater, TA5 1QB, 01278-732135, *Water:* Aprox 2 acre lake, *Species:* Mirror, Common, Leather Carp, Ghost Carp to 20lb, Tench to 5 lb, *Permits:* Self Service at fishing lodge, *Charges:* £5 per day, 2 rods, *Season:* Open all year 8am-9pm or dusk, *Methods:* Barbless hooks only, no nuts, only 'Carp mesh' keepnets allowed for smaller Carp, large Carp to be released immediately
Durleigh Reservoir
Contact: Wessex Water, 0845 600 4 600, *Water:* 80 acre reservoir, *Species:* Carp, Roach, Bream, Perch, Tench and Pike, *Permits:* Contact Ranger Paul Martin on 01278 424786, *Charges:* Day Ticket £5, Day Concession £3.50, Evening Ticket £3.50, Book of Tickets £40 for 10, *Season:* Open all year except Christmas day, Boxing day & New Years day
Summerhayes Fishery
Contact: Somerset Bridge, Bridgwater, 01278-781565/7661, *Water:* Several lakes - totalling 6 acres, *Species:* Carp, Bream, Tench, Roach, Rudd, Perch, Ghost Carp, *Permits:* Thyers of Highbridge (01278-786934). Somerset Angling Bridgwater (01278-431777), *Charges:* On bank £4 day, £3 concessions; disabled access, *Season:* Open all year dawn to dusk, *Methods:* Barbless hooks, no peanuts

Taunton Road Ponds

Contact: Phil Dodds, Off Taunton Rd (A38), Bridgwater, 01278-444145, *Water:* 3.5 acres, *Species:* Large Carp to 28lb, Tench to 6lb, Bream to13lb 6oz, Perch to 3lb, Rudd to 2lb, skimmer Bream to 12oz & Roach to 8oz, *Charges:* On site, £2 per day, *Season:* Closed May, open June 1st - April 30th; dawn to dusk, *Methods:* No night fishing, barbless hooks only, no live bait, no large Carp in keepnets, no Carp sacks

The Sedges

Contact: Pat & John, River Lane, Dunwear, Bridgwater, TA7 0AA, 01278-445221, *Water:* 2 lakes totalling 7 acres, *Species:* Tench, Rudd, Roach, Bream, Chub, Carp to 32lb, *Charges:* On bank: £4 adult day, children accompanied by adult £2.50, *Season:* Open all year dawn to dusk, *Methods:* No keepnets in summer months, no Carp sacks, barbless hooks, unhooking mats

Bristol

Alcove Angling Club

Contact: Mr K.Davis (Membership Secretary), 6 Ashdene Ave, Upper Eastville, Bristol, BS5 6QH, 01179 025737, alcoveacbristol@yahoo.co.uk, *Water:* 4 lakes in Bristol & South Glos, *Species:* Carp, Bream, Roach, Tench, Rudd, Pike, Perch, *Permits:* As above, *Charges:* Adult £35, OAP/Disabled £20, *Season:* No close season, *Methods:* As specified in membership card, Night fishing at Alcove Lido only

Bagwood Lake

Contact: Trench Lane, Woodlands, Patchway, Bristol, 01454 619319, *Water:* One coarse lake, *Species:* Carp, *Permits:* On site, pay in shop, *Charges:* £5 per day, £5 per night, *Season:* Open all year - night fishing by arrangement

Bitterwell Lake

Contact: Mrs M Reid, The Chalet, Bitterwell Lake, Ram Hill,, Coalpit Heath, Bristol, BS36 2UF, 01454 778960, *Water:* 2.5 Acres, *Species:* Common, Mirror, Crucian Carp, Roach, Bream, Rudd, Perch, *Charges:* £3.00./rod - £1.50 O.A.P's, Reg. disabled and arrivals after 4 pm, *Season:* Closed for spawning 4 - 6 weeks May - June, *Methods:* Barbless hooks size 8 max, No bolt rigs, No boilies, No nuts, hemp or groundbait

Bristol, Bath & Wilts Amalgamated Anglers (Lakes)

Contact: Jeff Parker, 16 Lansdown View, Kingswood, Bristol, BS15 4AW, 0117 9672977, *Water:* See entry under Avon - Various stillwaters, too much to list here, please contact the secretary for full details; Stillwaters at Lyneham, Calne, Malmesbury, Bath and Pawlett near Bridgwater, *Species:* All coarse species, *Permits:* Full membership 2000-2001 *Season:* Adult £30, concessions (ladies juniors OAPs) £10. Day permits for rivers and some lakes. Veterans over 70 apply to the secretary, include £2 with s.a.e. Discount if puchased prior to 31st March 2001. Limited to 100 permits. Limited night fishing only available for full members, permits £50 per season, apply to the secretary, *Methods:* Max. 2 rods; no metal cans or glass allowed on banks; no freshwater fish to be used as livebait. Full rules and maps available

Frome Vale Angling Club (Coarse Pond)

Water: 1 acre lake at Brimsham Park, Yate Bristol. See entry under Bristol Frome

Ham Green Fisheries

Contact: Mr Hunt, Ham Green, Chapel Lane, Pill, 01275-849885, *Water:* 2 lakes, 1 acre each, match facilities 25 peg, *Species:* Carp to 32lb, Roach, Rudd, Perch, Pike, Bream, Skimmers, Golden Tench, *Permits:* Mr Hunt, 21 Station Rd, Portishead, Bristol; also on lake side by arrangement, *Charges:* Day £4, half day £2.50, *Season:* No closed season, open dawn-dusk, night fishing by arrangement, *Methods:* No live bait, barbless hooks preferred, no keepnets for fish over 1lb, Carp sacks allowed

Paulton Lakes

Contact: Trevor Francis, Paulton, Bristol, BS39 7SY, 01761 413081, *Water:* 2 lakes totalling 2.5 acres, *Species:* Carp, Tench, Roach, Grass Carp, Rudd, Chub, *Permits:* Only from Paulton Builders Merchants, Paulton and A.M. Hobbs, Midsomer Norton. lel (01761) 413961, *Charges:* £5 per day ticket, *Season:* Open all year, Dawn to dusk, *Methods:* Barbless hooks, No ground baiting, Unhooking mats must be used.

Tan House Farm Lake

Contact: Mr & Mrs James, Tan House Farm, Yate, Bristol, BS37 7QL, 01454 228280, *Water:* Quarter mile lake, *Species:* Roach, Perch, Carp, Bream, Tench, Rudd, *Permits:* Day tickets from Farm House, *Charges:* Adult £3 per rod or £5 for 2 rods, Children & O.A.Ps £2, *Season:* closed April 17th - May 28th, *Methods:* No Ground bait, Dog & cat food, Boilies, Barbless hooks only

Chard

Chard & District Angling Club (Coarse Lakes)

Contact: Mr Braunton, Planet Video & Angling, 19a High Street, Chard, TA20 1QF, 01460 64000, *Water:* Perry Street Pond - 1.5 acres. Chard Reservoir - 48 acres. Also 3 miles on Isle see entry under associations, *Species:* Roach, Bream, Carp, Tench, Perch, Eels, Rudd, *Permits:* Planet Video & Angling, 19a High Street, Chard, Somerset TA20 1QF. Tel: 01460 64000.. Perry Street Ponds - members only, details from secretary, *Charges:* Chard reservoir £5 per day (£3 club members). Perry Street ponds members only, membership £12, *Season:* Open all year, *Methods:* Full list of rules from fishery notice board and membership book

Cheddar

Blakeway Fisheries

Contact: Mark Durston-Sweet, Blakeway, Nr Wedmore, BS28 4UB, 01934 713833, *Water:* 2.5 acres, *Species:* Carp, Bream, Tench, Roach & Rudd, *Permits:* Broadway House Caravan Park and at the Fishery, *Charges:* £4 per day. Junior/OAP £2.50, *Season:* All year, *Methods:* No keepnets, barbless hooks only.

Cheddar Angling Club

THE DIRECTORY

SOMERSET - STILLWATER COARSE

Cheddar Angling Club
Contact: Cheddar Angling Club, P.O. Box 1183, Cheddar, BS27 3LT, 01934 744595, *Water:* 200 acre Cheddar reservoir, *Species:* Pike, Perch, Tench, Roach, Eels, *Permits:* Permits are NOT available at the reservoir. Only from: Broadway House Caravan Park, Axbridge Road, Cheddar, Somerset. Bristol Angling Centre, 12-16 Doncaster Road, Southmead, Bristol. Thatchers Pet and Tackle, 18 Queen St, Wells. Veals Fishing Tackle, 61 Old Market St, Bristol. Thyers Fishing Tackle, Church St, Highbridge, *Charges:* Seniors season permit £30, Juniors season permit £15, Seniors day permit £5, Juniors day permit £3, *Season:* 16th June 1999 to 14th March 2000 inclusive, *Methods:* No live baiting, Moderate ground baiting, No dead baiting until 1st July. No night fishing, dawn to dusk only. Unhooking mats recommended. Rod limits: seniors maximum 2 rods, juniors one rod only

Stone Yard Fisheries
Contact: Thatchers Angling, 18 Queen St, Wells, BA5 2DP, 01749 673513, *Water:* Small Ponds (15 Anglers) at Litton near Chewton Mendip, *Species:* Carp to approx 18lb, small Tench, *Permits:* Thatchers Angling 01749 673513. 5 tickets per day available from A.M. Hobbs Angling 01761 413961, *Charges:* Day £5 Senior, £2.50 Junior, *Season:* March 1st - October 31st, *Methods:* Barbless hooks only. No Boilies

Clevedon
N. Somerset Association of Anglers (Coarse Lakes)
Contact: 01275 856107, *Water:* See entry under Yeo. Apex Lake, Newtown Ponds and Walrow Ponds, *Species:* Roach, Rudd, Carp, Tench, Bream, Eels, Perch, *Permits:* Local tackle shops, purchased in advance of fishing, *Charges:* £2.50/day, £7/week, £16/season, junior-OAP-disabled £7, *Season:* Apex + Newton Lakes 1 June - 28 Feb. (incl.), Walrow Pond 16 June - 14 March (incl.), *Methods:* Apex & Newton Lakes: Barbless hooks, min. 2.5lb BS line, no live or dead bait, no floating bait

Congresbury
Silver Springs Coarse Fishery
Contact: Liz Patch, Silver Street Lane, Congresbury, BS49 5EY, 01934 877073, *Water:* 4.5 acres, *Species:* Carp to 17lb, Rudd, Roach, Tench, *Permits:* On Site, *Charges:* £5 / £3.50 conc, *Season:* All year dawn till half hour before dusk, *Methods:* Barbless hooks

Corfe
Taunton Angling Association (Coarse Lake)
Contact: Mr. D. Bridgwater, 3 Laurel Villas, Bishops Hull, Taunton, 01823 271835, kgregson@compuserve.com, *Water:* Wych lodge Lake, 5 acre large Carp lake, *Species:* Large Carp up to 25lb, Roach, Rudd, *Permits:* Only from Topp Tackle, Taunton (restricted to 10 pegs), *Season:* Open all year, *Methods:* Barbless hooks, no Carp in keepnets

Crewkerne
Highlands Dairy Lake
Contact: J.Wyatt, Highlands Dairy Farm, Hewish, Nr Crewkerne, 01460 74180, *Water:* 1 acre lake, *Species:* Carp, Tench, Rudd, Roach, Perch, *Permits:* At house, *Charges:* £4 per day including night fishing. £3 day ticket, *Season:* Open all year, *Methods:* No keepnets for Carp. Barbless hooks only.

Water Meadow Fishery
Contact: Mr. Pike, Pitt Farm, North Perrott, Crewkerne, TA18 7SX, 01460 72856, *Water:* 2 coarse lakes totalling approx 1.75 acres, *Species:* 16 different varieties of coarse fish, *Charges:* On site - £4 day - £2 half day/evening, *Season:* Open all year - dawn to dusk, *Methods:* No boilies or keepnets, barbless hooks only, ground baiting in moderation.

Frome
Edneys Fisheries
Contact: Richard Candy, Edneys Farm, Mells, Frome, BA11 3RE, 01373 812294, *Water:* 2 lakes, *Species:* Carp, Tench, Roach, Rudd, Perch, Common, Mirror, Linear, Leather and Ghost Carp, *Charges:* Adults £5, Under 14 yrs £3. Evening tickets only available weekdays after 5pm at £3

Frome Angling Association (Lake)
10 acre lake. See entry under Bristol Frome.

Mells Pit Pond
Contact: Mr M.Coles, Lyndhurst, Station Road, Mells, Nr Frome, BA11 3RJ, 01373 812094, *Water:* 1 acre lake, *Species:* Various Carp, Rudd, Roach, Tench, Perch, *Permits:* Tickets issued at bankside, *Charges:* £4/day, Season tickets £50, *Season:* Open all year, *Methods:* Barbless hooks. No keepnets

Parrots Paddock Farm (Coarse)
Contact: Mr. Baker, Wanstrow Rd, Nunnery Catch, 01373 836505, *Water:* 90yd x 75 yd pond, *Species:* Rainbow Trout & Coarse fish, *Permits:* Please phone first, *Season:* Open all year, dawn to dusk, *Methods:* No night fishing, keepnets only for small fish, barbless hooks only, ground bait in moderation.

Witham Friary Lakes
Contact: Mr. Miles, Witham Hall Farm, Witham Friary, Nr Frome, BA11 5HB, 01373 836239, *Water:* Two lakes totalling approx. 2 acres, *Species:* Carp, Roach, Tench, Perch, Gudgeon, *Permits:* On site, *Charges:* £4 a day - £6 night ticket (dusk - 8 am), *Season:* All year, *Methods:* Barbless hooks only.

Highbridge
Emerald Pool Fishery
Contact: Mr Alan Wilkinson, Emerald Pool Fishery, Puriton Road, West Huntspill, Highbridge, TA9 3NL, 01278 794707, *Water:* 1.5 acre lake, *Species:* Bream, Golden Orfe, Roach, Rudd, Tench, Perch, Carp to low-mid 20's, Sturgeon to 4 feet long, Barbel 5lb, *Permits:* Enviroment Agency rod licence required on this water, *Season:* All year, *Methods:* Barbless hooks only, No Carp sacks, No peanuts or ground bait, All Sturgeon to be released immediately, No fish over 3lb to be retained at all

Keynsham
Avon Valley Country Park (Coarse Pond)
Contact: Bath Rd, Keynsham, Bristol, BS31 1TP, 0117 9864929 Fax:0117 9864041, *Water:* Small Coarse pond, *Species:* Carp to 12lb, *Permits:* From above, *Charges:* £3.95 Adult entrance to park (includes ticket to fish), £2.95 Child, £3.45 Senior Citizen, *Season:* Park open: Easter - 1st November 10am-6pm, *Methods:* Barbless hooks only, no keepnets

Keynsham Angling Association (Coarse Lake)
Contact: Mr K. N. Jerrom, 21 St Georges Road, Keynsham, Bristol, BS31 2HU, 01179 865193, *Water:* Century Ponds 0.25 acres. See also entry under River Chew, *Species:* Mixed Fishery, *Charges:* Day ticket for club members £2.50, *Season:* Open all year dawn to dusk. Closed alternate Sunday mornings until 1pm, *Methods:* Barbless hooks and no Boilies

Kingston Seymour

Bullock Farm Fishing Lakes
Contact: Phillip Simmons, Bullock Farm, Kingston Seymour, BS21 6XA, 01934 835020, *Water:* 4 Lakes totalling 4.75 acres, including specialist Carp lake, *Species:* Carp - Common, Mirror, Ghost, Crucian, Grass, Purple and Koi. Tench, Roach, Rudd, Chub, Bream, Skimmer Bream, Golden Orfe, Golden Tench, *Permits:* Only at lakeside, *Charges:* £5.00 day ticket, £3.00 O.A.P's / Under 14s / Disabled. Season tickets & Match rates available, *Season:* Open all year round Dawn - Dusk, *Methods:* No boilies, Barbless hooks, No keepnets on Carp lake, No dogs, u14s to be accompanied by an adult, no loose-fed pellets, Common sense!

Plantations Lake
Contact: Mr or Mrs W.Travis, Middle Lane Farm, Middle Lane, Kingston Seymour, Clevedon, BS21 6XW, 01934 832325, *Water:* 0.75 acre Carp lake, 2.5 acre Coarse lake. New Silver fish lake open Spring 2001, 1.75 acre, *Species:* 12 Species of coarse fish incl. Barbel, Crucian Carp. 3 Species of Carp in Carp lake, *Charges:* £5.50 Adult (£1 extra rod), £4.00 Juniors/O.A.P's/ Disabled. Half days (from 2pm) available: adult £3.50, juniors/OAPs £2. Please enquire for membership details. New price as from April 1st, *Season:* All year, *Methods:* No boilies, Barbless hooks

Langport

Langport & Dist. Angling Association (Coarse Lake)
Water: Coombe Lake - 2.75 acres. See entry under Parrett, *Species:* Carp to 21lb, Tench 6.5lb, Roach 1.5lb, Perch 2lb plus, Bream 7lb, Chub 4lb, *Permits:* See entry under Parrett, *Charges:* See entry under Parrett, *Season:* No closed season. No night fishing, *Methods:* Barbless hooks, no boilies, no Carp in keepnets.

Thorney Lakes
Contact: Richard or Ann England, Thorney Farm, Muchelney, Langport, TA10 0DW, 01458 250811, thorneylakes@langport.totalserve.co.uk, *Water:* Two 2 Acre lakes, *Species:* A selection of coarse fish including large Carp, *Permits:* On the bank, *Charges:* £5/day, £3/half day after 4 p.m, £3 for O.A.Ps + Children under 16, *Season:* 16th March - 31st January, *Methods:* Barbless hooks, No boilies, nuts or pulses, All nets to be dipped on site, No night fishing

Shepton Mallet

Bridge Farm Fishery
Contact: John Thorners, Bridge Farm Shop, Pylle, Shepton Mallet, BA4 6TA, 01749 830138, *Water:* 0.25 mile long x 30m wide lake, approx 3 acres, *Species:* Common Carp to 15lb, Roach, Rudd and other coarse fish, *Permits:* From farm shop on arrival, *Charges:* Adults £5, Juniors u.16 £2.50, *Season:* Open all year, dawn to dusk, *Methods:* Barbless hooks only, no keepnets, for Carp, no night fishing

Somerton

Miners Ponds
Contact: Lower Vobster, Coleford, Somerton, *Water:* 2 ponds totalling 1.5 acres approx, *Species:* Carp 28.25lb, Roach, Tench, Perch and Bream, *Permits:* AM Hobbs Angling, Midsomer Norton, Bath, Tel: 01761 413961; Haines Angling, 47 Vallis Way Frome, Tel: 01373 466406, *Charges:* Day tickets on bank, £5 per day, *Season:* Open June 16th - beginning March, dawn to dusk, *Methods:* No keepnets, no boilies, barbless hooks

Viaduct Fishery
Contact: Mr Steve Long, Viaduct Fishery, Cary Valley, Somerton, TA11 6LJ, 01458 274022, *Water:* Six Coarse Lakes including one specimen lake, *Species:* Mirror Carp 27lb, Crucian Carp, Common Carp 23lb, Perch 5lb, Roach 1.5lb, Bream 6lb, Tench 8lb and Golden Tench, Rudd, Ruffe, *Permits:* Fishery Shop or Pre-Payment Office; EA Rod licences available, *Charges:* Day ticket £5, Under 16 £4, Summer Evening ticket £3, Winter Half day ticket £3. Specimen lake £13/day; Match bookings taken, *Season:* All year, *Methods:* All nets to be dipped, no nuts or boilies, barbless hooks size 10 max, no fixed rigs, no braid, fishing from pegs only. Specimen lake has specific rules available from fishery office

Street

Godney Moor Ponds
Contact: Nick Hughes, Street Angling Centre, 160 High Street, Street, BA16 0NH, 01458 447830, *Water:* Approx 4 acres, *Species:* Coarse fish including Carp, *Permits:* Only from Street Angling Centre, *Charges:* £4 per day (All genders), *Methods:* No nuts, 2 rods maximum.

Taunton

Frog Lane Carp Fishery
Contact: Frog Lane, Durston, Taunton, 07771-993135, *Water:* 4.5 acre lake, *Species:* Carp to 31lb, Tench, Bream and Rudd, *Permits:* On site, *Charges:* Day: £3.50, 24hrs: £5, *Season:* Open all year, night fishing allowed, *Methods:* Barbless hooks only, no tiger nuts, no keepnets

Ilminster & District A.A. (Coarse Lake)
Contact: P. Lonton, Marshalsea, Cottage Corner, Ilton, Ilminster, 01460 52519, *Water:* Thurlebeare - 1.5 acres, *Species:* Carp 18lb, Bream 6lb, Roach 1.5lb, Perch 2.5lb, Tench 6lb - mixed fishery, *Permits:* Enterprise Angling, Taunton and Ilminster Warehouse. Membership details from the secretary. Annual membership tickets from Ilminster Warehouse, Yeovil Angling Centre, The Tackle Shack, Chard Angling, Enterprise Angling, Taunton, *Charges:* £12 annual membership. Day tickets £3. Junior £2, *Season:* Open all year

SOMERSET - STILLWATER COARSE / STILLWATER TROUT

Taunton Angling Association (Coarse Lakes)

Contact: Mr. D. Bridgwater, 3 Laurel Villas, Bishops Hull, Taunton, 01823 271835, kgregson@compuserve.com, *Water:* King Stanley Pond and Maunsell Lake; Wellington Basins, 2 lakes of mixed coarse fish; Walton Ponds (Street) mixed fishery, *Species:* Bream 6lb, Carp 24lb, Roach 2lb, Tench 2lb, Rudd 3lb, *Permits:* Topp Tackle Taunton (01823 282518), Enterprise Angling (01823 282623); Club membership details from the secretary, *Charges:* £4/day, *Season:* Open all year, *Methods:* Barbless hooks only

Wedmore

Lands End Farm Fishery

Contact: Martin Duckett, Heath House, Wedmore, BS28 4UQ, 07977 545882, *Water:* Match Lake and specimen Lake, total 3 acres, *Species:* Carp to 22lb (Common, Mirror, Ghost, Crucian) Grass Carp to 17lb, Bream to 8lb, Tench and Roach 2lb, Rudd, Chub, Ide, Perch, Barbel, Golden Orfe to 4lb, *Permits:* From offfice on site, *Charges:* £5/day, £3 after 4pm, £4 juniors, £4 conc, *Season:* Open all year. 7am to dusk in the summer, *Methods:* Barbless hooks only, No keepnets, No dog biscuits, boilies or nuts

Wellington

Langford Lakes

Contact: Mr. Hendy, Middle Hill Farm, Langford Budville, Wellington, 01823 400476, *Water:* 4 lakes totalling 3.5 acres, *Species:* Carp, Roach, Perch, Tench, Bream, *Charges:* Prices on application, *Season:* Open all year dawn to dusk, *Methods:* Natural baits only, keepnets permitted only on 2 lakes, barbless hooks, full list at fishery.

Wells

Emborough Ponds

Contact: Thatchers Tackle, 18 Queen Street, Wells, BA5 2DP, 01749-673513, *Water:* 3.5 acre lake, *Species:* Carp to 25lb, Tench 8lb, small Roach, *Charges:* Limited membership, please enquire at Thatchers Tackle, *Season:* 1 March - 31 December

Winterbourne

Frome Vale Angling Club (Coarse Lake)

Water: Half acre lake at Winterbourne. See entry under Bristol Frome

Wiveliscombe

Oxenleaze Farm Caravans & Coarse Fishery

Contact: Richard & Marion Rottenbury, Chipstable, Wiveliscombe, TA4 2QH, Tel/Fax 01984 623427, enquiries@oxenleazefarm.co.uk, *Water:* 3 Lakes 2 acres, *Species:* Carp, Tench, Roach, Rudd, Bream, *Permits:* At above address, *Charges:* £5/person/day (2 Rods max), Spectators 50p/person/day, *Season:* 1st April - 31st October, *Methods:* Barbless Hooks, No ground bait

Yeovil

Ashmead Lakes

Contact: Steve Maynard, Stone Farm, Ash, Martock, TA12 6PB, 01935 823319, *Water:* 11 acres, *Species:* Carp, *Charges:* Syndicate water. Please phone for details, *Season:* Closed January to mid February, *Methods:* No restrictions.

Hardington Lake

Contact: Peter David, Hardington Lake, Hardington Marsh, Nr Yeovil, *Water:* 1.5 acre Lake, *Species:* Wild Carp to 8lb, Common Carp to 22lb, Crucian, Grass, Ghost, Mirror and Leather Carp. Tench to 8lb, Bream to 7lb, Rudd and Roach, *Permits:* Micks Tackle and Guns, 67 Princess St, Yeovil, Somerset and Micks Tackle and Guns, 9 Abbotsbury Road, Weymouth, Dorset, *Charges:* £30 per year (June to June). £5 deposit key, *Season:* Open all year, *Methods:* No large Carp in keepnets, Please take all rubbish home. Barbless hooks preferred.

Stoke Sub Hamdon & District AA

Water: Bearley Lake (no night fishing) - See entry under River Parrett

The Old Mill Fishery

Contact: Mike Maxwell, Tucking Mill Farm, Stoford, Yeovil, BA22 9TX, 01935 414771, rosalind.maxwell@btinternet.co.uk, *Water:* Three 1.5 acre lakes plus fishing on a tributary of the River Yeo, *Species:* 21 different species of coarse Fish. River contains Roach, Dace, Chub and Barbel, *Permits:* On the bank, *Charges:* Permit for lakes and river £5/day (£2.50 accompanied juniors u.16yrs). £2 evening ticket 5pm onwards in summer, *Season:* Open all year 7am to dusk, *Methods:* No keepnets. Barbless hooks only

SOMERSET Stillwater Trout

Bridgwater

Burton Springs Fishery (Trout Lake)

Contact: Tony Evans, Lawson Farm, Burton, Nr Stogursey, Bridgwater, TA5 1QB, 01278-732135, *Water:* Aprox 1.5 acre lake, *Species:* Brown, Rainbow, Tiger & Blue Trout, *Permits:* Self service at fishing lodge, *Charges:* 4-fish ticket £22, 3-fish £18, 2-fish/ 5hr £15, sporting ticket £10 (catch & release permitted after limit), *Season:* Open all year 8am-9pm or dusk, *Methods:* Barbless hooks only, only Rainbow Trout may be taken

Hawkridge Reservoir

Contact: Wessex Water, 0845 600 4 600, *Water:* 32 acre reservoir, *Species:* Brown and Rainbow Trout, *Permits:* Ranger Gary Howe Tel 01278 671840, *Charges:* Day Ticket £13, Season Ticket £390, Day Concession £11, Season Concession £290, Evening Ticket £8 (no concessions). Book of Tickets - £70 for 6 available only from the ranger. Concession book of tickets £60, *Season:* 17 March -14 October 2001

Quantock Fishery
Contact: Sue & Neil Bruce-Miller, Quantock Fishery, Stream Farm, Broomfield, Bridgwater, TA5 2EN, 01823 451367, quantock@quantockforce9.co.uk, *Water:* 1 x 2 acre spring fed lake + 1 x 0.5 acre spring fed lake, *Species:* Brown + Tiger Trout, Rainbow Trout to 20lb, *Charges:* Prices on application and booking advisable, *Season:* Open every day all year dawn to dusk, *Methods:* Barbless hooks only, Two fish limit - then catch + release, all fish over 6lb to be returned

Bristol

Blagdon Lake
Contact: Bob Handford, Blagdon Lake, Park Lane, Blagdon, BS40 7UD, 01275 332339 Fax:01275 331377, bob.handford@bristolwater.co.uk, *Water:* 440 Acre Lake, *Species:* Rainbow Trout best 16lb 4oz, Brown Trout best 10lb 4oz, *Permits:* Woodford Lodge, Chew Valley Lake, Blagdon Lodge and Blagdon Lake, *Charges:* Day bank £15, O.A.P. £13, Junior £7.50, Evening Bank £12 - Day boat £22.50, O.A.P. £20.50, Junior £16, Afternoon £18.50, Evening £15 - Season £540, O.A.P. £340 (Valid at Chew and Barrows also), *Season:* 22 March - 25 November 2001, *Methods:* Fly fishing only

Bristol Reservoir Flyfishers Association
Contact: Roger Stenner, 18 Stafford Place, Weston-Super-Mare, BS23 2QZ, 01934 417606, *Water:* Fishing on Bristol Waterworks reservoirs. Blagdon, Chew Valley and Barrows. Competitions organised from bank or boat. Tuition offered. Full winter programme of activities including: tackle auctions, fly tying sessions, beginners and improvers casting sessions, *Species:* Rainbow and Brown Trout, *Permits:* Day tickets direct from Bristol Water. Club does not sell day tickets, *Charges:* £3 joining fee. Annual membership £5 full members, £3 pensioners and registered disabled, £1 juniors in full time education (no joining fee)

Cameley Lakes
Contact: J Harris, Hillcrest Farm, Cameley, Temple Cloud, BS18 5AQ, 01761 452423, *Water:* One 2.5 acre lake and three 1acre lake plus fishing on the River Cam, *Species:* Rainbow Trout, Brown Trout 1 - 5lb, *Permits:* Car park, *Charges:* £18 incl VAT Day ticket 4 fish, £15 incl VAT 1/2 Day ticket 2 fish, *Season:* Open all year - 8.00 till sundown, *Methods:* Fly fishing only. Hooks no larger than 1 inch

Chew
Contact: Bob Handford, Woodford Lodge, Chew Stoke, Nr.Bristol, BS40 8XH, 01275 332339 Fax:01275 331377, bob.handford@bristolwater.co.uk, *Water:* 1,200 Acre lake, *Species:* Rainbow Trout to 14lb 6oz, Brown Trout to 13lb 3oz, *Permits:* Woodford Lodge, Chew Lake, *Charges:* Day bank £13, O.A.P. £11, Junior £6.50, Evening bank £10 - Day boat £28.50, O.A.P. £26, Junior £21, Afternoon £23, Evening £17.50 - Season £440, O.A.P. £290 (Valid at Barrows also), *Season:* 22 March - 25 November 2001, *Methods:* Fly fishing only

Litton Lakes
Contact: Bob Handford, 01275-332339, Fax:01275-331377, bob.handford@bristolwater.co.uk, *Water:* 7 acre lake + 11 acre lake at Coley, Nr Chewton Mendip, *Species:* Brown & Rainbow Trout, *Permits:* Woodford Lodge, Chew Valley Lake, *Charges:* £83 permit for two rods, fishing both lakes exclusively, *Season:* 22 March - 15 Oct 2001, *Methods:* Fly fishing only

The Barrows
Contact: Bob Handford, The Barrows, Barrow Gurney, Nr. Bristol, 01275 332339, Fax: 01275331377, bob.handford@bristolwater.co.uk, *Water:* Three lakes of 25 acres (No. 1), 40 acres (No. 2), 60 acres (No.3), *Species:* Rainbow Trout (8lb 5oz) Brown Trout (9lb 1oz), *Permits:* Woodford Lodge, Chew Valley Lake, *Charges:* Day bank £10.50, O.A.P. £9, Junior £6, Evening bank £8.50, Season £330, O.A.P. £217, *Season:* 22 March - 25 November 2001, *Methods:* Fly fishing only

Congresbury

Silver Springs Trout Fishery
Contact: Liz Patch, Silver Street Lane, Congresbury, BS49 5EY, 01934 877073, *Water:* 2.5 acres, *Species:* Rainbows, *Permits:* On Site, *Charges:* 4 Fish £20 - 3 @ £17 - 2 @ £14 - O.A.P./ u16 £18, £15 & £12 resp, *Season:* All year, *Methods:* Fly only

Dulverton

Exe Valley Fishery
Contact: Andrew Maund, Exebridge, Dulverton, 01398 323328, enquiries@exevalleyfishery.co.uk, *Water:* 3 Lakes fly only (2 + 1 + 3/4 acre lakes), 1 Small lake any method half acre, *Species:* Rainbow Trout, *Permits:* Day Tickets, *Charges:* £5.50 per day + £3.50 per kilo, Evenings (after 5) April - September 3 fish limit, £3.30 plus £3.50 per kilo, *Season:* All year, *Methods:* See above

Wimbleball
Contact: South West Lakes Trust, 01837 871565, info@swlakestrust.org.uk, *Water:* Information Office Hours 01398 371372, *Species:* Premier Rainbow Fishery - Boat & Bank (boats may be booked in advance: 01398-371372). Rod average for 2000: 3.4 fish/rod/day. Biggest fish: Rainbow 11lb 9oz, *Permits:* Self service at Hill Barn Farm, *Charges:* Full day £15.75, Season £385. Reduced day £12.50, Season £290, Child/Wheelchair £3, Season £90. Evening Monday - Friday £12.50. Season Permits can be used on any Premier Fishery only. Boats £9.50 per day inc. 2 fish extra to bag limits. 'Wheelie Boat' available for disabled anglers (must be booked at least 48 hrs in advance), *Season:* Opens 24 March 2001 - 31st October, *Methods:* Fly fishing only. No child under 14 years may fish unless accompanied by an adult over 18 years

Frome

Parrots Paddock Farm (Trout)
Contact: Mr. Baker, Wanstrow Rd, Nunnery Catch, 01373 836505, *Water:* Rainbow Trout. See entry under Stillwater Coarse

SOMERSET - STILLWATER TROUT / WILTSHIRE - RIVER FISHING

St. Algars Farm Lake
Contact: Mr.A.M. Mackintosh, St Algars Farm, West Woodlands, Nr Frome, BA11 5ER, 01985 844233, *Water:* 2 Acre Lake, *Species:* Rainbow Trout, *Charges:* April - May (£14, 4-fish limit) (£8.50, 2-fish limit) June - October (£12, 4-fish limit) (£8.50, 2-fish limit), *Season:* 1st April - 31st October, Dawn to dusk

Taunton
Hawkridge Fly Fishing Club
Contact: Mrs Sally Pizii, Tumbleweed Cottage, Curry Mallet, Nr. Taunton, TA3 6SR, 01823 480710, *Water:* Primarily fishing on Hawkridge Reservoir. Club meetings 8pm second Tuesday of the month at The Blake Arms, Bridgwater. Visiting speakers & monthly competitions in season. Club trips, fly tying and social evenings
Otterhead Lakes
Contact: M.G. Woollen, *Water:* See main entry for Taunton Fly Fishing Club under River Axe, Somerset

Wiveliscombe
Clatworthy Fly Fishing Club
Contact: Mr F Yeandle, 51 Mountway Rd, Bishops Hull, Taunton, TA1 3LT, 01823-283959, *Water:* 130 acre Clatworthy reservoir on Exmoor, *Species:* Rainbow and Brown Trout, *Permits:* On site from Lodge, *Charges:* Day Ticket £13/5-fish limit, Concessions £11 OAP's. Evening Ticket £8. 6 Days £70, Concessions £60. Season £390/4-fish limit (only 4 visits/week allowed), Concession £290. Boats £10/day, £6 evening, *Season:* Open 17th March -14th October, *Methods:* Fly Fishing Only
Clatworthy Reservoir
Contact: Wessex Water, 0845 600 4 600, *Water:* 130 acre reservoir, *Species:* Rainbow and Brown Trout, *Permits:* Contact ranger Dave Pursey on 01984 624658, *Charges:* Day Ticket £13, Season Ticket £390, Day Concession £11, Season Concession £290, Evening Ticket £8 (no concessions). Book of Tickets - £70 for 6 available only from the ranger. Concession book of tickets £60, *Season:* 17 March - 14 October 2001

Yeovil
Sutton Bingham Reservoir
Contact: Wessex Water, 0845 600 4 600, *Water:* 142 acre reservoir, *Species:* Rainbow and Brown Trout, *Permits:* Contact ranger Ivan Tinsley on 01935 872389, *Charges:* Day Ticket £13, Season Ticket £390, Day Concession £11, Season Concession £290, Evening Ticket £8 (no concessions). Book of Tickets - £70 for 6, available only from the ranger. Concession book of tickets £60, *Season:* 17 March - 14 October 2001

WILTSHIRE River Fishing

AVON HAMPSHIRE
For detailed description of the Avon, see under Hampshire river fishing.

Chalk Stream Angler Fishery
Contact: Simon Cain, Salisbury, 01722-782602, info@chalkstreamangler.co.uk, *Water:* Approx. 2 mile upper Avon consisting of main river and carrier streams, *Species:* Wild Brown Trout and Grayling, *Charges:* Trout Season £70-£94/rod/day; Grayling period £35/rod/day, *Season:* Trout 15 April - 15 October, Grayling 16 Oct - 15 Dec, *Methods:* Upstream dry fly and nymph, Barbless hooks, catch & release, Long trotting for Grayling in the 'Grayling period'
Salisbury & District Angling Club
Contact: RW Hillier - Secretary, Inverleith, 29 New Zealand Avenue, Salisbury, SP2 7JX, 01722 321164, *Water:* Several Stretches on River Avon at Little Durnford, Amesbury, Ratfyn Farm & Countess Water. Also fishing on Dorset Stour, River Wylye, Nadder, Ebble, Bourne & Ratfyn Lake at Amesbury, *Species:* All species Coarse and Game, *Charges:* Full or Associate Membership available. Details from the secretary. Coarse £65.00. Concessions for Senior Citizens & Juniors; Game £105, *Season:* Lakes: 1st June - 31st March. Rivers: 16th June - 14th March

Services Dry Fly Fishing Association
Contact: Major (Retd) CD Taylor - Hon Secretary, c/o G2 Sy,HQ 43 (Wessex) Brigade, Picton Barracks, Bulford Camp, Salisbury, SP4 9NY, 01980 672161, *Water:* 7 miles on River Avon from Bulford upstream to Fifield, *Species:* Brown Trout & Grayling, *Permits:* Fishing Restricted to Serving & Retired members of the Armed Forces. for membership details apply to Secretary, *Charges:* On Application, *Season:* 1st May - 15th October. Grayling until 31st December, *Methods:* Only upstream fishing permitted, dry fly exclusively during May & dry fly/nymph thereafter
Wroughton Angling Club
Contact: Mr T.L.Moulton, 70 Perry's Lane, Wroughton, Swindon, SN4 9AP, 01793 813155, *Water:* 1.25 miles Rivers Avon and Marden at Chippenham, Reservoir at Wroughton, *Species:* Roach, Perch, Bream, Pike, Barbel, Chub, Carp, Tench, *Permits:* Mr M. Shayler, 20 Saville Crescent, Wroughton, Swindon, WILTS, tel.: 01793-815000, *Charges:* £12.50 per season (day tickets £5 seniors), *Methods:* Restrictions - No Boilies, Peanuts, Particle baits, Dog biscuits or Nuts of any description

AVON WILTSHIRE

Avon Springs Fishing Lake (River)
Contact: BJ Bawden, Recreation Road, Durrington, Salisbury, SP4 8HH, 01980 653557, barrie@fishingfly.co.uk, *Water:* 1 mile Wiltshire Avon at Durrington, *Species:* Brown Trout + Grayling, *Permits:* Also *Contact:* mobile 07774 801401. Email barrie@fishingfly.co.uk, *Charges:* £40 day ticket, *Methods:* Fly only

BRISTOL AVON
Malmesbury to Chippenham
Coarse fisheries predominate in this section, although Trout are stocked by fishing associations in some areas. Arguably one of the best fisheries in the country, this section contains a wide range of specimen fish. Local records include: Roach 3lb 2oz, Perch 3lb 3oz, Tench 8lb 5 1/2oz, Bream 8lb 8oz, Dace 1lb 2oz, Chub 7lb 10oz, Carp 20lb 8 1/4oz and Pike 33lb 3oz. Also many Barbel to 12lb have been reported.

Avon Angling Club (Bristol Avon)
Contact: R.P. Edwards, 56 Addison
Road, Melksham, SN12 8DR, 01225-
705036, *Water:* 4 miles of Bristol Avon.
see also entry under Kennet and Avon
Canal, *Species:* Roach, Bream, Tench,
Chub, Barbel, Perch, Pike, Eels, *Permits:*
Haines Tackle, Frome; Robbs Tackle,
Chippenham; Wiltshire Angling,
Trowbridge; Melksham Angling Centre
01225-793546 or call 01225-705036,
Charges: Day ticket £2. Full Licence
£12. Junior Licence £4, *Season:* Current
EA Byelaws apply, *Methods:* No
restrictions

Bradford-on-Avon & District A.A
Contact: Mr P O'Callaghan (sec), 4
Fitzmaurice Close, Bradford-on-Avon,
01225-863163, *Water:* 7 miles River
Avon at Staverton and Bradford-on-
Avon. 2 miles River Frome at Langham
Farm nr Tellisford. 1 mile River Biss at
Trowbridge. 5 miles Kennet & Avon
Canal, *Species:* Barton Farm: Mainly
quality Bream, big Chub, Roach, Tench
& Dace. Nets of Bream in excess of
100lb. Canal: mainly Tench, Bream with
good Perch & Roach. Frome: large
Bream, Chub, Tench. Quality Roach,
Dace and Perch. Avon: Large Bream
shoals, big Chub, Carp, Roach and
Perch. Biss: (mainly junior water) mixed
fishery with some good fish, *Permits:*
Club weekly and day/weekly permits
from Wiltshire Angling (5 Timbrell St.
Trowbridge, 01225-763835), St.
Margarets News Bradford-on-Avon,
Haines Angling, Frome. Season/ week/
day permits available from most tackle
outlets in the area, *Charges:* Senior:
Season: £20 / week: £10 / day: £3 -
Junior, OAP, disabled: *Season:* £9 /
week: £5 / day: £1.5, *Season:* June
16th - March 14th inc, *Methods:* Not
more than 2 rods at any one time, no
more than 4 mtrs apart. Keepnets
allowed; Bloodworm allowed from
October 31st

Calne Angling Association
Contact: Miss JM Knowler, 123a
London Road, Calne, 01249 812003,
Water: River Avon, River Marden and a
lake, *Species:* Barbel to 8lb, Pike to 8lb,
Carp to 10lb, Bream to 6lb, Rudd to 8oz,
Roach to 2.5lb; Wild Carp in lake,
Permits: T.K.Tackle, *Charges:* Please
enquire at T.K.Tackle, *Season:* River:
June - March, Lake: open all year,
Methods: No restrictions

Chippenham Angling Club
Contact: Mr Duffield, 95 Malmesbury
Road, Chippenham, SN15 1PY, 01249
655575, sw1/964952@aol.com,
Water: 8 miles on River Avon + Carp
lake at Corsham, *Species:* Barbel, Chub,
Roach, Bream, Perch, Pike, Tench,
Permits: Robs Tackle, Chippenham - Tel:
01249 659210, *Charges:* Please
telephone for prices, *Season:* June 16th
- March 14th, *Methods:* No boilies or
keepnets on Carp lake

Swindon Isis Angling Club (Bristol Avon)
Water: Two miles of the Bristol Avon at
Sutton Benger near Chippenham. See
also entry under Thames, *Species:*
Bream 9.9.0, Perch 4.0.8, Tench 8lb,
Barbel 11lb, Pike 28lb, Roach 2lb 7oz
and usual species, *Permits:* Tackle
shops in Swindon, Chippenham,
Cirencester and Calne, *Charges:* As per
Thames entry, *Season:* From 16th June
to 14th March, *Methods:* No Bans

KENNET AND AVON CANAL

*There are some 58 kilometres of canal
within the Bristol Avon catchment area
which averages one metre in depth and
thirteen metres in width. The Kennet &
Avon Canal joins the River Avon at Bath
with the River Kennet between Reading
and Newbury. The canal was opened in
1810 to link the Severn Estuary with the
Thames. The canal, now much restored,
provides excellent fishing with Carp to
25lb, Tench to 5lb also Roach, Bream,
Perch, Rudd, Pike and Gudgeon.*

Airsprung Angling Association
Contact: Alan Lampard, 6, Hewitt Close,
Trowbridge, BA14 7SG, 01225 764388,
Water: Two kilometres on Kennet and
Avon Canal from Beehive Pub to
Avoncliffe aquaduct at Bradford-on-
Avon, *Species:* Carp, Bream, Chub,
Roach, Rudd, Dace, Tench, Perch, etc,
Permits: St Margarets News, 45 St
Margarets Street, Bradford-on-Avon,
Wilts.; Wiltshire Angling, 01225-
763835; West Tackle, Trowbridge,
Charges: Day ticket £2. Full licence
price on application, *Season:* Open all
year, *Methods:* No night fishing, No
fishing on match days in pegged areas.
No radios etc. No fishing within 25
metres of locks etc. No bloodworm or
joker; be aware of overhead cables !

Avon Angling Club (Kennet and Avon)
Contact: R.P. Edwards, 56 Addison
Road, Melksham, SN12 8DR, 01225-
705036, *Water:* 1 mile of Kennet and
Avon Canal. See also entry under Bristol
Avon, *Species:* Bream, Tench, Roach,
Carp, *Permits:* Haines Tackle, Frome;
Wiltshire Angling, Trowbridge; Robbs
Tackle, Chippenham or call 01225-
705036, *Season:* All year

Devizes A.A
Contact: T.W. Fell, 21 Cornwall
Crescent, Devizes, SN10 5HG, 01380
725189, *Water:* 15 miles from
Semington to Pewsey, also 6.5 acre
lake, *Species:* Carp 15 - 23lb, Roach,
Tench, Pike to 26lb, Bream, *Permits:*
Angling Centre, Snuff St, Devizes,
Wiltshire. Tel: 01380 722350. Local
tackle shops in Devizes, Melksham,
Trowbridge, Chippenham, Calne,
Swindon. Wiltshire Angling: 01225-
763835, *Charges:* Adult £20 per
season. Junior £7.50. Day tickets £3.50
(not sold on the bank). 14 day ticket £8,
Season: E.A. byelaws apply, *Methods:*
Please use barbless hooks

Marlborough & District A.A
Contact: Mr.M.Ellis, Failte, Elcot Close,
Marlborough, SN8 2BB, 01672 512922,
Water: Kennet & Avon Canal (12 miles
approx), *Species:* Roach, Perch, Pike,
Tench, Bream, Carp, *Charges:* Full
membership £23 + £5 joining fee,
Junior up to 16 £5, Ladies £5, O.A.P's
£5, *Season:* Open all year in 2000.
Membership from 1st Jan - 31st Dec,
Methods: No live baiting, No bloodworm
or joker

Pewsey & District Angling Association
Contact: Don Underwood, 51 Swan
Meadow, Pewsey, SN9 5HP, 01672
562541, *Water:* 4 Miles Kennet & Avon
canal, *Species:* Roach, Tench, Carp,
Bream, Perch, Pike, *Permits:* The Wharf,
Pewsey, *Charges:* Day tickets Senior £3
/ Junior/OAP £2. Prices may change for
2001, *Season:* No closed season,
Methods: Rod and line

NADDER

The River Nadder rises near Tisbury draining the escarpment of the South Wiltshire Downs and Kimmeridge Clay of the Wardour Vale. The River Wylye joins the Nadder near Wilton before entering the main River Avon at Salisbury.
The Nadder is well known as a mixed fishery of exceptional quality; there is a diverse array of resident species including Chub, Roach, Dace, Bream, Pike, Perch, Brown Trout and Salmon. Much of the fishing is controlled by estates and syndicates although two angling clubs offer some access to the river.

Tisbury Angling Club

Contact: Mr E.J.Stevens, Knapp Cottage, Fovant, Salisbury, SP3 5JW, 01722 714245, *Water:* 3 miles on River Nadder. 3.5 acre lake and 2.5 acre lake, *Species:* Roach, Chub, Dace, Pike, Bream, Perch, Carp, Brown Trout, *Permits:* Phone for details, *Charges:* Adult £4 joining fee and £24 per season. Juniors £7.50 per season. OAPs £12.50 per season. Seniors £5 per day (dawn to dusk) Juniors £3 per day (dawn to dusk). New members welcome, *Season:* 16th June to 14th March, *Methods:* General

SEMINGTON BROOK

The Semington Brook is spring fed from Salisbury Plain and flows through a flat area to its confluence with the River Avon downstream of Melksham. In the upper reaches and in some of its tributaries Brown Trout predominate. Downstream of Bulkington coarse fish prevail with sizeable Bream, Chub, Roach, Dace and Perch.

Lavington Angling Club

Contact: Mr Gilbert, Gable Cottage, 24 High Street, Erlestokes, Nr Devizes, SN10 5TZ, 01380 830425, *Water:* Baldam Mill section of Semington Brook, *Species:* Coarse and Game, *Permits:* Membership details from Mr Gilbert, *Season:* Current EA byelaws apply

STOUR

See description under Dorset, river fishing

Stourhead (Western) Estate

Contact: Sonia Booth, Estate Office Gasper Mill, Stourton, Warminster, BA12 6PU, (01747)840643, Fax: 841129, enquire@stourheadest.u-net.com, *Water:* 10 ponds and lakes, largest 10 acres, on the headwaters of the Stour, *Species:* Wild Brown Trout, Perch, Tench, Bream, Roach, Carp, *Charges:* Season permit for fly fishing £100

THAMES

Swindon Isis Angling Club (Thames)

Contact: Peter Gilbert, 31 Havelock St, Swindon, SN1 1SD, 01793 535396, *Water:* 2 mile of River Thames at Water Eaton near Cricklade, Swindon, *Species:* Barbel 9lb, Chub 4.5lb, Roach 2lb, Bream 7lb, Perch 2lb, *Permits:* Tackle shops in Swindon, Chippenham, Cirencester and Calne, *Charges:* Club *Permits:* Senior £29.50. OAP and disabled £12. Juniors £8. The club permit contains two free day tickets and more day tickets can be obtained for £5 each; 1/2 year starts 1 November, £12 & £6 all others, *Season:* From 16th June to 14th March, *Methods:* No bans

WYLYE

The River Wylye rises near Kingston Deverill and flows off chalk, draining the western reaches of Salisbury Plain. The river confluences with the River Nadder at Wilton near Salisbury, then joins the main River Avon which flows south to Christchurch.
This river is best described as a 'classic' chalk stream supporting predominantly Brown Trout; hence most fisheries here are managed for fly fishermen. The fishing is predominantly controlled by local syndicates and estates.

Langford Fisheries

Contact: Paul Knight, Duck Street, Steeple Langford, Salisbury, 01722 790770, paul@knight2.supanet.com, *Water:* Wylye - 1 mile, *Species:* Brown Trout, Grayling, *Charges:* £35/2-fish limit + catch & release. Grayling fishing £17/day catch & release, *Season:* April 15th - Oct 14th Trout season. Oct 15th - March 14th Grayling season, *Methods:* Fly Only

Sutton Veny Estate

Contact: Mr & Mrs A.Walker, Eastleigh Farm, Bishopstrow, Warminster, BA12 7BE, 01985 212325, *Water:* 4 miles on River Wylye, *Species:* Brown Trout, *Charges:* £50/day (no beats), Season tickets upon request, *Season:* 15th April - 15th October, *Methods:* Dry fly + upstream nymph only

WILTSHIRE Stillwater Coarse

Calne

Blackland Lakes

Contact: J. or B. Walden, Blackland Lakes Holiday & Leisure Centre, Stockley Lane, Calne, SN11 0NQ, 01249 813672, fishing@blacklandlakes.co.uk, *Water:* One 1 acre, One 0.75 acre, *Species:* Carp (to 30lbs), Tench, Roach, Bream, Perch, *Charges:* 1 rod £6, extra rods £1, concessions OAP's and children, special rates for campers, *Season:* Open all year, *Methods:* Barbless hooks, No ground bait, No large fish or Bream in keepnets

Chippenham

Chippenham Angling Club (Coarse Lake)

Contact: sw1/964952@aol.com, *Water:* See entry under Avon. Carp Lake, *Permits:* Members only, no day tickets

Ivy House Lakes & Fisheries

Contact: Jo, Ivyhouse Lakes, Grittenham, Chippenham, SN15 4JU, 01666 510368 Fax:01666 510368, *Water:* 1 Acre + 6 Acre lakes, *Species:* Carp, Bream, Roach, Tench, Chub, Perch, *Permits:* On the bank day tickets, No night fishing, *Charges:* Day tickets £5 per day (1 rod). £3 Ladies O.A.Ps etc. Match booking £4, *Season:* All year, *Methods:* Boilies & Tiger nuts banned, Ground bait in moderation.

Sevington Lakes Fishery

Contact: R.J. Pope, Wellfield House, Parkhouse Lane, Keynsham, Bristol, BS31 2SG, 0117 9861841, *Water:* 2.5 acres in 2 lakes, *Species:* Mirror & Common Carp to 26lb, Crucians, Roach, Perch, Tench & Rudd, *Charges:* Day Ticket: Adult £5, Junior £2.50, *Season:* Open all year - Dawn to dusk, *Methods:* Barbless hooks please.

Silverlands Lake

Contact: Mr & Mrs King, Wick Farm, Lacock, Chippenham, SN15 2LU, 01249 730244, *Water:* One spring fed 2.5 acre lake, *Species:* Carp, Tench, Bream, Pike, *Permits:* Only from the fishery, *Charges:* Day/Night tickets £5, Season tickets 12 months - £100 Adult, £65 1/2 year. £8 - 24 hour ticket, *Season:* Open all year, *Methods:* No nuts, Dogs to be kept on a lead at all times

Wyatts Lake

Contact: L. Beale, Wyatts Lake Farm, Westbrook, Bromham, Nr Chippenham, SN15 2EB, 01380 859651, *Water:* 2 acre lake approx, *Species:* Mirror and Common Carp to 15lb, *Permits:* On site, *Charges:* £4 per person (unlimited rods), *Season:* Open all year 24 hours a day. Night fishing available, *Methods:* Good fishing practices required and expected.

Devizes

Devizes A.A

Contact: T.W. Fell, 21 Cornwall Crescent, Devizes, SN10 5HG, 01380 725189, *Water:* New 6.5 acre lake opening June 2001, Crookwood Lake well stocked, *Permits:* Angling Centre, Snuff St, Devizes, Wiltshire. Tel: 01380 722350. Local tackle shops in Devizes, Melksham, Trowbridge, Chippenham, Calne, Swindon. Wiltshire Angling: 01225-763835, *Charges:* Please phone for details

Lavington Angling Club (Coarse Lake)

Contact: Mr Gilbert, Gable Cottage, 24 High Street, Erlestokes, Nr Devizes, SN10 5TZ, 01380 830425, *Water:* Two acre lake, *Species:* Carp, Tench, Roach, Rudd, Bream and Perch, *Permits:* Members only, details from club secretary, *Season:* Closed season from March 14th to June 15th, *Methods:* Keepnet limits. Full details of rules in Club handbook

Malmesbury

The Lower Moor Fishery (Coarse)

Contact: Geoff & Anne Raines, Lower Moor Farm, Oaksey, Malmesbury, SN16 9TW, 01666 860232, *Water:* 7 acre coarse fishing lake, *Species:* Carp, Pike, Perch, Tench, Mirror, *Permits:* At lakeside, *Charges:* £5/day, *Season:* We observe close season for coarse fishing, *Methods:* Barbless hooks

Melksham

Burbrooks Reservoir

Contact: A.J. Mortimer, 17 Sarum Avenue, Melksham, SN12 6BN, 01225 705062, *Water:* 0.75 acre Lake between Melksham & Calne, and Devizes and Chippenham in the village of Bromham (New Road), *Species:* Mirror, Common & Crucian Carp, Bream, Tench, Roach, Perch, Gudgeon, Chub, *Permits:* Please contact Melksham Angling Centre, Melksham House, Melksham: 01225-793546, or the Spar Shop in Bromham Village: 01380-850337, *Charges:* £4 Adults. £2 ladies, juniors and OAPs, *Season:* Open all year dawn to dusk, *Methods:* No night fishing, Only one rod per person, No hooks above size 8

Salisbury

Salisbury & District Angling Club (Coarse Lakes)

Contact: Ron Hillier, Inverleith, 29 New Zealand Avenue, Salisbury, SP2 7JX, 01722 321164, *Water:* Peters Finger Lakes, Steeple Langford and Wellow. See entry under Avon Hampshire, *Species:* Carp, Tench, Bream, *Charges:* £65.00 per season. Concessions for Senior Citizens & Juniors, *Season:* 1st June - 31st March

The Longhouse Fishery

Contact: Jonathan Burch, Tinca, The Longhouse, Teffont, Nr. Salisbury, SP3 5RS, 07790-694757, *Water:* 3x 0.25 acre pond; 0.75 acre lake; 15 pegs in total, all deep, *Species:* Common+Mirror+Ghost+Koi+Crucian Carp (23.6lb), Roach+Rudd (2.6lb), Perch (3.9lb), Tench (3lb), *Permits:* Lakeside only, *Charges:* £5/day, £6/night, £7/24hrs, *Season:* All year 24hrs/day, only 10 days closed for pheasant shoot (Oct.-Jan.), *Methods:* Only bans are no particles (pulses) other than hemp or corn

Tisbury Angling Club (Coarse Lakes)

Contact: Mr E.J.Stevens, 01722 714245, *Water:* See also entry under Nadder. Old Wardour Lake (3.5 acre), 2 miles south of Tisbury and Dinton Lake (2.5 acre), 2 miles north of Tisbury

Waldens Farm Fishery

Contact: David & Jackie Wateridge, Waldens Farm, Walden Estate, West Grimstead, Salisbury, SP5 3RJ, 01722 710480, *Water:* 5 Lakes for approx 10 acres, *Species:* All coarse fish, *Permits:* From the bank, *Charges:* Day (dawn to dusk) tickets Adult £6, Junior - O.A.P. £4, Evenings 5 p.m.on £3.50, Match peg fees £4, *Season:* Open full 12 months, *Methods:* Barbless / Micro barb hooks, Net dips to be used, Limited Groundbait, No boilies, nuts or cereals

Witherington Farm Fishing

Contact: Tony or Caroline Beeny, New Cottage, Witherington Farm, Downton, Salisbury, SP5 3QX, 01722 710021, *Water:* 3 Well stocked lakes, *Species:* Carp, Tench, Roach, Bream, Rudd, Chub, Perch, *Permits:* On bank, *Charges:* Full day £5, Half day £3, Full day Junior U16 / Disabled / O.A.P. £3, *Season:* All year Dawn - Dusk, *Methods:* No Boilies, Barbless hooks, All nets to be dipped, No night fishing, No keepnets only in matches.

Trowbridge

Rood Ashton Lake

Contact: Marlene Pike, Home Farm, Rood Ashton, Trowbridge, BA14 6BG, 01380 870272, *Water:* 7 acre lake available for matches - please enquire for details, *Species:* Carp, Tench, Roach, *Permits:* Home Farm and Lake View, *Charges:* 6a.m. - 6p.m. £4.50, O.A.P.'s / Juniors £3.50. 6 p.m. - 11 a.m. £3.50, O.A.P.'s / Juniors £2.50. Please enquire for match bookings, *Season:* Open all year, *Methods:* No keepnets (only competitions). No tin cans or boilies, Barbless hooks only. No nuts. No night fishing

Tucking Mill

Contact: Wessex Water, 0845 600 4 600, *Water:* Free coarse fishing for disabled anglers from 16 June 2001 - 14 March 2002, *Species:* Roach, Chub, Tench and Large Carp, *Permits:* The site is regularly used by disabled angling clubs including Kingswood Disabled Angling Club. For more information please contact the club secretary Mr H Morris, 86 North Street, Downend,

Bristol BS16 5SF, *Season:* 8am to sunset throughout the year except in the close season

Warminster

Longleat Lakes & Shearwater
Contact: Nick Robbins, Longleat Estate Office, Longleat, Warminster, 01985 844496, *Water:* Longleat 3 Lakes, Top lake Carp up to 32lb, Shearwater 37 acres, Carp up to 25lb. Longleat, 20 Carp over 20lb, *Species:* Carp, Roach, Bream, Tench, Perch, Rudd, *Permits:* From bailiff on the bank, *Charges:* Upon request, *Season:* Upon request, *Methods:* No keepnets or Carp sacks, no boilies except Longleat. No nuts, peas, beans on all lakes, no bolt rigs. Barbless hooks only

Southleigh Lake
Contact: Mr John Shiner at on-site sub Post Office, Crockerton Out Of Town Shopping Centre, Crockerton, Warminster, BA12 8AP, 01985 846424, *Water:* Private 2 acre lake, *Species:* Mirror, Common Carp, Bream, Roach, Tench, *Charges:* £4 Day ticket, *Season:* Mon.-Sat. 7a.m. - 6 p.m. Sunday matches only (by advanced booking), *Methods:* Barbless hooks only, No Carp in keepnets, No boilies.

Westbury

Clivey Ponds
Contact: Mr Mike Mortimer, Lakeside Clivey, Dilton Marsh, Westbury, BA13 4BA, *Water:* 1 acre lake, *Species:* Roach, Rudd, Bream to 2lb, Perch, Carp to 12lb, Crucians, Tench to 3lb and Gudgeon, *Permits:* On the bank or from Haines Angling Centre, 47 Vallis Way, Frome, *Charges:* £3/Day Ticket. Juniors OAPs etc. £2/day, *Season:* All year, *Methods:* Barbless Hooks only. No Groundbait

Eden Vale A.A
Contact: A.E.D. Lewis, Secretary, Station Road, Westbury, 01373-465491, *Water:* 5.25 acre lake, *Species:* Carp (Common-15lb, Mirror-10lb), Bream-3lb, Roach-1.5lb, Perch-1lb, Rudd-0.75lb, Pike-15lb, *Permits:* Railway Inn opposite lake (max 8/day), Haines Angling, Badcox, Frome available from July 1st, Mon.-Fri. only, *Charges:* Day: £4 adult - £3 junior / Members

(restricted to 15 mile radius of Westbury) at present £15 may increassae in 2001 / New Members + £2.50 joining fee / Applications to Sec. with S.A.E, must be sponsored by two existing members, *Season:* members only May 1st - March 15th, day tickets July 1st - March 15th, *Methods:* No fixed rigs, no keepnets before June 16th, no Carp or Tench in keepnets

Woodland Park
Contact: Mrs S.H.Capon, Brokerswood, Westbury, BA13 4EH, 01373 822238, woodland.park@virgin.net, *Water:* 5 Acre lake within 80 acre country park, *Species:* Carp, Roach, Tench, Perch, Dace, *Charges:* Adults £4.50, Children £3, *Season:* Closed 17th April - 16th June, *Methods:* Barbless hooks, No boilies, No keepnets

WILTSHIRE Stillwater Trout

Chippenham

Pheasant Fly Fishers
Contact: Paul Maslin, 17, Ducks Meadow, Marlborough, SN8 4DE, 01672 514970, alan.tonge@agresso.co.uk, *Charges:* £15 Annual membership, £20 adult + junior. A small friendly Social Club open to new adult and junior membership.

Devizes

Mill Farm Trout Lakes
Contact: Bill Coleman, Mill Farm Trout Lakes, Worton, Devizes, SN10 5UW, 01380 813138 mob 0771 8892385, *Water:* 2 Waters of 3.5 acres each, *Species:* Rainbow & Brown Trout, *Permits:* Great Cheverell Post Office. One mile from fishery and open on Sunday mornings, *Charges:* 5 Fish £25, 4 Fish £22, 3 Fish £17, 2 Fish £12, 1 Fish £6 (2hrs before dusk only), *Season:* All year, 7.30am to dusk. December and January 8am to dusk, *Methods:* Fly fishing only

Malmesbury

The Lower Moor Fishery (Trout)
Contact: Geoff & Anne Raines, Lower Moor Farm, Oaksey, Malmesbury, SN16 9TW, 01666 860232, *Water:* 2 Lakes, 34 acre Mallard lake, 8 acre Cottage lake, *Species:* Rainbow 6lb 5oz & Brown Trout 13lb 4oz, *Permits:* At lakeside, *Charges:* 4 Fish ticket £20, 2 Fish ticket £12, Junior 2 Fish ticket £10, *Season:* March 17th - Jan 1st 2002, 8 a.m. to dusk, *Methods:* Mallard lake - any type of fly fishing, Cottage lake - nymph or dry fly on floating line

Pewsey

Manningford Trout Fishery
Contact: Alastair McPhee, Manningford Bohune, By Pewsey, SN9 6JR, 01980 630033, *Water:* 3.5 acre lake, *Species:* Rainbow Trout to 15lb. Brown Trout to 9lb, *Permits:* From the Woodbridge Inn, 200yds from the lake, *Charges:* Full day £20 - 4 fish. Half day £12 - 2 fish. Junior £8 - 2 fish, *Season:* Open all year from 9am to dusk, *Methods:* Fly fishing only.

Salisbury

Avon Springs Fishing Lake (Stillwater)
Contact: BJ Bawden, Recreation Road, Durrington, Salisbury, SP4 8HH, 01980 653557, barrie@fishingfly.co.uk, *Water:* One 4 acre lake, One 3 acre lake. One mile of upper Avon chalk stream, *Species:* Brown Trout 17lb 4oz, Rainbow Trout 15lb 11oz, *Permits:* EA fishing licences available on site. Also *Contact:* mobile 07774 801401, fax 01980-655267. Email barrie@avonsprings.freeserve.co.uk or barrie@fishingfly.co.uk, *Charges:* £33 per day, £20 junior. 1/2 day £25, junior £16, eve £17, *Season:* Open all year 8.30am to dusk, *Methods:* Fly only no lures

Langford Fisheries (Trout Lake)
Contact: Paul Knight, Duck Street, Steeple Langford, Salisbury, 01722 790770, paul@knight2.supanet.com, *Water:* 12 acre Trout lake, *Species:* Rainbow Trout, *Permits:* From fishery, *Charges:* Day ticket £33 - 4 fish plus catch & release or £22 - 2 fish catch & release. 1/2 day £22 - 2 fish catch & release or £16 - 1 fish catch & release. Boats £68 - 4 fish each plus catch & release, *Season:* Open all year, *Methods:* Max size 10 hook.

Sea Fishing

National Federation of Sea Anglers
Contact: Head Office, 51a Queen Street, Newton Abbot, TQ12 2QJ, 01626 331330, nfsaho@aol.com
South West Federation of Sea Anglers
Contact: Colin Davies (chairman), 12 Ilton Way, Kingsbridge, TQ7 1DT, 01548 852706, *Water:* South West coastal waters. The Federation is on www.fishingworld.co.uk

CORNWALL
Cornish Federation of Sea Anglers
Contact: Mrs Camilla Perry, 7 Henwood Crescent, St Columb Minor, Newquay, TR7 3HG, 01637 876287, *Water:* Sea Fishing. Shore and boat. Tidal fishing in estuaries, excluding Bass, *Permits:* None required, other than possible harbour charges, *Charges:* C.F.S.A. affiliation £41 per annum per club. Personal members £7.50. Family membership (ie husband, wife and children under 16) £10. All memberships inclusive of third party insurance, *Season:* None, *Methods:* Two rods three hooks maximum. No netting.
Boscastle Peganina
Contact: Ken Cave, 01288 353565
Falmouth & District Sea Angling Club
Contact: Colin Hedger, 38 Truro Lane, Penryn, TR10 8BW, 01326-372410, *Water:* Sea angling club with Senior & Junior sections; Shore & boat fishing off cornish coast, *Species:* All sea species, *Permits:* Meetings held first Wednesday each month at Cross Keys Pub, Penryn at 8pm all welcome, *Charges:* £10 seniors, £5 juniors (u.16), £20 family membership, *Season:* All year, *Methods:* All sea angling methods
Treyarnon Angling Centre
Contact: Ed Schliffke, Treyarnon Bay, St Merryn, Padstow, 01841 521157, *Water:* Shore Fishing Trips

DEVON
Combe Martin Sea Angling Club
Contact: Wayne Thomas, The Shippen, Loxhore Cott, Nr Barnstaple, EX31 4ST, 01271 850586, waesox@shippen99.freeserve.co.uk, *Charges:* Family £10/Senior £6/Jun. £1

Falcon Charters
Contact: Dennis, 01237 473197 or 01271 861307, *Water:* Deep sea fishing trips to Lundy Island off Bideford Bay and North Devon coast (Ilfracombe - Bude), *Species:* Bass, Pollack, Skate, Conger, *Permits:* Fully licenced code of practice for up to 10 people, *Charges:* Call for details, *Methods:* Full range of safety equipment
Ilfracombe & District Anglers Association (Sea)
Contact: Des Clements, 56 Slade Valley Road, Ilfracombe, EX34 8LF, 01271 865051, idaa@btinternet.com, *Water:* Beaches and rock marks. Founded in October 1929, the oldest club in North Devon, *Species:* Bass, Pollock, Conger, Mullet, Ray, Coalfish, Cod and various other species, *Permits:* From Variety Sports, Broad Street, Ilfracombe, *Charges:* Fees per year: Family £10, Adult £8, OAP £4, Junior £2. 17 competitions per year and an annual fishing festival in July/August, *Season:* January to January
Plymouth Command Angling Association (Sea)
Contact: Mr Vic Barnett Hon.Sec, 5 Weir Close, Mainstone, Plymouth, PL6 8SD, 01752 708206, victor.barnett@talk21.com, *Water:* Boat & Shore Fishing, *Species:* All sea fish, *Permits:* Membership is open to all serving members of the Royal Navy and Royal Marines with associate membership for serving members of the Army and Air Force. Associate membership is also open to ex-serving members of the Armed Forces, no matter when the time was served, *Charges:* Costs for full membership or associate membership are available on application or enquiry at the above contact

SOMERSET
Bristol Channel Federation of Sea Anglers
Contact: Keith Reed, 27 St Michaels Avenue, Clevedon, BS21 6LL, 01275 872101, *Water:* Bristol Channel, Hartland Point. North Devon to St Davids Head, Dyfed (all tidal waters eastwards), *Species:* All sea fish, both boat and shore records,Yearly update (52 different species recorded in major (over 1lb) rec.list, 14 different species in minor (under 1lb) rec.list, *Charges:* £22.50 per CLUB per year inclusive of shore activities insurance, *Season:* All

year round activities, shore + boat contests, small boat section with inter-club activities, *Methods:* Fishing to specimen sizes, all specimen fish awarded certificate, best of specie annually, plus fish of the month.
Clevedon Breakaways Sea Angling Club
Contact: R. Addicott (Sec.), 12 Dampier Road, Ashton, Bristol, BS3 2AT, 0117 9660400, *Water:* Competitions in the Bristol Channel and South West. Affiliated to B.C.F.S.A. and N.F.S.A, *Species:* All species, *Charges:* Adult £12 plus £2 joining fee. Juniors £2. OAP £6 per year

DORSET
Swanage Angling Club
Contact: Swanage Angling Centre, 01929 424989, *Water:* Fishing around Swanage & Purbeck coastal areas, pier fishing at Swanage, close to Chesil beach, *Permits:* Swanage Angling Centre (01929) 424989
Sangina
Contact: Swanage Angling Centre, 01929 424989, *Water:* Deep sea fishing trips. Fully licenced for 12 anglers. Experienced Skipper

---

Every care has been taken in compiling this directory and all information is believed accurate at the time of printing. The publishers cannot however accept liability for any errors or ommisions. Fishery rules may change throughout the year, if in any doubt contact the owner.

Brian Hawker of Leicester with a Dutson double

I caught this, but I'm not sure where or what it is? Can you help? Editor.

Part of a 10 fish 41lb 10oz haul for Rob Gail and Brian Hearn at Temple Trout

Simon Pomeroy with a Pallington Tench. Photo - Brian Gay

Eggesford Ghillie Julian Zealy returns a 12lb Salmon.

Heavily scaled Elmfield Mirror

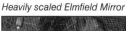

Rainbows to 5lb 8oz from Watercress Photo - Mike Weaver

ADVERTISERS INDEX

Coarse

Game

SERVICES

WHERE TO STAY
Hotels & Accommodation

Self Catering

Caravans

Camping

Tuition

Bed & Breakfast

186

Road Directions GAME

1. Angling 2000
Over 20 beats on the Tamar, Taw & Torridge. Please telephone 01566 784488.

2. Arundell Arms Hotel
Leave the A30 Dual Carriageway east of Launceston and follow signs for Lifton. The Arundell Arms is in the centre of the Village.

3. Avon Springs
Please telephone 01980 653557 or 07774 801401 for road directions.

4. Bake Lakes
A38 to Trerulefoot. At roundabout (half way between Plymouth & Liskeard) take minor road to Bake. Turn right at T junction, then take first left. Fishery is 200 yards on right hand side.

5. Bellbrook Valley Trout Fishery
From Tiverton roundabout on A361 head towards Barnstaple. Take 3rd right (6 miles) signposted Bellbrook & Spurway. Continue down lane for 2 miles then sharp right signed "To the fishery" then 200yds on the right. From Oakford leave uphill, bear left at Pinkworthy Post (signposted Rackenford). Follow lane down hill, cross stream then fork left. Fishery 200yds on right.

6. Blakewell Fishery
Take A39 from Barnstaple towards Lynton. 1.5 miles from Barnstaple turn left on to B3230 and follow signs to the fishery.

7. Bridge House Hotel
The fishing is located just upstream of Oakford Bridge on the A396 approx 15 miles from junction 27 on the M5. The Bridge House Hotel is in Bampton on the B3227 (A361 to Tiverton – A396 to Bampton). Please telephone 01398 331298.

8. Bristol Water Fisheries
a Barrows. b Blagdon. c Chew. d Litton. Bristol Water fisheries are well signposted from major roads. Telephone 01275 332339.

9. Cameley Lakes
0.5 miles off A37 Temple Cloud. Road marked Cameley Ilinton Blowitt.

10. Clinton Arms
Situated between Bideford and Great Torrington on the A386. Turn right to Frithelstock and follow signs to Clinton Arms.

11. Drakelands
From Exeter take the main road to Plympton. At Newnham Industrial Estate take the Cornwood Road to Hemerdon Village. Turn right past Miners Arms, the fishery is signposted 0.75 miles on the left.

12. Drift Reservoir
Take A30 towards Lands End. In Drift village, turn right (signposted "Sancreed"). Reservoir car park is approx 1/4 mile along this lane. Ticket sales enquiries: Adjacent.

13. Eggesford Country Hotel
At Eggesford on the A377 midway between Exeter and Barnstaple.

14. Environment Agency Fisheries
a-Exe & Creedy fisheries. b Watersmeet & Glenthorne fisheries. Directions are supplied with permits.

15. Exe Valley Fishery
M5 exit 27 to Tiverton on A361. Take A396 towards Minehead at Black Cat Junction, continue on A396 towards Minehead, at Exebridge turn left at garage on B3222, over bridge at the Anchor Inn take first right to fishery.

16. Fenwick Trout Fishery
From Bodmin take A389 toward Wadebridge, continue to village of Dunmere and turn immediate left off river Camel bridge. Fishery is signposted.

17. Flowers Farm Fly Fishery
Situated mid way Dorchester and Yeovil off A37. From Dorchester take A37, travel for approx. 7 miles look out for green dome on right, 0.5 mile turn right to Batcombe, 0.5 mile turn right at T junction marked to the Friary, take second left at fishing sign, then right at bottom of hill. The fishery is at the side of St Francis Friary. From Yeovil take A37 for approx. 6 miles, turn left at crossroads marked Batcombe, take 3rd left along top Batcombe Downs at fishing sign, right bottom of hill. Continue 0.5 mile to Fishery.

18. Fosfelle Country Manor
Please telephone 01237 441273 for directions.

19. Goodiford Mill Fishery
From Cullompton take the Honiton road, continue for over a mile past Horns cross. Turn left at signpost for Wressing, Goodiford, Dead lane. Right at end of lane, fishery on left.

20. Half Moon Hotel
Sheepwash lies 1 mile North of Highampton (A3072) between Hatherleigh & Holsworthy.

21. Nick Hart Fly Fishing
Junction 25 off M5, A358 out of Taunton. Pick up the B3224 just outside Bishop's Lydeard. Follow this road past Raleghs Cross Pub, turn right at small chapel close by and continue and continue on B3224 towards Wheddon Cross. Exford is 5 miles past Wheddon Cross.

22. Highbullen Hotel
Please telephone 01769 540561 for directions.

23. Higher Cownhayne Farm
Please phone for directions. 01297 552267.

24. Hollies Trout Farm
From Cullompton or Honiton take the A373 and follow signs for Sheldon.

25. Lower Bruckland Fishery
Turn into Bruckland lane 0.75 mile east of Colyford on A3052. Follow for 0.75 mile

26. The Lower Moor Fishery
From M4 junction 15 leave A419 for Cotswold Waterpark, straight across at crossroads, then road narrows, fishery on left after about 1.5 miles. From Wales and West, leave M4 at junction 17 (Chippenham/Cirencester), follow road towards Cirencester, in Crudwell turn right for Oaksey through village, over railway bridge, fishery is second drive on right, about 1 mile after bridge.

27. Manningford Trout Fishery
Please telephone 01980 630033 for directions.

28. Mill Leat Trout Lakes (Thornbury)
Take the A388 north from Holsworthy. Turn right following signs for Thornbury. The fishery is half a mile past Thornbury church.

29. Mill Leat Trout Farm (Ermington)
Take A38 dual carriageway to Ivybridge, then follow Ermington signs (B3211). Trout Farm is 1st property after Ermington village sign.

30. Newhouse Fishery
From Totnes take the A381 south towards Kingsbridge. After 5 miles turn right to Moreleigh on the B3207. After 2 miles turn right down the lane signposted Newhouse Farm Fishery.

31. Orvis Innis Fly Fishery
M5 to Exeter, A30 to Bodmin, A391 to Bugle. Turn left at lights in Bugle to Penwithick (B3374). In Penwithick left at Chapel. Fishery 1 mile on left.

32. Prince Hall Hotel
From M5 - pass Exeter, then take A38 signposted Plymouth. Take second Ashburton turn-off, the B3357 signposted Two Bridges and Princetown. Hotel is situated one mile from this point on the left and one mile before Two Bridges Junction. From Plymouth - Take A386 to Yelverton, follow signs for Princetown, continue towards Two Bridges, turn right and stay on B3357. Hotel is one mile on the right.

33. Quantock Fishery
M5, off at J24, follow A38 for Taunton. Turn right into "Old Road" in North Petherton, continue out of village for 4 miles. Turn left (First left turning since North Petherton), continue 0.5 mile, take first left. Fishery at end of lane.

34. Rising Sun Inn
The Rising Sun Inn is on the A377 opposite T junction with B3227 to South Molton.

35. Rockbourne Trout Fishery
Please telephone 01725-518603 for directions.

36. Roddy Rae's Fly Fishing School
Please telephone 01647 24643 for directions.

37. Rose Park Fishery
8 miles west of Launceston on the A30 turn off and follow signs for Altarnun. Drive through the village over the bridge and take next right. Follow the road, Rose Park is on right.

38. South West Lakes Trust - Game
a-Kennick, b-Siblyback, c-Wimbleball, d-Fernworthy, e-Colliford, f-Roadford, g-Burrator, h-Stithians, i-Crowdy, j-Wistlandpound, k-Meldon, l-Avon Dam, m-Venford, n-Tottiford. South West Lakes Trust fisheries are well signposted from major roads.

39. Stourhead (Western) Estate
From A303 come off at Mere and follow signs for Stourhead Gardens and House. Enter village and drive past Spread Eagle Pub. Approx 1 mile on turn right by a red phone box and post box. New Lake is on your right. Please phone before arrival.

40. Tavistock Trout Fishery
Entrance on A386 one mile from Tavistock.

41. Temple Trout Fishery
Travelling from Bodmin to Launceston along the A30 take the first Temple turning on the right Travel along this road over a chain ridge at the bottom of the hill, fishery entrance is just a little way along on the left. Travelling from Launceston to Bodmin along the A30 take second Temple turning at T junction, at the end of this road turn right back towards A30. The fishery is 300m on right.

42. The Chalkstream Angler
Please telephone 01722 782 602 for directions.

43. Valley Springs
Half a mile from Cider Press, follow official tourist signs from Frogmore or Totnes Road.

44. Watercress Fishery
Signposted from the B3344 Exeter to Chudleigh road just the Exeter side of the Highwaymans Haunt Inn.

45. Waterrow Touring Park
Leave the M5 at junction 25 (Taunton). Follow the A358 (signposted Minehead)around Taunton and then take B3227 (former A361 scenic route to N. Devon) signposted Wiveliscombe, Barnstaple. At Wiveliscombe cross straight over traffic lights towards Waterrow (3 miles) Park is on the left after passing the Rock Inn.

46. Wessex Fly Fishing School
In Tolpuddle turn off A35 signed Southover. You will see our signs 0.25 mile along lane.

47. Wessex Water - Game
a Clatworthy. b Hawkridge. c Sutton Bingham. Please telephone 0845 600 4 600 for further details.

48. Wiscombe Park Fishery
Leave A30 at Honiton, take A375 towards Sidmouth, turn left at the Hare and Hounds cross roads towards Seaton, after 3 miles turn left towards Blackbury Camp, fishery signposted on the left.

Road Directions
COARSE

1. Alcove Angling Club
Please telephone 0117 9025737 or 07941 168116 for directions.

2. Ashcombe Adventure Centre
From Exeter: at end of M5 fork left on A380 for 2mls. Turn left on B3192. After roundabout follow Teignmouth road for 1 mile then left at Ashcombe sign. From Plymouth: at Exeter

Racecourse turn left – then under bridge to join A380. Turn right as above. From Torquay: 3 miles after Newton Abbot turn left under bridge crossing A380. Turn right to B3192.

3. Avallon Lodges
From Launceston B3254 towards Bude town turn left at Langdon X (just before the Countryman Pub) then next right signed Clubworthy. Avallon is 1.5 miles along this road, up a short drive on the left.

4. Avalon Fisheries
Please phone 01278 456429 or 0966 363413 for directions.

5. Badham Farm Holidays
From Looe take road to Duloe, at Sandplace before crossing railway bridge take small road (not signposted) on right, Badham is 1 mile on right. From Liskeard take road to St. Keyne, through village, just before church take left turn signposted St. Keyne Well and Badham. Farm is about 1 mile on the left past Wellhouse Hotel.

6. Bakers Farm
Approx 0.75 miles from Torrington on the B3232 to Barnstaple. Bakers Farm is signposted on the right.

7. Bickerton Farm Fisheries
Please telephone 01548 511220 for road directions.

8. Braddon Cottages
From M5: take A30 dual carriageway at junction 31, signposted Okehampton / Bodmin, to Stowford interchange exit (34 miles). Turn towards Roadford Lake. Cross the dam. After 4 miles turn left at T junction (Ivyhouse Cross). Then immediately right. Cross stone bridge at Ashmill bearing right up hill signposted Holsworthy. After 2 miles turn right signposted Braddon and East Venn. Bear left at fork continue past Braddon Cottage crossing cattle grid to farmhouse.

9. Bridgwater Sports & Social Club
Please telephone 01278 446215 for directions.

10. Bristol, Bath & Wiltshire Amalgamated Anglers
Please phone 0117 9672977.

11. Bullock Farm Lakes
4.5 miles from J20 off M5 (Clevedon/Nailsea). Follow signs for B3133 for Yatton. Drive through village of Kenn. Turn right for Kingston Seymour (Fishing lakes signposted). In centre of village turn sharp right into Back lane and follow signs for Bullock Farm Fishing Lakes.

12. Bush Lakes
Halfway between Notterbridge A 38 & Pillaton or halfway between Hatt & Pillaton.

13. Christchurch Angling Club
Please telephone 01425 279710 for directions.

14. Clawford Vineyard
Take A388 from Holsworthy to Launceston. Turn left at crossroads in Clawton. After 2.5 miles turn left at T junction. Clawford is a further 0.6 miles on left.

15. Cofton Country Holiday Park
From Junction 30, M5 Exeter, take A379 signed Dawlish. Park is on the left half mile after small harbour village of Cockwood.

16. Cokerhurst Farm
Please telephone 01278 422330 for directions.

17. Coombe Fisheries
Leave the A386 (Plymouth to Tavistock road) at Yelverton and then follow signs to Buckland Abbey. The Fishery is signposted 100yds past the Abbey entrance on the left.

18. Coombe Water Fisheries
Half a mile from Kingsbridge on road to Loddiswell, B3210.

19. Coombelands & Stout
Only 15 mins. from junction 28 M5. Approx. 3.5 mls from Tiverton, .75 mls from Butterleigh on the Silverton Rd, 3.5 mls from Cullompton, 1ml from Bunniford X on the Silverton Rd and 3 mls from Silverton on the Butterleigh Rd.

20. Cranford Inn & Holiday Cottages
Please telephone 01805 624697 for directions.

21. Creedy Lakes
Travelling south down the M5 exit at junction 27. From Tiverton take the A3072 Exeter/Crediton road. At Bickleigh bear right towards Crediton. At Crediton town sign turn right. Follow blue and white fishery signs.

22. Darts Farm
Leave M5 at junction 30. Follow signs to Exmouth (A376). After 2 miles follow brown tourist signs to Darts Farm Shopping Village.

23. Diamond Farm
Fishing is on river Axe at Brean. Site can be found from M5 junction 22. Follow signs for Burnham-on- Sea, Brean. On reaching Brean turn right at junction for Lympsham and Weston Super Mare on the Weston road. Diamond Farm is approx half mile from junction on left hand side.

24. Dorchester & District Angling Society
Phone 01305 264873 or enquire at local Tackle Shops.

25. Dutson Water and Homeleigh Angling Centre
From Launceston take A388 to Holsworthy. Permits from Homeleigh Angling & Garden Centre, 1 mile from Launceston on A388 on right hand side.

26. East Rose Farm
From A30 take turning to St Breward opposite Temple where dual carriageway commences. Go north across Moor to Bradford and turn left at telephone box. Continue for 0.5 miles and turn right at junction signposted St Breward. East Rose is first property on right one mile from T junction. From Camelford follow St Breward signs, turn left after passing pub and Church. Continue over cross roads and cattle grid at Hallagenna, continue for half mile over second cross roads and the farm is on the left side.

27. Eastcott Lodges
From B3254 take turning signposted North Tamerton. As you come into village take first right to Boyton. Eastcott is 1.5 miles along on the left hand side.

28. Edneys Fisheries
Please telephone 01373 812294 for directions.

29. Elmfield Farm Coarse Fishery
From Launceston take the Egloskerry road found at the top of St.Stephens Hill. About 1 mile out of Egloskerry look for the Treburtle turn off to the right. Follow Fishing signs for 3 mls, signposted on the left.

30. Emerald Pool Fisheries

Off the A38 at West Huntspill, turn into Withy Road by the Crossways Inn. Take the next right Puriton Road. Travel along road for approx. 0.5 mile, over Huntspill river, take the next track on the left. Pool on the right at the top of the track.

31. Glenleigh Farm Fishery

From St. Austell take A390 towards Truro, after approx. 3 miles second hand car garage on left, turn left to Sticker, follow road to top of hill, immediately before bus shelter turn left, past mobile homes park, over by-pass to bottom of hill, car park on right.

32. Godney Moor Ponds

Please telephone 01458 447830 for directions.

33. Hardington Lake

Please telephone 01935 411087 for directions.

34. Hazelwood Park

Just off the A379 road from the Exeter bypass, travelling through Starcross, turn left at the Harbour Bridge at Cockwood. The park stands to the right of the Coast road approximately 0.75 mile from the bridge. If using the M5 leave at the exit for Dawlish (junction 30).

35. Hidden Valley

2 miles west of Launceston, turn off the A30 at Kennards, on to the A395 towards North Cornwall. Follow this road for half mile, then follow Hidden Valley brown signs.

36. Ivy House Lakes

From Swindon to Wooton Bassett, bottom of hill turn right down Whitehill Lane. Fishery is approx. 2 miles on the left hand side.

37. Kingslake Fishing Holidays

From Exeter at end of M5 take A30 to Okehampton, in the centre of Okehampton at the lights, turn right onto A386 to Hatherleigh. At Hatherleigh (7 miles) take left onto A3072 Holsworthy/Bude. Travel 7 miles then turn left at sign 'Chilla 2 miles' Kingslake is .75 mile along this road on left.

38. Lands End Farm

From M5 junction 22, turn left at first roundabout, then first left and follow road to T junction, turn left signposted Wedmore, continue through village of Mark, then into Blackford where you turn right by the school signposted Heath House, follow road to crossroads, turn right, then second right, fishery is at bottom of lane.

39. Legge Farm Fishery

From Hatherleigh take A3072 Holsworthy road for 2 miles, turning right (signposted Church Road), continue along lane for 1.75 miles. Legge Farm is on the right.

40. Little Allers

From Exeter: Take Wrangaton Cross exit off A38, take 2nd road on left. From Plymouth: Take Ivybridge exit off A38. Go through Ivybridge to Wrangaton. Turn right and take 2nd road on left.

41. Longleat & Shearwater

From Warminster take 362 towards Frome, follow signs to Longleat. Further information from the bailiff, Nick Robbins on (01985) 844496.

42. Luccombes Fishery

From Exminster, enter Exminster from Exeter on A379, pass the shops on right and Victory Hall on left, take first right into Days Pottels Lane, then next left into Towsington Lane, the fishery is situated approx. 0.5 mile on the left.

43. Mangerton Valley

Please telephone 01308 458482 for directions.

44. Martin's Farm Fishery

On the A31 Winchester to Ringwood road, take the left slip road after Ringwood Church – the B3081 to Verwood. Just past the golf course turn left towards Woodlands. After 600 yards turn left into New Road and through the housing estate. Go down track to end where you can park on left.

45. Meadowside Fishery

Located on A39, just south of the roundabout junction with B3274 at Winnards Perch, within the Cornish Birds of Prey Centre at St. Columb Major.

46. Mellonwatts Mill Coarse Fishery

From St. Austell take A390 Truro road to end of Sticker bypass, then road signposted Tregoney and St. Mawes. Turn left after 1 ml for Mevagissey. Fishery 2nd farm on rt.

47. Milemead Fisheries

From Tavistock take B3362 (old A384) towards Launceston. Take turning left just outside Tavistock signposted Mill Hill. Entrance is 1 mile down lane on right.

48. Mill Park Touring Site

Take A399 coast road between Ilfracombe and Combe Martin. Take turning opposite Sawmills Inn for Berrynarbor, Lake and touring site are on the left.

49. Millbrook

Approach Millbrook on B3247, follow brown Tourist Signs from Tregantle Fort.

50. Millhayes Fishery

2 miles from junction 28 (M5) on the A373 towards Honiton turn left at Post Cross to Kentisbeare. 1 mile to village centre, turn right at Post Office and go down hill for 300yds, turn right at sign for Millhayes.

51. Minnows Camping & Caravan Park

From the North or South exit M5 at junction 27 onto A361 signposted Tiverton. After about 600 yards take first exit signposted signposted Sampford Peverell. Turn right at next roundabout, cross bridge over A361. Straight across at next roundabout signposted Holcombe Rogus. Site is on left. From N. Devon on the A361 - go to end of A361 to junction 27 of the M5. Go all the way round and return back onto the A361. Then follow the above directions.

52. Nance Lakes

From A30 take the holiday route to St. Ives. Follow signs for holiday route for approx. 2 miles. Fishery is signposted on the right hand side.

53. Nanteague Farm

We are situated on the main A30 between the Chiverton & Carland Cross roundabouts. From South on main A30 pass Zelah on dual carriageway and 2 miles further on through the hamlet of Marazanvose on the brow of the hill opposite Town & Country Nissan Garage you will find our entrance.

54. New Barn Angling Centre
From Paignton bypass traffic lights, take the A385 to Totnes/ Plymouth. Turn left after 2 miles into farm track signposted New Barn Angling Centre. From Totnes take the A385 to Paignton, turn right 200 yards past the Texaco garage into farm track signposted New Barn Angling Centre.

55. New Forest Water Park
From Ringwood head towards Fordingbridge on A338. After 4 miles you will see signs on the left.

56. Newberry Farm Coarse Fishing
On A399 western edge of Combe Martin village.

57. Newcourt Ponds
Take junction 28 M5 into Cullompton town centre, follow B3181 towards Exeter for 2 miles. At Merry Harriers Inn turn left. After hump backed Bridge turn right, at top of road turn right. Ponds 100yds on left.

58. Northam Farm
Leave the M5 at junction 22. Follow signs to Burnham-on-Sea, Brean. Continue through Brean village and Northam Farm is on the right half a mile past Brean Leisure Park.

59. Nurston Lake
Turn off at Lower Dean or Buckfastleigh, take the South Brent road. Turn off at the Skerraton sign and take the next right hand turn.

60. Oakside Fishery
From Newquay take road to Quintrell Downs, at roundabout at Quintrell Downs take A3058, continue to Dairyland, first left, past Dairyland (signposted White Cross). Fishery is 1 mile down road on right hand side.

61. Oaktree Carp Farm & Fishery
From Barnstaple take the A361 to Newtown. Left onto B3227 Bampton Road for 2.5 miles and left at fishery signpost. Down hill and entrance signposted on right. From M5 junction 27 take A361 to Newtown, then as above.

62. Oldborough Fishing Retreat
Turn off A377 for Morchard Bishop, after 1.5 miles turn right for Oldborough, at T junction turn right down Sidborough Hill. Retreat is at bottom of hill on left.

63. Osmington Mills
Approaching from Wareham on the A352 Dorchester road turn left at the A353 Weymouth junction. At the Osmington Mills sign opposite the Garage, turn left and follow the lane to Holiday Park. Approaching from Weymouth, follow the A353 Wareham road. Pass through Osmington village and turn right at the sign for Osmington Mills. Follow lane to Holiday Park.

64. Pallington Lakes
On the unclassified road between Dorchester and Bovington Tank Museum (signposted) 1 mile east of Tincleton.

65. Peninsula Coarse Angling Association
Please telephone 01884 256721 for directions.

66. Penvose Fishery
From the A30 follow signs for Newquay Airport. Passing the Airport on your left and heading towards Watergate Bay. At the T junction turn left, we are the first turning on the left approx 200 yards.

67. Plantation Lakes
From Bristol - Weston-Super-Mare A370. Turn towards Yatton B3133 at Congresbury traffic lights. Go right through Yatton. Turn left towards Kingston Seymour. Just after the Bridge Inn. At village take middle lane. From M5. junction 20. Clevedon. Turn left at both roundabouts onto B3133 towards Yatton, after approx 3 miles turn right towards Kingston Seymour At village take middle lane.

68. Retallack Waters
Just off the A39 between Newquay and Wadebridge at Winnards Perch, signposted 'American Theme Park'.

69. Riverton House & Lakes
M5 junction 27 - Barnstaple via A361. Continue for 3 miles past junction A399 for Lynton then turn right towards West Buckland. 250m left signed Riverton. Barnstaple A361 - Exeter. 1 mile - Landkey & Swimbridge. Signed Riverton. Exeter A377 - Barnstaple. At Kingsnympton B3226 - South Molton - Barnstaple via B3226 & A361. Right - West Buckland. 250m left signposted Riverton.

70. Rood Ashton Lake
Leave A350 heading through West Ashton Village. Take next left signposted Rood Ashton, continue past East Town Farm, turn left. Home Farm is 0.5 mile on your left where you will see a sign.

71. Rosewater Lake
Take the A30, follow B3285 through Goonhavern to Perranporth. Continue for half mile, then turn right for Rose signposted from crossroads.

72. Royalty Fishery
Royalty & Winkton fisheries main entrance is on B3073, 200yds from its own junction with A35.

73. Salmonhutch Fishery
A377 to Crediton, turn left after Shell Garage, follow road signed Tedburn St Mary for 1.5 miles, right at junction marked Uton, follow fishery signs.

74. The Sedges
Please telephone 01278 445221 for directions.

75. Silverlands Lake
20 mins. from junction 17 on M4 - A350 between Chippenham and Melksham, turn into Folly Lane, west of the Laycock by-pass, 1.5 miles down lane.

76. Simpson Valley Fishery
1.5 miles from Holsworthy on main A3072 Holsworthy to Hatherleigh road.

77. South View Farm Fishery
From Bristol follow M5 onto A38. After 1.5 miles turn off into Kennford. Continue through village following Dunchideock signs until Shillingtord signs are seen. Follow Shillingford signs. Entrance to fishery on left at sharp bend before village. From Plymouth turn left off A38 following Dunchideock until sign for Clapham is seen on right heading down the hill. At Clapham follow signs for Shillingford. From Exeter follow signs to Alphington then Shillingford St. George. Fishery on right after village.

78. South West Lakes Trust - Coarse

a-Slade. b-Jennetts. c-Darracott. d-Melbury. e-Trenchford. f-Upper Tamar. g-Squabmoor. h-Old Mill. i-Crafthole. j-Porth. k-Boscathnoe. l-Argal. m-Bussow. South West Lakes Trust fisheries are well signposted from major roads.

79. Spires Lakes

Take the A3072 Holiday Route (HR) from Crediton. Spires Lakes are on the left after the first Winkleigh turn off.

80. Stafford Moor Country Park

Clearly signposted on the A3124, 3 miles North of Winkleigh, 9 miles South of Torrington.

81. Sunnyview Lake

Please telephone 01726 890715 for directions.

82. Sunridge Fishing Lodge

Travelling west on A38, just after South Brent take slip road for National Shire Horse Centre, turn left, travel 2 miles to crossroads, turn right onto B3210, continue 3 miles to T junction, turn right onto A379 towards Plymouth, continue 2 miles to second cross roads (just before garage) and turn right. Travel 1 mile and you will find the lodge on left.

83. Tan House Lake

M4 exit junction 18 onto A46 (Stroud) to Chipping Sodbury on to B4060 Wickwar. Take 4th left to Rangeworthy then Bury Hill Lane. Alternatively M5 to junction to Wickwar to Chipping Sodbury B4060 for 1.5 miles. Take 3rd road on right to Rangeworthy and Bury Hill Lane.

84. The Longhouse Fishery

7 miles west of Salisbury on the B3089

85. Thorney Lakes

Directions from A303 to Muchelney. Turn off A303 dual carriageway signposted Martock Ash. Follow signs to Kingsbury Episcopi, at the T junction in village turn right, through the village of Thorney, over river bridge & disused railway. Lakes are on left. Thorney Lakes & Caravan Park.

86. Todber Manor Fisheries

5 miles from Gillingham, Shaftesbury and Sturminster Newton. Telephone 01258 820384.

87. Town Parks Coarse Fishing Centre

We are half way between Totnes & Paignton along the A385 opposite the Texaco Petrol Station.

88. Trencreek Farm Holiday Park

The site is situated 4 miles southwest of St Austell. Take the A390 from St Austell to Truro. Approx. 4.5 miles out of St Austell take turning on left to Tregony & St Mawes (B3287) which is just after Pengelly plant centre. Do not turn for Sticker/Hewaswater. Trencreek is one mile on left.

89. Trevella

Proceed on A30 as far as Indian Queens, turn right onto A392, follow signs to Newquay until you come to Quintrell Downs roundabout, take signposted Crantock road which brings you to the Trevenper Bridge roundabout. Turn left onto A3075, the Redruth road, for 200yds and you will see Crantock signposted. If you are in Newquay, take A3075 to Redruth for 1.5 miles until you see Crantock signposted. If you are approaching us from the West, you will see Crantock signposted from A3075. Follow this road for 1 mile to T

junction signed to Newquay, where you turn right and then into Trevella entrance.

90. Upham Carp Ponds

From J30 on M5, take A3052 signposted Sidmouth. After approx 4 miles, after pasing White Horse Inn on right, sign to fishery will be seen on left. Turn left and after 700yds fishery will be found on left hand side.

91. Viaduct Coarse Fishery

From Yeovil take the A37 north towards Ilchester and then the B3151 to Somerton. Turn left onto the B3153 (Signposted Somerton) and go up hill to mini roundabout. Go straight over roundabout and take first right through housing estate to T - junction. Turn left and almost immediately first right onto track to fishery.

92. Waldens Farm Fishery

Off the A36 Salisbury to Southampton road near Whaddon. Phone for futher details (01722) 710480.

93. Warren Park Farm

A31, just past Ringwood take B3081, about 1 mile fork right to Alderholt. On entering Alderholt turn left into Ringwood Road, as road bears right farm on the left.

94. Week Farm

From Exeter leave A30 carriageway at Sourton junction. Cross A386 at Staggered crossroad (signposted Bridestowe) second right turning, over dual carriageway 1 mile to crossroad, turn left 0.5 mile signposted Week.

95. Wessex Water - Coarse

a Durleigh reservoir. b Blashford Lakes. c Tucking Mill. Please telephone 0845 600 4 600 for further details.

96. Witherington Farm Lakes

2 miles out of Salisbury on A36 fork right as duel carriageway starts, then first right again after about 0.5 miles. Follow signs for Downton and Stanlynch. Witherington Farm is about 3 miles on the right.

97. Wood Farm Caravan Park

7 miles west of Bridport on A35, entrance off roundabout with A3052 (access to fishing through caravan park).

98. Wooda Farm Park

From the A39 take the road signposted Poughill, Stampford Hill, continue 1 ml, through crossroad. Wooda Farm Park is 200yds on the right.

99. Woodacott Arms

Proceed north off the A3072 at Anvil Corner, turn right at Blagdon Moor Cross or proceed south off the A388 at Holsworthy Beacon, turn left at Blagdon Moor Cross. After approx 1.5 miles turn sharp left at Woodacott Cross, Woodacott Arms immediately right.

100. Woolsbridge Manor Farm

Please telephone 01202 826369 for directions.